ATTRACTING AND COMPENSATING AMERICA'S TEACHERS

ATTRACTING AND COMPENSATING AMERICA'S TEACHERS

Edited by
KERN ALEXANDER
Western Kentucky University

and

DAVID H. MONK
Cornell University

**Eighth Annual Yearbook of the
American Education Finance Association
1987**

BALLINGER PUBLISHING COMPANY
Cambridge, Massachusetts
A Subsidiary of Harper & Row, Publishers, Inc.

International Standard Book Number: 0-88730-203-3

Library of Congress Catalog Card Number: 87-30830

Printed in the United States of America

Library of Congress Cataloging-in-Publication Data

Attracting and compensating America's teachers / edited by
  Kern Alexander and David H. Monk.
    p.   cm. — (Annual yearbook of the American Education
  Finance Association : 8th)
    Includes index.
    ISBN 0-88730-203-3
    1. Teachers—Salaries, etc.—United States. 2. Teachers—
  United States—Supply and demand. I. Alexander, Kern.
  II. Monk, David H. III. Series.
  LB2842.2.A93   1987
  331.12'313711'00—dc19   87-30830
                                                        CIP

CONTENTS

LIST OF FIGURES

LIST OF TABLES

PREFACE

During the 1980s U.S. public education, both K–12 and higher education, experienced enormous societal pressure. Realizing that the nation was losing its supremacy in international economic system, Americans scrutinized and criticized all facets of society and proferred recommendations for substantial changes. A series of national, regional, and state commissions was established for the purpose of reforming public education. Buttressed by a variety of other societal forces, including political, economic, legal, and equity issues, these study commissions often provided the focus and unity necessary to encourage and rationalize school reform initiatives in state legislatures.

Most of the state school reform programs recognized that the classroom teacher was the key component in the educational process, and legislative actions included provisions designed to attract and retain high-quality instructional personnel. State legislatures commonly addressed a variety of instructional personnel issues. Many of these issues concerned establishing or increasing academic eligibility standards for candidates seeking admission into the teaching profession. Others included working conditions, administrative and instructional support services, and teacher education programs. Nearly all state legislatures addressed issues of teacher compensation. Merit pay plans, career ladder programs, and other teacher compensation systems were widely debated and occasionally enacted by state legislatures. This yearbook reviews and reflects upon the recent upheaval and its effects upon teacher compensation, supply and demand of classroom teachers, quality of instructional personnel, teacher retirement systems, and related issues.

Chapter 1, by Patricia Anthony, analyzes teachers in the economic system of the nation. Anthony provides a historical perspective of the economic status of teachers as well as an in-depth examination of teacher salaries during the 1980s. She also addresses issues directly related to the economic status of teachers, including marital status, outside employment, and working conditions. The issue of teacher supply and demand is integrated with issues affecting the current economic status of teachers. Anthony concludes with a discussion of the long-term effect that inadequate teacher salaries may have upon the quality of public education.

In Chapter 2 K. Forbis Jordan discusses teacher education recommendations derived from the series of national school reform reports, focusing on the recommendations regarding teacher preparation and the role of the teacher in the school. Specifically, he analyzes eleven major school reform reports in regard to composition of reform group, recommended teacher preparation program, certification/licensing/career ladders, recruitment, salaries, and teacher role and environment. Jordan concludes with a discussion of the consistencies and inconsistencies of the reports plus an identification of unresolved problems and issues.

The perennial debate regarding the supply of teachers for public elementary and secondary education is presented in Chapter 3 by James N. Fox. He discusses both research reports providing evidence that there will be a considerable shortage of teachers in the late 1980s and continuing into the 1990s, and studies suggesting that there will be no shortage of teachers for the foreseeable future. Fox persuasively argues that three problems hobble the accurate projection of teacher supply: elusive demand, complex supply, and varied definitions of teacher quality. Regardless of whether these problems can be overcome, he observes that over one million teachers will be hired during the next several years and challenges policymakers to employ a backward-linking strategy to identify and attract quality teachers into the profession.

In Chapter 4 Stephen B. Lawton poses the question: "Why is it that the United States is experiencing a shortage of teachers, particularly in mathematics and science, yet Canada has a surplus of teachers and has experienced little difficulty in finding qualified teachers in all areas?" In striving to answer that question, Lawton broadened his study to include several other countries. While he concludes that Canadian teachers receive significantly greater compensation than do their American counterparts, which partially accounts for Canadian university graduates seeking entry into teaching, Lawton suggests that a review of international data shows that well-qualified people can be attracted to teaching, even in areas of relatively short supply.

Restructured teacher compensation systems are analyzed and discussed in Chapter 5 by Betty Malen, Michael J. Murphy, and Ann Weaver Hart. The authors evaluate three incentive strategies—merit pay, expanded jobs, and redesigned jobs—regarding their central features, initial effects, and potential for achieving the desired outcomes. Also highlighted are the implications for those responsible for allocating resources for the purpose of reforming teacher compensation systems. Malen, Murphy, and Hart raise compelling questions about the use of merit pay while suggesting other strategies that are fiscally prudent and defensible.

In Chapter 6, Lloyd E. Frohreich reviews the issues and potential solutions relating to implementation of merit pay systems by school districts. He defines merit pay systems, discusses an array of theory and merit pay issues, and presents a proposed teacher incentive and compensation decision model. While Frohreich indicates that research generally favors the perspective of those who are opposed to merit pay systems, he suggests that the issue is not as bleak as has been indicated by several literature sources. Frohreich recommends that considerable additional research should be conducted in such areas as teacher motivation and satisfaction and how participatory management relates to motivation and organizational productivity within schools.

Stephen L. Jacobson provides in Chapter 7 a theoretical analysis of merit pay and its effects upon teaching as a career. According to Jacobson, merit pay proposals are based on two assumptions: (1) that teachers are motivated primarily by monetary rewards, and (2) that the opportunity for extra compensation can motivate teachers' behavior throughout their teaching careers. Jacobson uses Herzberg's two-factor theory and Vroom's expectancy theory to examine these assumptions and also reviews the *Holmes Group Report* and *The Report of the Carnegie Task Force on Teaching as a Profession* regarding merit pay issues. Contrary to certain assumptions supporting merit pay, he finds that teachers appear to be motivated largely by intrinsic rewards rather than by monetary benefits. He suggests that reflecting experience-related differences in teacher preferences is more likely to effect meaningful change than implementing merit pay schemes.

In Chapter 8 Bruce A. Peseau presents a compelling argument that most teacher education programs are funded at poverty levels by the nation's colleges and universities. Peseau develops an analogy of the concepts of adequacy and equity between the funding of K–12 and higher education programs. He suggests that state legislatures have failed to provide budget oversight in higher education appropriations as they affect teacher education. Peseau believes that with the absence of external program review agencies, higher education administrators will continue to fund teacher education programs meagerly.

In Chapter 9 Joseph C. Beckham reviews federal statutes and case law from federal and state courts regarding wage and salary equity for both public and private employees. Beckham suggests that federal statutory law has not been judicially interpreted to compel widespread reform of wage inequities among professional employees in educational institutions. He maintains that the difficulty in establishing proof of discriminatory intent and judicial acceptance of employer defenses predicated on the influence of market forces have virtually eliminated discrimination suits based upon theories of comparable worth. However, Beckham believes that studies of comparable worth will continue to be conducted by state legislatures for the purpose of eliminating gender-based discrimination.

Eugene McLoone discusses teacher retirement systems in Chapter 10 and provides a historical review of major studies conducted in the area. He also gives an in-depth analysis of the current issues and potential problems facing many state teacher retirement programs, addressing policy issues, integration of social security and state teacher retirement systems, benefit levels, portability and vesting, investment policy, inflation retirement plans, and the ratio of dependent aged to working population.

In Chapter 11 Richard G. Salmon discusses teacher compensation during the recent era of public school reform, providing an analysis of teacher salary data from both a national and a regional perspective. He indicates that although average annual salaries paid classroom teachers have grown significantly from 1976–77 to 1986–87, adjustment for price inflation reduces the gain to a modest 5.95 percent. Over that same eleven-year period the fiscal effort made by the nation and most states has declined. Salmon also notes that the fiscal position of teachers relative to other occupations has remained remarkably constant over considerable time.

The editors of this yearbook want to extend special thanks for assistance given in preparation of manuscript by Faye Finney of Western Kentucky University. Ms. Finney's contributions included technical editing of the entire manuscript, coordination with the various authors, and communication with the publisher. Without her tireless devotion, the task would not have been completed.

Bowling Green, Kentucky   K. A.
September 10, 1987   D. M.

INTRODUCTION
Observations on Teachers' Economic Subsidies

Kern Alexander

Myriad economic and social constraints affect the adequacy of compensation of public schoolteachers in America today. One predominant and underlying factor is the citizenry's general view of the importance of the public school system. At the heart of that system is, of course, the quality of the teaching staff, the single most important element in determining the level of learning. Because they are dependent on government tax support for their well-being, however, teachers receive only marginal compensation—marginal in that most public schools are so precariously fiscally balanced that a slight shift in funding can deprive the students of an efficient level of teaching knowledge and expertise. This book examines the flow of capital between the state and the teacher.

The quality of the teaching force is largely determined by the pay that teachers receive. Whereas employment in other sectors can yield a net gain in income over a lifetime, teachers must consider the costs of "alternatives forgone" when deciding whether to remain in the public schools. The problem of determining the level and adequacies of pay, endemic to the issue of public school finance, is not new. In 1927 Ellwood Cubberley observed that "it has always been easier to secure adequate pay for policemen, firemen, city hall clerks, and general municipal employees than for teachers."[1] He noted that during the post-World War I era, the nation's economy developed in such a way that wages of carpenters, plumbers, painters, bricklayers, and other private-sector employees rose steadily, without a corresponding increase in wages for teachers. Cubberley concluded that the increased cost of education, while real, was actually being absorbed in a lowering of the teachers' standard of living: "In the purchase of what we eat and wear and in the rent we pay the increased cost, but not for education, as the teachers there help pay the increased cost of producing an output—teaching—which the public enjoys at a lower relative cost than it does almost any other thing it buys."[2]

Cubberley's point is obvious, yet quite cogent, motivating us to think not only about the economic status of public schoolteachers, but also about improvement in the quality of the schools, generally. Importantly, it compels us to consider how much should be paid and who should pay it. Since the early 1980s several states have launched drives to improve the effectiveness of the public schools through a host of legislative requirements. Some legislatures have increased funding, but many have done little to raise the general level of support. On one hand, they modify the system to give the public better schools yet, on the other hand, they fail to provide a corollary or commensurate increase in funding. Thus the public school, as an entity, may absorb the increased costs by making internal organizational adjustments or, alternatively, the schoolteachers themselves may absorb the added costs. Effectively, then, to some undefined extent, *public school teachers personally subsidize the improvements in education* from which the taxpayers benefit but do not choose to ameliorate through increased taxes.

Much has been said about the lack of productivity of the public schools. Recently, federal governmental leaders and the business community, in particular, have expressed the need for and expectation of greater efficiency and productivity. If teachers' compensation is to be increased, they argue, there should be a corresponding increase in the marginal value of the education received. The assumption is that higher salaries will motivate teachers to work harder and enable the public schools to hire better educated teachers, both of which will result in measurable educational gains. It is on this basis that merit pay is rationalized, the idea being that by providing categorical pay increases for teachers who exhibit measurably better performance, educational productivity will improve. Thus merit pay assumes that improvements in education will result from subsidizing some—but not all—teachers for their outstanding efforts. The inevitable corollary assumption is that other teachers will strive to be meritorious but will fall short of the predetermined merit goal so will not be rewarded. These are the teachers who must personally subsidize the improvements and attendant costs they make to public education. Therefore, the costs of increased educational productivity are borne by both the state and the meritorious or nonmeritorious teachers who receive no financial incentive.

In a larger sense, macroeconomic forces have considerable influence on the balance between the costs of education supported by the public and private sectors. There is always a high degree of receptivity to distributing the costs of public operations among various segments of our society. Sometimes these costs are shifted to the "workers," as in the aforementioned case of teachers. At other times the costs may be shifted to the "users" of the public service, for example through increasing public college tuition or charging fees for the use of school labs and textbooks. In other instances shifts occur as costs of government are channeled from economic class to class through changes in the tax structure; the federal government's recent tax reforms moved the burden from the more affluent to persons in lower income levels. It is difficult to determine precisely where the burden of costs of a governmental service will finally rest. But, as Musgrave observed, "it must be recognized that in the end, the entire tax burden must be borne by individuals."[3] Seldom does altruism overcome the innate propensity of individuals to push the burden off to someone else in society. Because increases in public school costs require greater outlays of public funds, and sometimes tax increases, there is a strong tendency for taxpayers to shift the burden away from themselves to either the users (students) or the workers (teachers).

This type of cost shifting has occurred in several states where the legislatures have attempted to lengthen the school day without providing a corresponding increase in funding. In 1983, for instance, the Florida senate proposed to lengthen the school day from six to seven periods but with no increase in funding for teachers' salaries and other operations. Apparently the rationale was that teachers were at school during that time anyway, and it would not inconvenience them to teach one additional hour each day.

Annually, legislators propose bills that would require students (or parents) to pay for fees for labs, transportation, use of library, textbooks, and other services and materials. Attempting to shift costs to students in this fashion shows the legislators' failure to understand

and value education as a public good, meriting the allocation of state resources derived from general taxation. Some lawmakers believe that the student as user or consumer should bear a large portion of the costs of public education. To correct this, the citizenry must be of the general conviction that the "externalities" or "social spill-overs" from education are sufficient to justify total financing of public schools from tax sources.

A reluctance to provide teachers with higher pay may also occur as a result of shifting the tax burden from the more affluent, better educated to the poorer, less educated segment of the population. Reinhold Niebuhr has noted that universal education by its very assumption and nature has caused discomfort among the more affluent and propertied classes of our society: He observes that ". . . it has always been the habit of privileged groups to deny the oppressed classes every opportunity for the cultivation of innate capacities . . .;"[4] and, if government does actually redress the needs of the lower class, the tendency is for the upper classes to structure a tax system in which the lower and middle classes pay for the services.

Most state tax structures are regressive, and much of public school revenue is dependent on the even more regressive property tax. Moreover, the middle and lower classes often reject funding for public schools that would go toward providing reasonable compensation for teachers. For so long as teachers' pay is closely linked to regressive tax structures, which generally make the most demands of the poorly educated, low income segment of the population, little change is likely to come about in the overall economic status of teachers.

In *The Next American Frontier* Robert Reich notes that Americans tend to divide the dimensions of our national life into two broad areas, the realm of government and politics and the realm of business and economics, restricting our concerns about social justice to the first realm and our concerns about economic prosperity to the second.[5] Within the former realm lies our civic concern for welfare, democratic participation, sharing of wealth, and the commonwealth. On this aspect the public common schools are premised. The business culture, on the other hand, calls for individualism, freedom, and competition. The profit motive is the holy grail, and collectivism is an anathema. To provide incentives for the aggressive and competitive spirit is the desired goal of government. Reich observes that these two spheres are becoming less distinguishable in our society, as aspects of each spill over to the other. This phenomenon applies to the public schools in numerous ways, the most obvious of which is the ageless issue of whether education should be a public- or private-sector activity.

Some Americans maintain that complete privatization of education is desirable and that society should be deschooled or that education should be left to a market economy to be purchased at whatever price supply and demand will permit. Others advocate some government financing supplemented with individual financing to be purchased at prices established by competitive schools operating in a largely unregulated economy. This is the voucher, or tuition tax credit, school of thought, which represents a peculiar amalgam of public financing and private entrepreneurial initiative. With certain of these mixtures of funding and control, the private and the public spheres may become largely indistinguishable. But whether the schools are public or private, there persists the issue of funding and ultimately the relative importance of the human resources provided by the knowledge and skills of the teacher. The extent to which the teacher is forced to subsidize the educational enterprise is present regardless of the nature of the school.

Teachers' subsidization of public education is largely passive. When educational costs rise, either through inflation or additional services, and teachers do not receive a corresponding increase in wages or benefits, then their subsidization of the public schools automatically rises. To shift increased costs of public education to the taxpayers, local school boards or legislatures must levy taxes that will address the rising costs. Legislative or constitutional provisions requiring referenda at the state or local level further increase the difficulty of public assumption of costs.

Whether the citizenry is willing to subsidize its appropriate share of educational costs is speculative and dependent on one's philosophical view of public education in the economy. That which is "appropriate" may vary greatly on a broad spectrum between the liberal and conservative views of education. The more liberal viewpoint, as enunciated by John Kenneth Galbraith, asserts that the affluent society has been undermined by a calculated starvation of the public sector. He observes that Americans have viewed some of the most trivial commodities "with pride," while conversely viewing "some of the most significant and civilizing services," such as education, as a "burden to be discharged or paid for with regret." Galbraith condemns the "failure to keep public services in minimal relation to private production" and maintains that there is a necessity to maintain a "social balance" between the two.[6]

The appropriate balance is seen to be entirely different by those on the more conservative end of the ideological spectrum. Milton and Rose Friedman maintain that the effectiveness of education is reduced as the government's role increases. They argue that education is "another example, like Social Security, of the common element in authoritarian and socialist philosophies. . . . The establishment of the school system in the United States is an island of socialism in a free market sea reflected only to a very minor extent the early emergence among intellectuals of a distrust of the market and of voluntary exchange."[7] In their view, more government financing leads to objectionable governmental control, which can be remedied only by vesting authority over the schools almost exclusively with the parents or private school authorities.

Whether schooling takes place in public or private schools, though, teachers subsidize the educational program. The Friedmans fail to recognize this important point when they state that "in schooling, the parent and child are the consumers, the teacher and school administrator the partners."[8] Actually, the teacher may be not only a producer of educational services but a financier of them as well. This is even more true in private schools than in public. Traditionally, in many parochial schools nuns taught for little or no pay, making teacher subsidization of the educational program almost complete. In private schools, the extent of teacher subsidization often varies even more than in public schools, ranging in inverse proportion from very low pay (high subsidization) in some parochial schools to relatively high wages (lower subsidization) in some elite prep schools. Of course, with their proposed voucher system, the Friedmans seek to establish a system of financing whereby public tax dollars would be used to help reduce the "in kind" subsidies contributed by private school teachers for the conduct of the private schools.

The extent of the individual subsidy varies depending on the teacher's potential for alternative employment, personal costs incurred in academic preparation to become a teacher, and attendant costs related to experience or internships required in becoming a teacher. The Friedmans note that the cost per pupil in private schools is far less than in public schools "even after account is taken of the free services of those who are nuns." . . . That's because teachers and parents are free to choose how their children are taught. Private money has replaced tax money. They further point out that many teachers in these private schools "did not have the right pieces of paper to qualify for certification to teach in public schools."[9]

In reality, public school teachers are required by the state to attend school and to participate in internships in order to be certified so as to assure the public of a minimal level of qualification. This certification process may be quite costly, particularly for a public schoolteacher who holds a bachelor's or master's degree, as required for certification, as opposed to a private schoolteacher who is not required to hold either. In short, the cost of a teacher's personal investment of time and money in becoming a teacher tends to increase the personal subsidy that teacher will give to the school. Uncertified teachers in private schools are usually paid less than public schoolteachers; but, because they generally have lower levels of training, their personal subsidy to education is less. The greatest subsidy would be provided by highly trained nuns in parochial schools who receive no pay, and the least subsidy would probably come from highly paid elite prep schoolteachers who have only a four-year liberal arts education and are not certified. The subsidy provided by public schoolteachers would fall somewhere in between.

When discussing public and private schoolteachers as a group, it is important to distinguish to whom or to what the benefits of the subsidy accrue. Public schoolteachers' subsidies go to the general public benefit, to all children in common, and to the public enterprise or commonwealth, generally. On the other hand, the beneficiaries of the subsidy in private schools, usually some general social benefit or individual students, may also be a church, a particular social or economic group, a race, or another individual. The subsidy contributed by the nun to the parochial school benefits the student and the church; it goes without saying that a relatively high percentage is for religious purposes.

It is probably impossible to establish the exact economic balance at which teacher compensation could minimize the required subsidy. Historically, teachers have been paid wages lower than those given to artisans and even day laborers. Dan Lortie observes that "economists may argue that teachers have been paid the 'going rate,' but many in our society have considered teacher incomes as somehow inappropriate given the importance of education."[10] To some this suggests that a "just wage" would provide teachers with greater income. In this regard it could be maintained that the difference between the going rate and a just wage is the amount by which the teacher personally subsidizes the public school (just wage – going rate = subsidy).

The monetary value of a subsidy is mitigated by trade-offs such as job security, a predictable and steady income, relative autonomy, and intellectual stimulation. Where these factors are sufficient to offset the net subsidy loss of the teacher, a balance is reached that will keep the teacher from seeking alternative employments. But from a purely economic viewpoint, the teacher's subsidy contributed to the public school may be most nearly assessed by the traditional benefit-cost ratio or rate of return approach to determine whether the costs incurred in becoming a teacher are offset by lifetime earnings.

In a recent study, Edlow Barker found that the benefit-cost ratio and the internal rate of return for a teacher who studied full-time for a master's degree are both negative. In other words, the costs of earning a master's degree on a full-time basis exceeded earnings. For example, he shows that on the average a person will lose .745 percent a year on the educational investment of a full-time master's degree. The benefit-cost ratio was found to be .6565, or less than a one-to-one ratio, indicating that earning a master's degree by full-time study is not economically feasible for a teacher.[11]

Such a negative result indicates that the teacher who returns to the university full-time to study for a master's degree will incur a net loss in income upon reentering the teaching ranks. It may be concluded that the extent of this net loss is the degree to which the teacher with the master's degree (earned full-time) subsidizes the public school program. A benefit-cost ratio at a breakeven one-to-one ratio would indicate that the teacher does not fiscally subsidize the public school operation but, receives no benefits either. To the extent that teachers are willing to absorb the uncompensated costs of their own training, which improves the overall quality of education, they are subsidizing the schools while taxpayers enjoy a public school program at a cost substantially below its actual monetary value. Recent proposals for five-year teacher training programs will suffer from this economic reality.

If state proposals for the improvement of education are to have a practical and lasting effect on the quality of education, policymakers must necessarily regard each in relation to its economic impact on the teacher. Programs that shift the burden of costs toward greater teacher subsidization will likely fail. To determine the proper balance requires substantial analysis, and to that end the remaining chapters in this book are devoted.

NOTES

1. Ellwood P. Cubberley, *State School Administration* (Boston: Houghton Mifflin Company, 1927), pp. 651–52.
2. Ibid., p. 652.
3. Richard A Musgrave and Peggy B. Musgrave, *Public Finance in Theory and Practice* (New York: McGraw-Hill Book Company, 1980), p. 259.
4. Reinhold Niebuhr, *Moral Man and Immoral Society* (New York: Charles Scribner's Sons, 1932), p. 118.
5. Robert B. Reich, *The Next American Frontier* (New York: Times Books, 1983), pp. 4–5.
6. John Kenneth Galbraith, *The Affluent Society* (New York: Houghton Mifflin Company, 1958), pp. 127–28.
7. Milton and Rose Friedman, *Free to Choose* (New York: Harcourt, Brace, Jovanovich, 1980), p. 154.
8. Ibid., p. 157.
9. Ibid., p. 159.
10. Dan C. Lortie, *School Teachers, A Sociological Study* (Chicago: The University of Chicago Press, 1975), p. 7.
11. Edlow Garrett Barker, "A Cost-Benefit Analysis of Investment in Graduate Education by Virginia Public School Teachers" (Ph.D. dissertation, Virginia Tech University, 1987).

1 TEACHERS IN THE ECONOMIC SYSTEM

Patricia Anthony

Benjamin Rush presents an interesting paradox concerning the U.S. schoolteacher (Runes 1947: 114):

> He is, next to mothers, the most important member of civil society. Why then is there so little rank connected with that occupation? Why do we treat it with so much neglect or contempt?

Although Rush pondered this subject in 1790, his query is relevant to us today.

In the 1985–86 school year teachers averaged an annual salary of $24,559, ranking them slightly below mail carriers in terms of occupational wages. When teacher salaries are compared with those of other occupations requiring a four-year degree, the wage gap widens significantly; in several instances, teachers are no better off financially than individuals working in occupations for which a college degree is unnecessary (Task Force 1986).

How important are the earnings of teachers in the overall reshaping of the U.S. teaching force? In responding to this question, this chapter will address several issues related to teacher salaries: (1) the current economic status of teachers; (2) factors affecting this status; and (3) the subsequent impact of economic status on this nation's public education system. First, however, a retrospective look at the economic status of teachers in the United States is provided.

A HISTORICAL PERSPECTIVE

The economic condition of the teacher has varied little since 1637, when forty-five of Boston's wealthiest citizens banded together and raised enough funds to found the Boston Latin School. By 1665 financial support for the school had become the responsibility of the town, and in fulfillment of this trust a headmaster was employed for the sum of "60 pounds per annum for his services in the school, out of town's rates and rents that belong to the school" (Small 1969: 4). Between 1636 and 1700 thirty-five grammar schools were founded in the Massachusetts Bay and Connecticut colonies, and for each school the services of a schoolmaster whose recompense amounted to between twenty and forty pounds a year were sought.

Even with the allocation of these meager wages, towns more often than not had difficulty meeting their obligations. Forced by the Massachusetts School Act of 1647 to hire schoolmasters, towns-people of many communities bade their selectmen to procure the schoolmaster's services for "as cheap as they can," a practice that resulted in schoolmasters underbidding each other when applying for a position (Small 1969).

Being hired for the job did not guarantee payment of wages, nor were salaries always paid in the form of currency. Typically, a teacher's contract called for partial payment in money, with the remaining sum to be delivered throughout the year in the form of wheat, corn, or other commodities.

Payment was often delayed, depending on the financial straits of each particular community. Schoolmasters, in some cases, had to hound town fathers in an effort to receive what was due them. One such incident resulted in a lawsuit lodged against the selectmen of Hampton, New Hampshire, by schoolmaster John Legat who sought to recover payment "for schooling and other writings done for the town" (Small 1969: 157).

In exchange for his humble wages, the schoolmaster agreed to perform a variety of tasks, which included acting as court messenger, conducting certain ceremonial services of the church, leading the Sunday choir, ringing the bell for public worship, and digging graves. One additional responsibility, by far considered the most important, was preaching to the congregation on Sundays when the resident minister was indisposed or out of town.

The eighteenth-century teacher saw little improvement in his financial situation. Most communities still paid their schoolteachers an annual salary of approximately $40. In some instances, depending on a particular community's finances, various perquisites were bestowed on teachers, such as a horse, land, or even a dwelling. By the late eighteenth century, teacher salaries in several communities had risen to $70 a year, but the effect of the Revolutionary War was evident; many towns were unable to meet their commitments to schoolteachers, forcing them to live on credit and the goodwill of their neighbors (Small 1969).

The gradual acceptance of women into the teaching ranks occurred during the early nineteenth century, and although this movement increased employment opportunities for women, it accomplished little to bolster teacher salaries.

In 1832 the state of Connecticut paid its male teachers $11 a month and its female teachers $4 (Knight and Hall 1951). The common practice of paying female teachers less than their male counterparts was soundly denounced by some educational thinkers such as Henry Barnard, who said, "I have no hesitation in saying that, in the schools which I have visited, the female teachers were as well qualified, as devoted to their duties, and really advanced their pupils as far as the same number of male teachers" (Barnard 1839: 38). Yet the practice persisted through the remainder of the nineteenth century.

By the early 1920s teachers were earning an annual salary of approximately $500 (Stuart 1949). The extension of boarding privileges to teachers was no longer a popular practice; many teachers saw half of their monthly pay consumed in meeting these needs. Twenty years later, in 1946, the average salary for teachers nationwide had risen to $2,254 with California leading the states in teacher salaries at $3,304 and Mississippi bringing up the rear with an annual salary of $984 (Knight and Hall 1951).

TEACHER SALARIES IN THE 1980s

In 1985 teachers averaged $23,500 in annual wages, a salary that places them at the lower end of the professional salary spectrum. When comparing salaries for eleven selected occupations, only plumbers, airline ticket agents, and secretaries earn less in annual wages than teachers (Task Force 1986).

A more significant contrast is noted when teacher salaries are compared with those of other professions requiring a four-year degree, such as buyers, accountants, and systems analysts. In comparing teacher salaries with this group, teachers earn roughly $9,000 less in annual wages than individuals working in these occupations (Task Force 1986).

An earlier study of thirty-five occupations arrived at similar conclusions (Feistritzer 1985). Again, teachers ranked at the bottom of the salary scale, twenty-sixth out of thirty-six occupations. With the exception of possibly two—social workers and Catholic priests— the ten occupations ranking below teachers in annual wages were all occupations for which a college degree is not a requirement.

Further comparisons between teachers and individuals with identical educational levels but who work in occupations other than the teaching field reveal similar wage discrepancies. For the 1985–86 school year, male teachers earned $26,517; female teachers earned an average of $23,543, which is substantially less (Feistritzer 1986). The average age for male teachers is forty-three; for females, forty-one. Eighty-five percent of male teachers have achieved an educational level of five or more years of college; 78 percent of female teachers have attained a similar level of education.

When teacher salaries are compared with those of other workers in an identical age range and possessing a similar educational level, teachers earn $11,726 less than their peers (Feistritzer 1986). For male teachers, the salary differential is even more pronounced. Male workers in the 35 to 44 age range, with five or more years of college, earn an average of $41,234; male teachers falling into the same age and educational level category average an annual income of $27,105 or $14,129 less than their fellow workers. A wage disparity for female teachers is also evident; however, because female workers in general do not earn salaries competitive with their male counterparts, the discrepancy between female teachers and the rest of the female working population is not as great. Female workers in the 35–44 age range, who have completed five or more years of college, earn an average salary of $26,509; female teachers in this category earn $24,102 or $2,407 less.

Is a teacher's salary adequate for supporting a family? A closer look at the teacher's economic situation in regard to (1) marital status, (2) the prevalence of "moonlighting," and (3) the continual exodus of experienced teachers to more lucrative careers would suggest that it is not.

Marital Status

Eighty-four percent of male teachers and 72 percent of all female teachers are married. These statistics are relatively unimportant by themselves; but when data on spouse employment are considered, then the economic impact of teacher marriage patterns is evident.

Ninety-one percent of the husbands of female teachers are employed in full-time positions. For married male teachers, however, the percentage for full-time employment of spouses is considerably lower. Only 54 percent of the spouses of male teachers work full-time outside the home (Feistritzer 1986). Consequently, two divergent economic patterns exist in regard to married teachers. For the married female teacher, the family's chief income provider is the male head of the household. The female teacher's salary, in many cases, is considered a second income.

The married male teacher, on the other hand, is usually the main contributor to his family's household income; and in 20 percent of the marriages, he is the sole supporter (Feistritzer 1986). Translated into dollars, this figure means that for 46 percent of all married male teachers their average annual salary of $26,517 provides the main basis of financial support for their family; and for 20 percent, this salary is the only support.

Although married female teachers generally are partners in two-income marriages, an increasing number of women teachers head households alone. As of 1980 a little over 9 million families in the United States—one out of every seven—were supported by single mothers (Feistritzer 1983); and in 1985 thirteen percent of all female teachers reported their marital status as "divorced." This high rate of female heads of households has a detrimental effect on the teaching profession because it forces good female teachers to seek more lucrative employment elsewhere. As Feistritzer and her associates observe, "sheer economic necessity is driving women . . . into higher paying professions." (Feistritzer 1983: 34).

After-School-Hours Employment

Roughly 4.8 percent of all U.S. workers hold part-time jobs in addition to their regular positions of employment. In several occupations—education, local and state government, the postal service—the rate for after-hours employment exceeds 8 percent; and of those fields teachers represent the highest number of moonlighting employees (Wisniewski and Kleine 1984). A 1982 survey conducted by the National Education Association (NEA) found that approximately half of the teachers surveyed held another job from which they earned around $2,462 annually (Toch 1982).

Male and female teachers differ significantly in their patterns concerning employment after school hours. Seventy-two percent of all male teachers hold jobs in addition to their teaching position, whereas only 33 percent of all female teachers hold such supplementary employment. When questioned as to why they moonlight, the majority (81 percent of male teachers) responded that it was for financial reasons rather than for personal satisfaction (Feistritzer 1986).

In their recent study on teachers and moonlighting, Wisniewski and Kleine (1984) found substantial evidence that a large number of teachers are forced to supplement their teacher earnings, and that in doing so they jeopardize the already fragile image of teachers as professionals. It is their contention that teachers are paid wages that do not reflect the level of professionalism accorded to other occupations requiring similar educational backgrounds; and because the majority of teachers engaged in moonlighting take jobs in nonprofessional occupations, rather than education-related types of work, these activities further demean the status of teachers.

Exodus of Experienced Teachers

According to the National Center for Education Statistics (NCES), an estimated 6 percent of the teaching force leaves the profession annually. One of the reasons most frequently cited for abandoning a teaching career in favor of another occupation is lack of adequate financial compensation. When asked if they would leave teaching for another position paying at least $5,000 more than their current job, over half (53 percent) of all teachers answered in the affirmative (Feistritzer 1986).

The younger a teacher, the greater the likelihood that he or she will leave teaching for any advancement in salary. When teachers in the 25 to 34 age group were asked if they would leave teaching for another position paying an additional $2,000 in salary, only 38 percent said that they would not. In contrast, a slim majority of teachers age 55 and over, when asked the same question, replied in the negative. Considering the age of the latter teachers, this statistic is not surprising. At age 55 and over a teacher has reached the top end of the salary scale, is tenured, and does not foresee many years left before retirement. An interesting fact about this statistic, however, is that almost an equal number of teachers (45 percent) in this age bracket would leave in order to earn an additional $2,000.

FACTORS AFFECTING THE CURRENT ECONOMIC STATUS OF TEACHERS

Emily Feistritzer (1983:1) profiles the typical U.S. teacher as

> a woman approaching her 40th birthday. She has taught 12 years, mostly in her present district. Over those dozen years she returned to . . . college . . . to acquire enough credits for a master's degree. She is married and the mother of two children. She is white and not politically active . . . teaches in a suburban elementary school, staffed largely by women . . . the principal is male . . . she [the teacher] puts in a work week slightly longer than the typical laborer, and brings home a pay check that is slightly lower.

In her description of the individual most likely to be engaged in the business of teaching, Feistritzer touches on several troubling aspects of the teaching profession:

1. The majority of teachers are married middle-aged females;
2. Although the typical teacher is armed with a master's degree, she earns less than a common laborer;
3. The salary of a typical teacher is, more often than not, a family's second income; and
4. A complacency or willingness to accept the status quo is a characteristic attributable to teachers.

These four aspects directly influence the economic situation of teachers and, in a larger sense, the condition of public education in the United States.

A Woman's Profession

Teaching is often characterized as a woman's profession and for good reason. Sixty-nine percent of the teaching profession is female. Of that 69 percent, 78 percent of all female teachers have completed five or more years of college, making them the largest single group of females in the U.S. working force with such a level of education. In fact, female teachers with five or more years of college constitute 49 percent of all female workers fitting this description.

An advanced degree is not an entrance requirement for teaching; however, over half of the teaching force has earned a master's degree. Because 69 percent of all teachers are female, the majority of teachers holding an advanced degree are women. In all fields for which an advanced degree is a prerequisite for entry, males predominate: Eighty-two percent of all lawyers are men, 83 percent of all doctors, 94 percent of all dentists, and 56 percent of all certified public accountants (Feistritzer 1986). The average annual salary for individuals in these professions is approximately $60,000 (Task Force 1986; Feistritzer 1986). Considering female teachers who have completed five or more years of college and who have an average annual salary hovering at $24,000, it is evident that a huge wage discrepancy between male- and female-dominated professions exists.

A Need for Professionals

One factor contributing to the low earning capacity of teachers is that, unlike with other professions requiring four or more years of education, there appears to be an unwillingness on the part of the public, and teachers themselves, to view the field as one that should be accorded a high degree of respect and esteem. This credibility problem is partly due to the perception that teaching is a feminized occupation that "took its current form in the 1930s and 1940s when women were expected to subordinate their career aspirations to their childrearing responsibilities and their salary expectations to the man's role as breadwinner" (Task Force 1986: 36). Other factors, however, also play a role. In recent years a series of national reports, largely negative in nature, have focused the public's attention on this nation's schools and its schoolteachers. Unfortunately, when assessing what measures need to be taken to introduce more quality into U.S. public schools, the individuals least likely to become actively involved in initiating reform are teachers. Conversely, with male-dominated professions such as medicine and law, professional standards are proposed, defined, and redefined by members of the professions themselves. Teachers play no significant role in establishing overall goals for education or in developing standards for their field.

When teacher involvement in instigating educational reforms has occurred, it has developed primarily through the teaching field's chief professional association—the union. The choice by teachers in adopting the union as their main representative body may further demean the image of the teacher as a professional. In the minds of many Americans, unions are equated with blue-collar jobs, employment for which a college degree is unnecessary. Doctors and lawyers, on the other hand, belong to associations that exude professionalism: They set professional standards for their fields, censure offending members by meting out punishments ranging from a simple reprimand to stripping individuals of their licenses to practice, and publish highly regarded professional journals.

According to Darling-Hammond (1984: 16), any semblance of this type of professionalism existing in teaching was abandoned during the 1970s in preference to the adoption of what was considered a more progressive model for education:

> Based on a factory model of schooling in which teachers are semi-skilled, low-paid workers, at least two-thirds of the states enacted policies . . . that sought to standardize and regulate teacher behaviors. Elaborate accountability schemes such as management-by-objectives, competency-based education, minimum competency testing, and other efforts to develop a teacherproof curriculum were imposed.

The authors of *A Nation Prepared* (Task Force 1986: 39) strongly suggest that teachers of the 1980s are still perceived in this light, citing the diminished role that teachers play in making decisions even within their own academic subject areas and the passive reliance of teachers on "rules made by others [to] govern their behavior at every turn" as examples of the prevalency of this factory-worker mentality in the field of teaching.

This perception of teachers provides a stark contrast to the professional status accorded to individuals in other fields and probably directly affects teacher salaries. A vicious cycle evolves: (1) Teachers—although their field requires the same educational level as others engaged in business, law, or medicine—are compensated at semi-skilled employment wages; (2) the low salaries paid within the teaching profession fail to attract individuals who would bring to teaching a sense of professionalism, initiative, and confident expertise; and therefore, (3) persons most likely to enter teaching are those individuals who will perpetuate the factory worker syndrome and (4) will be content with the status quo—that is, stultifying working conditions and low wages. The end result is that neither teacher salaries nor the public's respect for the teaching profession is significantly elevated, and the cycle continues.

Undesirable Working Conditions

Coupled with the public's perception of teaching as a feminized occupation and the corresponding lack of esteem for teaching as a profession, there is a third element that may influence teacher salaries—the working conditions. State efforts to entice higher-achieving college graduates away from other professions into teaching will probably be unsuccessful unless the environment in which teachers work undergoes significant changes.

Authors of *A Nation Prepared* contrast the working conditions for teachers and those for other professionals, citing how "decisions made by curriculum supervisors, teacher training experts, outside consultants and authors of teachers' guides determine how a teacher is to teach," while an "endless array of policies succeed in constraining the exercise of the teacher's independent judgment on almost every matter of moment" (Task Force 1986: 38–39). On the other hand, individuals who occupy positions within the upper levels of other professions are given a great deal of latitude in which to operate:

> Those people are, and tend to think of themselves, as professionals. Professional work is characterized by the assumption that the job of the professional is to bring special expertise and judgment to bear on the work at hand. Because their expertise and judgment is respected and they alone are presumed to have it, professionals enjoy a high degree of autonomy in carrying out their work.

Not only may lack of autonomy tend to discourage some candidates from considering teaching as a career, but such conditions also may drive superior teachers out of the teaching ranks and into school administration. Such a career move has the effect of immediately providing for the individual the three prerogatives lacking in the field of teaching: (1) a higher salary, (2) increased respect and esteem, and (3) more professional discretion. Furthermore, because the vast majority of educational leadership roles are occupied by men—83 percent of all principals are men; 98 percent of all superintendents; 82 percent of all college deans; and 74 percent of all state education officials (Metropolitan Life 1986)—the female teacher who leaves the profession for the more prestigious administrative position has the additional satisfaction of having entered a male-dominated profession.

When teacher salaries are compared to those of administrators, it becomes more evident why more superior teachers make the career jump into administration. According to a recent U.S. Bureau of Labor Statistics *Occupational Outlook Handbook* (1984–85 edition), the average school principal's salary is $33,000. For this same year, teaching salaries were $13,000 less. Even accounting for a shorter work year, this difference is significant. Talented teachers are undoubtedly tempted to leave the classroom and to enter administration even if their professional interest lies in working directly with students in the classroom.

Supply and Demand

A final element affecting teacher salaries is a free-market economy issue—that of supply and demand. Parents desire quality education for their children. In order to attract qualified individuals to teaching as a profession, higher salaries must be paid. As salaries increase, people who would not normally consider teaching as a career possibility become interested and decide to enter the teaching field.

During the past decade, a relative wage increase for teachers has not occurred; in fact, quite the opposite has taken place. The teaching profession has remained unattractive to bright, qualified college students, and colleges of education have witnessed a considerable decline in their enrollments. The National Center for Education Information (NCEI) reports that in 1983 there were approximately 135,000 graduating new teachers in contrast with the 289,000 students who graduated from teacher programs ten years earlier. State education officials across the country have been predicting a teacher shortage into the twenty-first century. Individual state needs vary, but data from the National Center for Education Statistics (NCES) have indicated that the demand for teachers will exceed the supply for at least the remainder of this decade, particularly in the areas of preprimary and elementary education (Feistritzer 1984).

In 1984 seven states were already experiencing a teacher supply shortage in elementary and one in preprimary. Twenty-eight states reported shortages of secondary teachers, particularly in math and science teachers. Most significantly, ten states project that they will experience teacher shortages for all grade levels during the middle 1990s, and nineteen states predict that across-the-board shortages will occur within the next five years (Feistritzer 1984). These current and projected shortages have spurred some states to enact programs that pay particular disciplines, such as science and math, salaries competitive with other professions in order to entice qualified individuals.

Because the determination of teacher salaries is not purely controlled by the fluctuations of the marketplace, supply and demand does not completely govern the amount of salary paid to a teacher. Three other factors exert varying degrees of influence on state salary scales: (1) the increase or decline of student populations; (2) an individual state legislature's posture on the worth of its teachers; and (3) the types of programs prioritized by the legislature and then implemented through state education laws. The effect of two of these factors—pupil enrollment and state educational priorities—may very positively affect teacher salaries.

Pupil Enrollment

The largest increase in pupil enrollment is predicted for children under age 5, whose numbers have increased by 9 percent during the past three years. In previous years, children under age 5 would not be considered a school-related problem; however, due to the pervasiveness of poverty within the ranks of the very young, these children do and will continue to require educational services prior to first grade. Such services are provided through government- and state-sponsored programs such as Head Start. Coinciding with the jump in the preprimary population, there has been projected a 12.2 percent increase in the school-age population for the next fifteen years. The college-age population will decline by 14.4 percent up to the end of this century (Feistritzer 1985).

In response to these shifts in the school-age population, additional teachers will be needed almost immediately at the elementary level, and secondary education will experience a shortage during the 1990s. If teacher salaries are elevated to a level where they are competitive with other professions currently attracting academically capable college students, the anticipated teacher shortage might serve as a conduit for funneling quality persons into the field of education.

State Educational Priorities

With the passage of major education legislation in many of the states, a new need for qualified teachers has appeared. Subjects recently shunted aside as unnecessary (such as foreign languages, music, and art), have been reinstated, and others (such as advanced math and science courses) have gained in popularity due to stricter state laws governing high school credit and requirements necessary for college entrance. Only eight states report that they are experiencing no teacher shortages in the math and science areas, and fifteen states lack enough foreign language teachers to supply their needs (Feistritzer 1986). In the face of the growing shortage of these specialized teachers, several states have enacted programs whereby emergency teaching certificates are being issued to individuals meeting specific requirements for teaching a particular subject. In addition, several states have offered stipends to teachers willing to become certified in a subject area experiencing a teacher shortage or are offering higher salaries to individuals interested in teaching those particular subjects as a means to attract qualified people who might normally put their mathematical or scientific skills to use in industry.

STATE TEACHER SALARY SCALES:
THE CURRENT STATUS

The average teacher salary for the 1985–86 school year was $24,559. Male teachers earned an average annual wage of $26,517, and female teachers earned less: $23,543 (Feistritzer 1986). These averages mask substantial diversity in the wages earned by individual teachers among the fifty states.

Of all teachers in the United States, one-third work in only five states, of which three—New York, California, and Illinois—rank among the top ten states in teacher salaries (Feistritzer 1985). The other two, Texas and Pennsylvania, rank fourteenth and eighteenth, respectively.

For the 1984–85 school year, average teacher salaries across the United States ranged from a high in Alaska of $39,751 down to a low of $15,971 in Mississippi (Feistritzer 1986). Considering that the majority of U.S. teachers have taught for fifteen years, the average salary for all teachers is skewed toward older persons in the teaching force. Beginning salaries for teachers are much lower; in 1982 the average entry wage in teaching was approximately $14,000 (Feistritzer 1985).

State Effort for Teacher Salaries

How do individual states compare in their efforts to adequately compensate teachers? In order to achieve a true comparison of state efforts in paying teacher salaries, the fiscal capacity of each state must be considered. One viable method for calculating state fiscal capacity is the representative tax system that applies national average tax rates to all potential standardized tax bases within a state. This method provides a reasonably accurate picture of any state's level of economic resources (Johns, Morphet, and Alexander 1983).

The relative amount of a state's average teacher salary is directly contingent on the fiscal capacity of a state and its electorate's propensity to utilize that capacity for education. Tax capacity figures (Advisory Commission on Intergovernmental Relations 1986) provide a basis for comparison regarding the willingness of particular states to commit a larger share of state funds toward better teacher salaries.

As evidenced in Table 1–1, high salaries do not necessarily denote high effort; in fact, the three states that put forth the least amount of effort—Alaska, Nevada, and Wyoming—pay above the national average in teacher salaries. Alaska, which leads the nation in the amount it pays its teachers, is the most fiscally able state in the country, with a tax capacity almost three times the national average. In comparison with other states, Alaska's average teacher salary for the 1982–83 school year—$33,953—is quite high.

On the other hand, the five states exhibiting the greatest effort in teacher salaries—Rhode Island, Michigan, New York, Wisconsin, and Oregon—all fall below the national average in tax capacity. Rhode Island, which is at the national average for per capita income, but below for tax capacity, puts forth the highest effort in teacher sal-

Table 1-1. State Effort for Teacher Salaries and Rank among the Fifty
States, 1983.

	Average Salary	Effort Index	Capacity as Percentage of U.S. Average[a]	Effort Rank
Highest five states:				
Rhode Island	$23,175	22.97	88.5%	1
Michigan	23,965	22.59	90.2	2
New York	25,100	22.37	95.4	3
Wisconsin	20,940	20.43	87.2	4
Oregon	22,334	19.89	88.2	5
Lowest five states:				
Texas	$19,500	13.41	124.0%	46
New Hampshire	15,353	12.13	107.6	47
Nevada	20,944	12.10	147.2	48
Wyoming	24,000	11.19	182.4	49
Alaska	33,953	10.62	271.9	50

a. Halstead's representative tax system is used as the measure of capacity (Halstead 1978).

aries. Alabama, a poor state when measured by either the representative tax system or per capita personal income, is ranked seventh. The poorest of the fifty states, Mississippi, ranks well above the more fiscally able states of Florida and Massachusetts. Mississippi ranks twenty-second, whereas Massachusetts and Florida rank thirty-seventh and thirty-fourth, respectively.

Caution must be exercised when comparing state effort indexes. As an earlier study conducted on state effort for instructional staff salaries noted, "Economic circumstances, economic growth rate, educational values, and social characteristics differ across the country. . . . Regional comparisons are much more valid since the economic and social characteristics within a region are not likely to be so extreme" (Richardson and Williams 1981: 198).

As evidenced in Table 1-2, when the forty-eight contiguous states are clustered into eight different regions, the Great Lakes region exhibits the highest effort in teacher salaries. The Southwest puts forth the least amount of effort of all eight regions.

Intraregion comparisons reveal differences in effort among states that by virtue of proximity share a more common heritage in relation

Table 1-2. Regional Effort for Teacher Salaries and Rank among the Eight Regions, 1983.

Region	Effort Index	Percentage of National Effort Index
United States	17.46	—
Great Lakes	20.46	116.6
Mideast	18.43	105.6
Southeast	17.37	99.5
Far West	16.60	95.1
Plains	16.08	92.1
New England	15.24	86.5
Rocky Mountains	15.11	86.5
Southwest	14.78	84.7

to economic ability, educational values, and social characteristics. In the New England region, New Hampshire exerts the least amount of effort for teacher salaries, although its tax capacity and personal income measures are above the national average. Connecticut, with both tax capacity and per capita personal income well above those indexes for the nation as a whole, ranks fourth out of the six New England states in effort for teacher salaries. Massachusetts in 1979 led the fifty states in effort; Massachusetts ranks second in the region and, as previously noted, now ranks thirty-seventh in the nation. Undoubtedly, reduction in revenue caused by Proposition 2½ (the tax limitation measure passed by Massachusetts voters in 1980) has contributed to this relative decline in effort.

In the Southeast, Florida is last when its effort is compared with that of the other eleven states in that region. This is in spite of the fact that Florida ranks second within the region in both personal income and tax capacity.

TEACHER COMPENSATION: ITS IMPACT ON U.S. PUBLIC EDUCATION

Nowhere is the impact of inadequate teacher compensation more apparent and its deleterious effect on the future of this nation's public education system more compelling than in the current class enrollments of colleges of education. Fox (1984: 215), in describing the present plight of teacher education programs, asserts, "A compelling body of data indicates that our children, on the average, are being taught by individuals who do not score well on tests of academic ability."

It is an unfortunate truism that prospective education majors lag far behind other college-bound high school seniors when it comes to scoring well on college entrance examinations. In 1973 potential education majors scored twenty-seven points below other high school seniors on the verbal section of the Scholastic Aptitude Test (SAT) and thirty-two points below all other seniors in math. By 1981 this margin had widened to thirty-four points below the average on the verbal and forty-eight points below in math (Fox 1984). Because college acceptance and acceptance into the college of a student's choice depend largely on the score earned on the college entrance examination, this continued low performance of potential education majors clearly suggests that the bulk of this nation's future teachers are being drawn from the lower academic ranks of senior high school classes, whose members have discovered that schools of education act as a mecca for the less academically able student.

A further substantiation of this trend—the weaker academic student considering teaching as a career—is apparent when the current high school pool of students is examined. Although the number of high-caliber students who are willing to commit themselves to a teaching career has decreased, the percentage of potential education majors being drawn from general and vocational-oriented high school programs has risen dramatically. At the present time, approximately half of future U.S. teachers have graduated from secondary programs that are not geared for college preparation (Task Force 1986). This fact is of significant import in view of the findings reported from a group of early 1970s studies investigating the relationship between teacher verbal ability and student achievement (Hanushek 1972; Michelson 1970; Bowles 1970). Each of these studies reported a positive relationship between the two variables; therefore, the current influx of academically weak students into the field of teaching should be a source of concern in light of present state efforts to upgrade the quality of education in public schools.

An additional cause for concern has been cited by Vance and Schlechty (1982) in their study examining the academic quality of the U.S. teaching force. Vance and Schlechty discovered that teachers most likely to leave the teaching profession are those individuals who previously were identified through their SAT scores as being among the most academically able within their field. Consequently, the teaching profession faces continual devitalization; as the best and the brightest teachers leave the field for greener pastures, their vacant positions are replenished with below-average or mediocre recruits.

SUMMARY: OBSERVATIONS ON TEACHER SALARIES AND THE QUALITY OF EDUCATION

In their examination of what connotes an appropriate teacher salary, Richardson and Williams (1981: 193) state that

> teacher salaries should reflect (1) the social and educational contribution each teacher makes to students in the educational environment; (2) the value and significance that the public places on education; and (3) the number of qualified individuals available for employment as teachers.

Perhaps the pivotal point about which the entire teacher salary question revolves is contained in the second clause of the above observation—exactly how important is public education to the U.S. people? If education is of little significance to most Americans, then it stands to reason that our public school systems will be, at best, mediocre institutions staffed by individuals unable to obtain more advantageous employment in other professions, with the final product being, by and large, average-thinking students.

To some extent, this supposition is a valid one. When U.S., Japanese, and Taiwanese mothers were queried concerning how satisfied they were with their eighth graders' performances in mathematics, U.S. mothers asserted that they were satisfied, although U.S. scores in mathematics fell far below those of the other students. In a companion study examining twelfth graders' scores in algebra and calculus, Americans were found to be deficient again, with the lowest score out of twelve countries (Walberg 1986).

Recognizing the widening educational gap and its resultant effect on this nation's economy, educational leaders, government officials, and concerned citizens have lobbied for educational reforms. Such reforms have touched on all facets of education, and, for many, the center of concentration has been the U.S. teaching force. Throughout all the ensuing debates and buried beneath all the statistical data, one concept has withstood the battering of both the pros and cons: In order to attract and retain quality teachers, the financial compensation for the job must in itself be rewarding. If that is indeed the case, then an appropriate teacher's salary will reflect the social and educational contribution that each teacher provides for his or her students, and the number of qualified persons seeking positions in the teaching force will increase.

REFERENCES

Advisory Commission on Intergovernmental Relations. 1986. *1983 Tax Capacity of the States.* Washington, D.C.: U.S. Government Printing Office.

Barnard, Henry. 1839. *First Annual Report.* Connecticut.

Bowles, Samuel. 1970. "Towards an Education Production Function." In *Education, Income, and Human Capital,* edited by W. Lee Hanson, New York: Columbia University Press.

Bureau of Labor Statistics. 1985. *Occupational Outlook Handbook, 1984–85 Edition.* Washington, D.C.: U.S. Department of Labor.

Darling-Hammond, Linda. 1984. *Beyond the Commission Reports.* Santa Monica, Calif.: Rand Corporation.

Feistritzer, C. Emily. 1983. *The Condition of Teaching.* Princeton: Carnegie Foundation for the Advancement of Teaching.

_____. 1984. *The Making of a Teacher.* Washington, D.C.: National Center for Education Information.

_____. 1985. *The Condition of Teaching.* Princeton: Carnegie Foundation for the Advancement of Teaching.

_____. 1986. *Profile of Teachers in the U.S.* Washington, D.C.: National Center for Education Information.

Fox, James N. 1984. "Restructuring the Teacher Work Force to Attract the Best and the Brightest." *Journal of Education Finance* 10 (2) (Fall): 214–37.

Halstead, Kent D. 1978. *Tax Wealth in Fifty States.* Washington, D.C.: U.S. Government Printing Office.

Hanushek, Eric A. 1972. *Education and Race: An Analysis of the Educational Production Process.* Lexington, Mass.: Lexington Books.

Johns, Roe L., Edgar L. Morpher, and Kern Alexander. 1983. *The Economics and Financing of Education.* Englewood Cliffs, N.J.: Prentice-Hall.

Knight, Edgar. W., and Clifton L. Hall. 1951. *Readings in American Educational History.* New York: Greenwood Press.

Michelson, Stephan. 1970. "The Association of Teacher Resourceness with Children's Characteristics." In *Do Teachers Make a Difference?* Washington, D.C.: U.S. Department of Health, Education, and Welfare, Office of Education.

Pipho, Chris. 1986a. "Education Reform—It Looks Like a Keeper." *Phi Delta Kappan* 67 (10) (June): 701–02.

———. 1986b. "Quantity vs. Quality: States Aim to Improve Teaching and Teachers." *Phi Delta Kappan* 67 (5) (January): 333–34.

Richardson, James, and Trent Williams. 1981. "Determining an Appropriate Teacher Salary." *Journal of Education Finance* 7 (2) (Fall): 189–204.

Runes, D.D. 1947. *The Selected Writings of Benjamin Rush.* New York: Philosophical Library.

Small, Walter H. 1969. *Early New England Schools.* New York: Arno Press and The New York Times.

Stuart, Jesse. 1949. *The Thread That Runs So True.* New York: Charles Scribner's.

Task Force on Teaching as a Profession. 1986. *A Nation Prepared: Teachers for the Twenty-First Century.* New York: Carnegie Forum on Education and the Economy.

Toch, Thomas. 1982. "Teachers Today Are Older, Poorer, and Much Less Happy with Career." *Education Week* (March 10): 7–10.

Vance, Victor, and Phillip C. Schlechty. 1982. "The Distribution of Academic Ability in the Teaching Force: Policy Implications," *Phi Delta Kappan* 64 (1) (September): 23.

Walberg, Herbert J. 1986. "What Works in a Nation Still at Risk." *Educational Leadership* 44 (1) (September): 7–10.

Wisniewski, Richard, and Paul Kleine. 1984. "Teacher Moonlighting: An Unstudied Phenomenon." *Phi Delta Kappan* 65 (8) (April): 553–55.

2 TEACHER EDUCATION RECOMMENDATIONS IN THE SCHOOL REFORM REPORTS

K. Forbis Jordan

Starting with *A Nation at Risk*—the report from Secretary of Education T. E. Bell's National Commission on Excellence in Education— in the spring of 1983, thirteen major national reform reports have presented a variety of recommendations for improving the education of teachers for U.S. public elementary and secondary schools. These reports on teacher education have addressed different types of problems and have had different orientations. Principal areas of concern have been teacher preparation, performance, pay, and working conditions. Interest also has been expressed in changes that might attract more able persons to teaching careers.

The 1983 reform reports, exemplified by *A Nation at Risk* (NCEE 1983) and *Action for Excellence* from the Education Commission of the States (ECS 1983), included recommendations related to high school graduation requirements, the school day, and student expectations. There was general agreement that teachers were critically important and needed to be better prepared; however, improvement of teaching forces was not the major focus. This pattern contrasts with later reports in 1985 and 1986—those from the Carnegie Forum (1986), Council for Economic Development (1985), American Association of Colleges for Teacher Education (1986), Southern Regional

The views expressed here are those of the author and should not be understood to represent the position of either the Library of Congress or the Congressional Research Service.

Education Board (1986), National Governors' Association (1986b), and the Holmes Group (1986). These later reports tended to focus on changes in teacher education programs, higher teacher pay, and improved working conditions for teachers as critical elements in the efforts to reform the schools.

This chapter summarizes and compares the principle reform report recommendations on teacher preparation and the role of the teacher in the school. It also summarizes information on state funding for education reform related to teachers and draws conclusions about the key issues highlighted in these reform reports.

COMPOSITION OF REFORM GROUPS

Efforts to understand the recommendations of the various reports, the context in which they were developed, and possible reasons for differences may be enhanced by a discussion of the composition of the various groups and commissions. The National Commission on Excellence in Education, the Carnegie Forum on Education, the Education Commission of the States (ECS), and the Committee for Economic Development (CED) groups consisted of a mixture of persons from the business community, public life, elementary and secondary education, and higher education. The National Science Board Commission on Precollege Education in Mathematics, Science, and Technology (NSB) was composed of individuals from scientific fields in the private sector and higher education. Except for the superintendent of schools from Las Vegas, the Twentieth-Century Fund task force consisted of persons from higher education; the past experiences and interests of the members would suggest a high level of interest in urban education issues. The membership of the National Commission for Excellence in Teacher Education (NCETE) consisted of college and university administrators, elected public officials, representatives from the national teachers' organizations, a past-president of the National School Boards Association, and a superintendent of schools. The Southern Regional Education Board (SREB) statement is a policy position from the board rather than from a study group or a commission.

The NGA report was prepared by the governors under the auspices of the National Governors' Association, but this report is different in that the recommendations were not adopted by the group. The chairman of the Task Force on Teaching was Governor Kean of New Jersey.

The Holmes Group consisted entirely of self-selected deans of schools and colleges of education. Some of these institutions have large teacher education programs; others do not, but the report indicated that research was a central responsibility of the institutions (Holmes 1986).

Even though others may have been involved in phases of the data gathering and analysis, the reports suggest that Ernest Boyer, John Goodlad, and Theodore Sizer were the principal authors of their reports. However, Goodlad and Boyer did have advisory groups composed of educators and public figures.

Among all groups, teachers, school administrators, and parents appear to have been minimally represented. However, employers of the schools' graduates and public officials were quite evident in the membership. On a few groups, college and university administrators were heavily represented.

TEACHER PREPARATION PROGRAM

Recommendations related to the preparation of elementary and secondary school teachers were contained in virtually all of the reform reports. Areas of concern included length and content of the program, entrance and exit requirements, performance standards, and clinical experiences.

Current Teacher Education Programs

The following brief review of current teacher education programs will provide background for the subsequent discussion. Programs for students desiring to be secondary school teachers are different from those for students preparing to be elementary school teachers. Most current teacher education programs are completed in the four-year course of studies leading to the baccalaureate degree, but a few institutions have initiated five-year programs.

Depending on the organization and policies of the institution attended, students completing teacher preparation programs for secondary school teachers may be designated as having an education major or a major in the subject to be taught. A very high percentage of the students preparing to be secondary school teachers receive a bachelor of arts or sciences degree related to the academic department offering the teaching field. The number of academic credit hours taken in the subject to be taught often is equivalent to the number of hours required for an academic major, but there may be some difference in specific courses. Prospective secondary school teachers average about 35 to 40 percent of their credit hours in the field in which they plan to teach, or in other liberal arts courses. Students preparing to be secondary school teachers also are required to take a series of professional education courses in teaching methods, educational psychology, and history and structure of education, and to complete an internship or "student teaching" clinical experience in a school setting. These professional education courses and clinical experiences often represent about 20 percent of the total credit hours required for the baccalaureate degree (NCETE 1985).

Those students preparing to be elementary school teachers usually are classified as majors in elementary education. Programs for these students typically consists of (1) a general education block of courses, (2) academic courses related to subjects taught in elementary schools, (3) professional education courses related to elementary education (teaching methods for elementary school subjects, educational psychology, and history and structure of education), and (4) an internship or "student teaching" experience in an elementary school. Professional education courses and clinical experiences for persons preparing to be elementary school teachers normally represent about 40 percent of the total credit hours required for the baccalaureate degree. Collegiate programs for persons preparing to be elementary school teachers often are highly structured, and the number of courses required for state licensing often provides limited opportunity for electives (NCETE 1985).

Report Recommendations

The reform reports took different approaches in their recommendations about ways to improve teacher education programs. Some addressed pedagogical (professional education) and subject matter content issues; others focused on the level at which teacher education programs should be offered; and still others identified the parties that should be responsible for initiating reforms in teacher education. CED called for the creation of a national commission to address the issue of standards for teacher education programs. (Both the Holmes Group and NCETE were to some degree "national commissions" whose primary function was to study teacher education programs.) NGA and SREB advocated that the governors appoint ad hoc groups to promote reforms or call on state boards of education and higher education institutions to form such groups.

As an indicator of its recognition of the importance of teacher education, NCETE recommended the creation of a National Academy for Teacher Education. Financial support could come from institutional and corporate memberships. Through the academy persons interested in teacher education from higher education institutions, the schools, and the private sector could be brought together to discuss common problems and assist in efforts to improve teacher education.

NGA did not propose a set of changes in teacher education programs but instead advocated that each state study the various reform reports. Governors were called on to create statewide advisory panels and to direct the chief state school officer to convene professional educators and parents and ask them to identify opportunities and obstacles related to improving the schools.

Location of Program.   The issue of the location of teacher education programs was addressed only by NCETE in its recommendation that teacher education programs be in colleges and universities rather than apprenticeship programs in schools. NCETE's contention was that teacher education programs should include not only development of teaching skills but also mastery of the subject to be taught and of the principles of teaching and learning.

Length of Program.   In those reform reports that provide sufficient detail, the general assumption appeared to be that teacher preparation programs should encompass five years; the chief differences were whether to maintain and reform or to abolish professional education courses in the baccalaureate degree program. (The Carnegie Forum appeared to recommend that the teacher preparation program should extend over six years.) The Holmes Group and the Carnegie Forum recommended abolition of the undergraduate education major and a strengthening of academic preparation. The Carnegie Forum also recommended that professional education be made a graduate-level enterprise. NCETE recognized that adequate prepara-

tion for teachers likely would require a year beyond the baccalaureate degree, and several NCETE members indicated that a minimum
of four years should be devoted to the liberal arts component of the
teacher education program with professional education coming in the
fifth year. Boyer appeared to have assumed continuation of professional education programs at the undergraduate level and extension
of the teacher preparation program into the fifth year.

SREB took a different position on length of program and contended that evidence does not show that extended programs will produce better teachers, attract more talented persons into teaching, or
be cost-effective. SREB recommended that extended teacher education programs should be considered only after careful examination of
the current four-year programs, that action to extend programs
should be based on improvements in the demonstrated teaching ability of the graduates, and also that such decisions should be shown to
be worth the cost. NGA also recommended that caution be exercised
on lengthening programs but advocated that governors encourage
competition among various teacher education approaches.

ECS (1983), NSF (1983), Twentieth-Century Fund (1983), Goodlad (1983), Sizer (1984), and NCEA (1983) reports were essentially
silent on this particular issue, but the ECS, NSF, and Goodlad reports did emphasize that increased attention should be placed on
mastery of content in the subjects to be taught.

The recommendations of the Holmes Group (1986) were the most
detailed; three professional career levels were recommended. First-
level persons would be required to have a bachelor's degree with a
major in the subject to be taught; second-level persons would have
received the master's degree. Third-level career professionals would
have to demonstrate outstanding professional practice and have further specialized study in an academic subject, student learning, or
pedagogy at the level of the doctorate or its equivalent.

Program Content. The interest in program content is illustrated in
the rather consistently stated or implied recommendation among the
reports that secondary school teachers should have a full academic
major in the discipline to be taught, supplemented by professional
education courses and an internship that would develop professional
knowledge and skills. The NCEE, Holmes Group, and SREB contended that teachers should demonstrate competence in their academic discipline. The Carnegie Forum and the Holmes Group recom-

mended that a bachelor's degree in the arts and sciences in the subject to be taught be a prerequisite for all teachers. Goodlad contended that teachers should be knowledgeable in the content of the subjects that they would be teaching. The ECS report recommended that greater emphasis be placed on academic knowledge in the training of teachers, and NCETE took a more expansive position in calling for teachers to have a liberal education equivalent to the best-educated members of the community. (Several members of NCETE, in a concurring comment, advocated that all teachers should have at least one academic major.)

Evidently, Boyer, NSB, and SREB assumed the continuation of the current baccalaureate degree program for preparing teachers. They recommended that the program should include a common core of liberal arts or general education. Under Boyer's recommendations, students would be required to complete a major in an academic discipline and to observe elementary or secondary classroom teaching during their junior and senior years.

The concept of pedagogy (the art or science of teaching) was also addressed by the various reports. The Holmes Group called for a reorientation of pedagogy so that students would develop an understanding of the discipline in the subject to be taught, the methods for teaching the subject, and the methods and techniques used to assess professional performance and evaluate instruction. ECS contained specific recommendations for a "renewed" teacher education curriculum and for steps to be taken to increase teachers' use and application of technology. SREB contended that there was not "common agreement" about the core of knowledge needed to be an effective teacher and recommended (1) that courses in teacher education programs should "measure up to university-wide standards" and (2) that colleges of education should reevaluate all programs to determine the needed content with special attention to reducing the number of methods courses for prospective elementary teachers. NSF advocated that prospective teachers be required to take a limited number of professional education courses, and the Carnegie Forum took a more general approach in its recommendation that graduate schools of education should develop a new professional curriculum with the focus on students' developing a systematic knowledge of teaching, including internships and residencies.

Goodlad possibly gave greatest attention to professional education or pedagogy by recommending that teachers should have an interest in both the learner and the subject to be taught and also that teachers should understand and practice the pedagogical techniques designed to keep the student overtly and covertly engaged in learning. To bring about greater institutional commitment and broader faculty involvement in teacher education, Goodlad recommended that faculties from the academic disciplines should be involved in the teacher education program by using a team-teaching approach in the methods courses. He also stressed that teachers should understand human development, be sensitive to individual differences, and be dedicated teaching. Goodlad further recommended that the content of teacher education programs should include components that would prepare teachers to use alternate teaching methods, diagnostic tests, evaluation feedback, and praise for students.

Admission, Performance, and Exit Standards.   Several reports included recommendations related to admission, performance, and exit standards for the teacher preparation program. The NCEE recommended that persons preparing to teach be required to meet high educational standards and demonstrate an aptitude for teaching. Boyer (1983), CED, ECS, NCETE, and SREB called for high standards for admission and retention into the teacher education program. Boyer would admit students into teacher education programs after careful selection at the start of their junior year only if they had attained minimum grade point average standards and had satisfactory recommendations from their professors in required courses. NCETE recommended that a person should demonstrate knowledge of subject to be taught, the process of teaching, and the ability to teach effectively before being graduated from a teacher education program. The Holmes Group recommended that entry-level teachers be required to pass a written test in each subject to be taught.

State legislatures and state boards of education have taken action to implement recommendations in this area. The American Association of Colleges of Teacher Education reported that by June 1986 as a result of state legislative or regulatory mandates the schools, colleges, or departments of education in forty-four states were using or developing statewide required entry, exit, and/or certification examinations for teachers (AACTE 1986).

Clinical Experiences.   Most current teacher preparation programs include clinical experiences such as classroom observation and internships or student teaching. Support for strengthening these clinical experiences for prospective teachers came from the Boyer, Carnegie Forum, Goodlad, Holmes Group, NSF, and SREB reports.

The Carnegie Forum advocated that the teacher education program should include systematic internships and residencies. After completion of the core curriculum and an academic major, Boyer's fifth year would consist of an instructional and internship experience including the core courses to meet the special needs of teachers. Boyer also recommended that the fifth year include seminars with professors in the disciplines; these professors would be expected to relate the knowledge in their fields to a contemporary political or social theme. Goodlad recommended that requirements for prospective teachers include a two-year program of professional studies and clinical experiences and an internship, prior to their receiving a regular license. He would limit internships to demonstration schools; involve university faculty members oriented to research and development in school organization, teaching, and curriculum in demonstration schools; and use clinical teachers from elementary and secondary schools on university faculties.

The Holmes Group advocated that new connections be established with the schools and that good elementary and secondary teachers be brought into universities to work with prospective teachers and with teacher educators. The Holmes Group also recommended that the clinical component be an integral part of the teacher education program with formal interaction between the institution and the clinical sites.

Continuing Education. The importance of continuing education programs in school improvement efforts was recognized in most of the reports. Boyer recommended that local school districts implement a continuing education program that would serve all teachers and meet tests of relevance and substance. The Carnegie Forum viewed continuing education programs as having two functions: keeping teachers current and assisting board-certified teachers in their efforts to qualify for an advanced certificate. Goodlad had a somewhat different perspective on continuing education; he called for staff development programs that would address problems that teachers perceive to be interfering with their teaching role.

ECS supported continuing education but viewed such programs more from a personnel management than from a curriculum or staff development perspective. The position was that teachers in difficulty should be given all possible encouragement and assistance to improve; however, if there were no progress, then the school district should dismiss the teacher.

The NSB supported continuing education and recommended that the federal government fund programs for retraining teachers and that each state establish at least one regional training and resource center for teachers. ECS also called for states to establish better inservice education programs; NCETE called on state boards of education to make the professional development of teachers a top priority. NSB called for states to develop teacher retraining programs in cooperation with colleges and universities.

NGA considered continuing education to be a part of the recognition program for teachers as well as a part of a staff development program. Teacher academies, summer symposia, and annual convocations on excellence in teaching were advocated as ways to improve teaching.

Responsibility for Implementation. The reports took different approaches in fixing responsibility for improving teacher education programs. Various positions are illustrated by the ECS report recommendation that states and local school boards improve the ways that teachers are trained and recruited (and paid), and the NSF recommendation that states develop teacher training programs in cooperation with colleges and universities. NGA called on governors to convene statewide panels to recommend the state's agenda and also advocated that higher education leaders in the state be convened for the purpose of identifying what should be done and how to proceed.

The complexities of reforming teacher preparation programs were illustrated in the NCETE recommendations. For example, NCETE recommended that higher education institutions study, design, and provide teacher education programs and that states be responsible for approving these programs. NCETE also urged that the federal government and the states increase their support for educational research and development. Specifically, NCETE called for states to provide higher education institutions with supplemental funding to design, test, and evaluate new approaches in teacher education.

A contrasting position on implementation is that the major responsibility for initiating and supporting reform of teacher preparation programs rests with the institutions of higher education. Goodlad recommended that undergraduate faculties redesign the curriculum to devise the best general education for elementary school teachers. The Carnegie Forum called for a reexamination of undergraduate "content area" programs to ensure their appropriateness for the preparation of professional teachers. NCETE contended that teacher education is an all-campus priority and urged college and university presidents to evaluate their teacher education programs and the graduates of the programs. SREB continued this general theme in its recommendations that the entire faculty should participate in a comprehensive examination of the entire higher education program related to teacher education and that faculty promotions and pay in colleges and universities should be related to the work that faculty members do with schools.

Differences in the recommendations from the various reports were minor, but subtle differences were found. Of those reports that offered a recommendation on the matters, the majority appeared to support the belief that higher education institutions have a function to perform in the preparation of teachers, that the current institutional preparation programs should be lengthened, and that current programs should be improved by placing additional emphasis on both knowledge in the subject to be taught and educational pedagogy.

Several potential problems may be encountered in efforts to reform teacher education. A variety of actors may become involved. State legislatures and governors may impose teacher preparation requirements on higher education institutions that have a tradition of faculty control over programs. Strong internal administrative support, possibly accompanied by professional or legislative mandates, may be necessary to implement teacher preparation reforms in colleges of education or to effect reforms in teaching content areas in other colleges or departments. Further, implementation of many of the reforms will require cooperation from local school districts as well as fiscal support and regulatory changes from state agencies and legislative bodies.

CERTIFICATION/LICENSING/CAREER LADDER

The lack of consistency in terminology is a common problem in analyzing recommendations from different reports and is especially noticeable in the use of the terms *certification* and *licensing* in the reform reports. Rather than being interchangeable, some distinction should be made between the two terms. The interest in creating a national board for professional teaching standards makes it necessary that efforts be made to differentiate between the role of the national board and the role of state educational agencies.

In this discussion, *certification* would be granted by a national board composed primarily of practicing professional teachers. The issuance of a certificate would indicate that a teacher had achieved a professionally recognized status based on criteria established by the national board or comparable professional body. In contrast, *licensing* of teachers *currently is and would continue to be* a state function; state legislatures, state boards of education, state educational agencies, or other designated agencies establish and enforce minimal requirements for public school teachers. Issuance of a teaching license is an indication that a person meets the state's legal requirements for teachers. States might incorporate the board's certification standards in their licensing requirements or provide that certification qualifies a person for a license, but licensure would not qualify a person for certification. (None of the reports proposed that the federal government should assume any role in either teacher certification or licensing.)

National Certification

The most comprehensive recommendations concerning teacher certification are from the Carnegie Forum. The report called for the creation of a national board for professional teaching standards to establish "high" standards for subject matter knowledge and performance and to certify teachers who meet those standards. State or regional organizations would oversee certification functions at those levels. Decisions to seek certification would be voluntary, and the Forum recommended that candidates for board certification be able to choose the means of professional preparation that best suits their needs. NGA supported the creation of a national board.

Licensing

As indicated earlier, licensing of teachers is a governmental function designed to protect the public interest by establishing and enforcing qualification standards for teachers in the public schools. NCETE and SREB contended that approval of a person to teach is, and should continue to be, a state responsibility; however, NCETE urged that professional educators should have the major responsibility for determining licensing standards and for ensuring that standards are set and met for those who prepare teachers and for those who seek to teach. SREB recommended that states examine the subjects in which they certify (license) teachers and align them more closely with the needs of the schools. The Carnegie Forum attempted to accommodate both licensing and certification by recommending that teacher licensing continue to be required function of a state agency and that board certification be voluntary.

In general, the reports advocated that prospective teachers be required to complete professional education requirements before receiving a regular license, but CED recommended that prospective teachers be able to complete licensing requirements on the job. ECS called for each state to structure its licensing programs so that some type of license could be used to encourage teaching service by "qualified" persons who have not completed professional education programs. NSF addressed the same issue by recommending that states adopt rigorous standards but not those that would create artificial barriers to entry of "qualified" persons. Boyer called for programs to recruit outstanding professionals from other fields to teach part-time.

NCETE also addressed the issue of license renewal for teachers by urging that staff development be recognized in the state requirements for renewal of teaching licenses. Specifically, NCETE recommended that recertification requirements (license renewal) should include satisfactory evidence of competency-based professional development that would be evaluated locally.

The Carnegie Forum recommended that, after a "set" date, no licensed teachers be permitted to teach subjects other than those in which they hold a license and no emergency licenses (for teachers who do not meet minimum state qualifications) be granted. However, the Forum also recommended that a nonrenewable teacher license be issued to persons with an undergraduate major in the teaching area and no professional education; this is one of the current types of emergency licenses. NGA followed the same theme by advocating that governors end emergency teacher licenses.

SREB contended that alternative programs should be developed that would permit liberal arts graduates to be certified without having to complete an undergraduate program in teacher education.

When liberal arts graduates (without professional education) are hired to teach, SREB recommended that they should receive assistance and supervision from the school and college faculty and also should have "instruction in teaching" as part of their preparation.

Career Ladder

Even though the concept of the career ladder for teachers does not have direct relevance to preservice education programs for teachers, recommendations concerning this change in teacher status typically have included requirements for continuing education and advanced training. The typical career ladder proposals called for a three-tier system of teacher licensing: instructor or apprentice, professional teacher, and master teacher or career professional. Typically, persons at the first level would have a three- to five-year nonrenewable license and would receive some type of assistance or supervision. Only the last two levels would be eligible for tenure appointments. (The Carnegie Forum appears to have contemplated a four-level career ladder.) The various reports are not clear concerning whether attainment of the third status—career professional—would be achieved by meeting quantitative state licensing standards, by participating in a voluntary peer review process, or by being recommended for the status after evaluation by a supervisor.

The career ladder concept for teachers was endorsed by the Carnegie Forum, CED, ECS, NCEE, Holmes Group, NSF, and SREB. The principal goal appeared to be the creation of a reward system for teachers that would permit them to move up the salary schedule without leaving the classroom. Reports also appeared to agree that pay and status should increase as teachers "move up" the ladder, but they did not all assume that levels of responsibility should change as teachers "move up." SREB stressed the importance of classroom performance as a key to advancement in a career ladder program.

CED perceived the career ladder as a means to attract and retain high-quality teachers. Acquisition of the status would not be based on increasing levels of responsibilities but on a person's role as a professional educator. This position was different from that of the Carnegie Forum and ECS reports, which advocated a restructuring of the teaching force with those teachers in the top level of the career ladder providing active leadership in curriculum and program development and helping colleagues.

NCETE did not recommend development of the typical career ladder approach but advocated that all new teachers complete a one-year induction or internship period for which compensation would be provided. During this period, interns would have a reduced teaching load so that they would have time to participate in professional development activities.

Active involvement and support from different institutions and agencies will be required to implement the proposed changes in teacher certification, licensing, and status. Such diverse entities as higher education institutions, local school boards, state educational agencies, national certification bodies, accreditation agencies, and teacher organizations all appear to have an interest in the deisgn and implementation of reforms; however, conflicts may arise when efforts are made to determine the role of each entity.

RECRUITMENT

A common theme of the reports was the need to recruit more able persons into teaching. ECS advocated scholarships and financial incentives to attract the most able youth to teaching. NCETE recommended that the states and the federal government launch a national campaign to recruit qualified candidates into teaching. The Carnegie Forum and the NCEE stressed the need for financial aid for highly qualified applicants and especially for those students interested in teaching in fields with critical shortages. The Carnegie Forum, NCETE, NGA, and SREB reports emphasized the need to attract minority youth into teaching careers; SREB also recommended that financial incentives be provided to attract minority students and that extra efforts be taken to ensure that disadvantaged students who want to teach are prepared to meet the higher standards required for teachers. The NGA emphasized the need to define and implement a comprehensive teacher recruitment strategy and to use strategies that include information, alternative programs, financial assistance, placement help, and attractive starting salaries.

The concept of the teacher service corps has been advocated as one way to attract more able persons into teaching. Volunteer programs such as the Peace Corps and VISTA have been examined as possible models for improving the teaching profession. The Holmes Group supported implementation of a system of national service for talented college graduates who lack professional education training and who could serve as "instructors" in the schools. Boyer also supported the service concept but advocated a somewhat different approach by calling for the creation of a national teacher service corps similar to the National Health Service Corps. Under the Holmes Group proposal, the persons would not have to be fully qualified as teachers. However, under the Boyer proposal, participants would receive scholarships while in school and would be fully qualified teachers on completion of the program.

SALARIES

Teacher pay was addressed in virtually all of the reform reports. NSF called for salary schedules that would foster competition for and retention of high-quality teachers in critical fields. The NCEE stated that salaries should be competitive, market sensitive, and performance based. NGA advocated that attractive starting salaries be established for teachers and that the total incentive program for teachers include professional growth opportunities, sabbaticals, and teacher recognition programs. CED, Carnegie Forum, and ECS recommended that salary schedules be designed to reward teacher performance. The Carnegie Forum and Goodlad recommended higher salaries for teachers with increased responsibilities because of differentiated roles. A major difference between these two reports is that Goodlad recommended that seniority not be recognized on the salary scale, but the Forum supported recognition of seniority. The Forum also advocated recognition of competency, as indicated by "national certification."

The Carnegie Forum, CED, and SREB reports advocated higher salaries for entry- and career-level teachers. The Carnegie Forum and NCETE also proposed that teachers' salaries and career opportunities be competitive with those in other professions. Sizer advocated that teachers' salary schedules be "steeper" to provide higher salaries for experienced teachers. The Forum and CED also supported the "merit school" concept by advocating bonuses to teachers for improving schoolwide performance. The latter position is consistent with Goodlad's position that the individual school is the unit for improvement.

TEACHER ROLE/SCHOOL ENVIRONMENT

In their discussion of teacher role and school environment, the various reports followed several themes. The first is illustrated by the recommendations from the Carnegie Forum and Sizer that teachers be held accountable for student progress. The second, supported by the Carnegie Forum, CED, NCETE, NSF, and Sizer, was that authority in schools should be decentralized, that teachers should be given more collective power and individual autonomy, and that efforts should be made to improve the working conditions for teachers by providing them with variations in work responsibilities and initiating efforts to ensure stability in schools. In a specific recommendation related to this area, the Carnegie Forum contended that the professional environment of the school would be improved by making "lead" teachers responsible for overseeing the work of others. SREB contended that career ladder programs have the potential of permitting teachers to play a larger role in decision making and to assume leadership roles in curriculum and teaching. On a related item, CED and NCETE recommended curtailment of nonprofessional responsibilities of teachers. NGA called for efforts to design more professional work environments for teachers.

NSB recommended that the teaching environment be improved by providing greater administrative and parental support of student discipline and attendance, reducing classroom interruptions, and enforcing higher standards. The report also recommended that teachers and students be provided with needed equipment, materials, and specialized support staff.

In the administration of schools, the Carnegie Forum, CED, ECS, NCEE, and Holmes Group advocated increased building level discretion in budgetary decisions. The Carnegie Forum recommended that school districts consider a variety of approaches to school leadership. The Holmes Group suported this latter position by recommending that greater power be given to teachers, especially in school and classroom management. These two positions appeared to be in contrast with the recommendations from CED, ECS, and NCEE that called for principals to assume a greater leadership role, to serve as curriculum leaders, and to have discretion over personnel and fiscal planning. NCETE stressed the educational leadership role of the principal, but it also advocated the creation of a collegial environment and greater delegation of managerial duties so that principals would have additional time for educational leadership. The NCEE also called for superintendents to exercise greater leadership.

Differences in emphasis also were noted in the recommendations concerning teacher role. The consensus appeared to be that efforts should be made to improve the day-to-day working conditions of teachers and to make the teaching job more professional, but differences were noted in the recommendations on the power-sharing arrangement that teachers and principals should have in administering the school.

STATE EDUCATION REFORM DOLLARS FOR TEACHERS

Most of the teacher education reports called for higher teacher salaries but were silent on the broader issue of general funding for education. Among the various reform reports, the issue of financing was addressed most directly in the NGA report's call for an analysis of current spending patterns and for sustained growth in funding for instructional support.

Isolation of specific funds for state education reform is a difficult task. Since 1983 the term *education reform* has been used to refer to a variety of actions. The problem is that one state's or local school district's reform may be another's standard method of operation or even a discarded practice. Thus, the operational interpretation of whether or not a practice is an education reform depends largely on the setting. Some reforms will be evident immediately; examples include five-year teacher education programs and screening tests for potential teachers. Other reforms may be viewed as investments in school improvement; they may not result in immediate changes but may have long-term effects on improving teaching and learning in the schools, such as higher teacher salaries or teacher/administrator training programs.

Summary information about 1985–86 funding for major education reforms was reported by the Education Commission of the States (ECS) (1986).[1] The intent of the survey was not to identify funding provided for all education reform efforts among the states but to secure information about the amount of funds provided for specific types of "education reforms" that have received most national attention. States were asked to report the new funding provided for each type of reform. Data from the forty-seven responding states were grouped into five categories. The following discussion includes information on funds for teacher initiatives, the reform category that received the most funds.

State actions under the category of teacher initiatives have included increased compensation for teachers as well as mandated changes in teacher training programs. Funding for teacher initiatives totalled $588.1 million for the 1984–85 school year and $795.6 million for the 1985–86 school year. Even though the amount increased, the percentage of total "reform" funds to be used for teacher initiatives declined slightly from 1984–85 to 1985–86. To place these amounts in some context, of the estimated $67 billion in total state revenues distributed to local school districts in 1985–86 (Sirkin 1986), state appropriations for "education reform," as reported by the responding states, totalled slightly less than $2 billion, or approximately 3 percent of the estimated total state revenues provided to local school districts.

Teacher Compensation

The major portion of the funds for teacher initiatives, $534.3 million in 1984–85 and $714.6 million in 1985–86, was targeted for teacher compensation. Funds were provided for career ladder plans, salary increases for all teachers, merit (or incentive) pay programs for teachers on a pilot basis, increases in the state minimum salary schedule for teachers, and higher salaries for beginning teachers. Salary increases for all teachers were provided in fourteen states, and salaries for beginning teachers were raised in eight states.

The focus of much of the state action in school reform appears to have been on salary increases for teachers. Several states have taken specific action to raise teachers' salaries. In Georgia $80 million of the $218 million in 1986–87 "reform" funding was earmarked for teacher salary increases (State Capitals 1986b). A portion of the new funds in Kentucky also was earmarked for teacher salary increases (State Capitals 1986c). This same trend was found in Mississippi where the state legislature voted $21 million for a $1,000 salary raise for teachers for the 1986–87 school year (Mississippi 1986). New Mexico enacted "education reform" legislation that provided for an across-the-board salary increase for all certified personnel. Of the

$63.7 million increase in state funds for the 1987 fiscal year, $33.7 million was for the salary increase (Snider 1986a). Arizona approved $15 million for teacher raises for FY 1987, but the availability of funds will be dependent on the outcome of a statewide referendum to raise revenues for general operation of schools (State Capitals 1986d).

For the 1986–87 biennium, Virginia allocated an additional $530 million in state aid; the bulk of these funds will be used to raise teachers' salaries. Under the reform legislation, local school districts will be required to raise teachers salaries by at least 10 percent (State Capitals 1986a).

Education Improvement Activities

In addition to the funding for teacher compensation, funds also were provided for teacher and administrator training programs. In 1985–86 the forty-seven responding states provided $81 million for summer institutes for teachers, teacher training centers, and academies for school administrators.

In response to concerns about implementation, Florida replaced the state's master teacher program with a career ladder program (Snider 1986b). The major new program in the 1985 fiscal year was the merit schools and master teacher programs, which received $30 million, but in the 1986 fiscal year school reform activities related to teachers included master teacher ($6.6 million) and merit schools ($10.0 million) (Florida Legislature 1984, 1986).

The $114 million in new state funds in Illinois for "education reform" in 1985–86 included $20 million for improvement of instruction in mathematics and the sciences, $3.5 million for a pilot program on career ladders for teachers, and over $4.1 million for staff development programs (ISBE 1985).

School reform funds in Texas have been subjected to the state's fiscal equalization provisions, and local school districts share in the costs of education reform. Of the total state funds for FY 1987 of $4.4 billion, reform-related items included $402.6 million in "education improvement" funds for the career ladder program, a prekindergarten program, and local district summer school programs (Texas Legislature 1985; TEA 1985).

The outlook for significant increases in state funds is somewhat bleak in many states because of a lack of economic growth and pressures for other state services. The National Governor's Association has indicated that the "general fund year-end balance" fiscal condition of the states is projected to decline in the 1986 and 1987 fiscal years. Using the Wall Street bond analysts' measure that state year-ending fund balances should be in excess of 5 percent of expenditures, only ten of the fifty states are projected to have in excess of the 5 percent benchmark at the end of their 1986 fiscal year, and only eight of forty-eight reporting states at the end of their 1987 fiscal year (NGA 1986a).

OBSERVATIONS AND CONCLUSIONS

Even though the reform reports advocated changes in teacher preparation programs, inconsistencies, unresolved issues, and vague recommendations were noted among the reports. An additional problem is that teacher-related "education reforms" in one state may be long-established programs in another and may even have been tried and rejected in other instances. Also, reforms that are highly visible mandated changes in one instance and may be hardly noticeable long-term program improvement investments in other cases. An overarching consideration is that the reform reports were national reports, but teacher education programs are provided in a wide range of higher educational institutions each of which has a degree of autonomy. Further, teacher licensing is a state function with voluntary cooperation among states. To add to the complexity, over 2 million teachers work in a decentralized setting involving fifty states, almost 16,000 local school districts, and approximately 80,000 individual public schools (Grant and Snyder 1986).

The unresolved issues or potential problems are of two types. First, on several key issues, the reports contained either different or contradictory recommendations. Second, in view of the ways in which changes in teacher preparation programs and teacher roles have the potential of interacting on higher education institutions, individual schools, local school districts, state educational agencies, and state legislatures, certain significant implementation problems are likely to develop. The following discussion includes observations and conclusions about common themes and points of difference or unresolved issues among the reports.

Decisionmaking Process

One of the unknowns in the reform of teacher education is the decision process that will be used in making and approving program changes. Issues include the role of practicing teachers in developing and policing standards, opportunities for individual institutions of higher education to pursue common or independent paths in structuring their teacher preparation programs, role of the voluntary accrediting agencies in reviewing and approving programs, the teacher certification role of the proposed national board for professional teaching standards, and the role of the individual state educational agencies in approving collegiate teacher preparation programs and issuing teacher licenses.

Another unknown element is the relationship between teacher licensing and certification. As these new relationships evolve, will teacher certification and licensure become discretely different or interrelated functions?

Most of the reports called for large-scale changes in teacher preparation programs, but the reports appeared to differ or were silent on how to implement or fund the changes. Changes in collegiate programs and offerings likely will require the cooperation of departments other than education as well as administrative support. This support will be especially critical in efforts to restructure course offerings throughout higher education institutions.

Program Content

Reports were rather consistent in considering mastery of knowledge in the subject to be taught, professional education courses, and a student teaching or internship experience to be important elements in teacher education programs. The consensus appeared to be that teacher education programs should be five years in duration, but the reports were not consistent concerning whether all professional education courses should be delayed until the fifth year. Virtually unanimous agreement was expressed that, during the undergraduate collegiate years, greater emphasis should be placed on mastery of the academic disciplines related to the teaching field, as opposed to increasing the number of professional education or pedagogical courses.

One of the unanswered questions was whether preparation programs for elementary and secondary teachers should be different or more alike. In the various reports, specific recommendations on this issue were limited.

Most of the recommendations anticipate a lengthened field experience component prior to final licensing, but no mention was made of incentives for local school districts to cooperate in implementing the proposed changes in teacher licensing patterns and lengthened teacher preparation and internship programs. Another unresolved issue is the role that local school districts will have in planning and providing the continuing education programs.

Emergency Licenses

The reports may have advocated that all new teachers have a major in the subject to be taught and that no more emergency licenses be issued, but local school districts may be faced with the options of denying students admission to school, having large classes, or hiring teachers with emergency licenses. The complexities of the licensing dilemma are evident in a recent statement by Wise (1986); he noted that state policymakers have given unprecedented attention to the education of teachers but simultaneously are permitting administrative actions that undercut the maintenance of standards. Emergency licenses are increasing; out-of-field placement for teachers is common; and eased entry in the form of alternative licensing is increasing. Thus, the rhetoric is calling for standards, but practices appear to be going in a different direction.

Career Ladder

Implementation of the career ladder recommendations likely will require a change in teacher role as well as a differentiated salary schedule with a greater range—both of which would appear to affect the operation and funding of local schools. One possibility is that implementation of the career ladder concept will result in the imposition of the higher education staffing model on elementary and secondary schools. Problems may arise because of the differences between elementary and secondary schools and higher education institutions (that is, faculty role in governance, teaching loads, and opportunities for interaction with other faculty), the small number of persons working in the same discipline or at the same grade level in many schools, and the range in salaries for persons with the same responsibilities.

Recruitment

The need to recruit more able persons into teaching was advocated in virtually all reports, aand some placed special emphasis on recruitment of minorities into teaching. With higher entrance and exit standards and a longer program, financial incentives likely will be needed to encourage college students to enter teaching. There was also general agreement that improvements will be needed in salaries and working conditions to attract quality persons.

Teacher Role and School Leadership

One of the operational challenges will be to reconcile the recommendations that call for enhancement of the leadership role of the principal in school improvement with those that call for schools to operate as collegial institutions and for teachers to have a greater role in school and classroom management. This latter recommendation also must be considered in the context of the recommendations that working conditions for teachers should be improved and that teachers should be relieved of tasks not directly related to teaching.

Teacher Salaries

Additional funds will be required to implement the recommendations for higher starting salaries and more competitive salaries for teachers. Pressures for higher entering salaries may develop because of the higher qualifications required of entering teachers, and additional funds will be required to implement differentiated salary schedules for teachers. The options are either to increase salaries significantly for both entering and practicing teachers or to restructure the educational process or the teaching force with pay differences as under a medical staffing model of orderlies, nurses' aides, technicians, nurses, interns, general practitioners, and surgeons.

Funding for Reform

Pressures for more funds likely will arise as higher education institutions attempt to design and implement program changes. Within institutions, either more funds will be provided to the affected departments, or the departments will be expected to fund the changes by reprogramming current funds.

States have not made significant increases in their spending for public elementary and secondary schools to support education reform; however, funding efforts must be considered in the context of the current economic conditions among the states. Relatively small percentages of total state funds have been targeted on specific reform activities. Also, among the states, patterns have varied in the approaches used to fund education reform. Some states have allocated funds for increased teacher salaries, implementation of career ladder or differentiated staffing programs, and reduced class size. Other states have enacted a series of relatively low-cost, but highly visible, programs.

The interaction of demographic developments through an aging teaching force and an increasing student population in concert with the increased interests in school improvement and student performance provide a setting that offers the possibility for dramatic changes in teacher preparation programs and teacher role and compensation. The overarching issue is whether interested parties will lay aside self-interest and devise creative ways to bring about lasting improvement in elementary and secondary education.

NOTES

1. Except where specific cites are used, this section has been summarized from a recent study by Dougherty (1986).

REFERENCES

AACTE. 1986. *Teacher Education in the States*. Washington, D.C.: American Association of Colleges of Teacher Education.

Boyer, E. L. 1983. *High School: A Report on Secondary Education in America*. New York: Harper & Row.

Carnegie Forum on Education and the Economy. 1986. *A Nation Prepared: Teachers for the Twenty-First Century.* Washington, D.C.: Carnegie Forum.

CED. 1985. *Investing on Our Children.* New York: Committee for Economic Development.

Dougherty, V. L. 1986. "Funding State Education Reforms." Unpublished paper. Denver: Education Commission of the States.

ECS. 1983. *Action for Excellence.* Denver: Education Commission of the States.

Florida Legislature. 1984. *Florida's Fiscal Analysis in Brief, 1984.* A House/Senate Appropriations Staff Report. Conference Report #63. Tallahassee: Florida Legislature.

_____. 1986. "Working Tables, Public School Budget, 1986–87." Unpublished tables. Tallahassee: Florida Legislature. May 20.

Goodlad, J. I. 1983. *A Place Called School: Prospects for the Future.* New York: McGraw-Hill.

Grant, W. V., and T. D. Snyder. 1986. *Digest of Education Statistics 1985–86.* Office of Educational Research and Improvement. Department of Education. Washington, D.C.: U.S. Government Printing Office.

Holmes Group. 1986. *Tomorrow's Teachers.* A Report of the Holmes Group. East Lansing: Michigan State University.

ISBE. 1985. *State, Local and Federal Financing for Illinois Public Schools.* Springfield: Illinois State Board of Education.

"Mississippi Hikes School Budget." 1986. *Education Week* 5, no. 31 (April 23): 16.

NCEE. 1983. *A Nation at Risk.* Washington, D.C.: U.S. Department of Education, National Committee on Excellence in Education.

NCETE. 1985. *A Call for Change in Teacher Education.* National Commission for Excellence in Teacher Education. Washington, D.C.: American Association of Colleges for Teacher Education.

NGA. 1986a. *Fiscal Survey of the States.* Washington, D.C.: National Governor's Association.

_____. 1986b. *Time for Results: The Governors' 1991 Report on Education.* Washington, D.C.: National Governor's Association.

NSF. 1983. *Educating Americans for the Twenty-First Century.* Washington, D.C.: National Science Foundation, National Science Board Commission on Precollege Education in Mathematics, Science, and Technology.

Olson, L. 1986. "State Ladder Plans in Several Places Moving Forward." *Education Week* 5 (33) (May 7): 1, 6.

Sirkin, J. R. 1986. "Education-Spending Rate Slows; Salary Gains Made, N.E.A. Finds." *Education Week* 5 (31) (April 23): 4.

Sizer, T. R. 1984. *Horace's Compromise: The Dilemma of the American High School.* Boston: Houghton Mifflin.

Snider, W. 1986a. "New Mexico Lawmakers Pass Wide-Ranging School-Reform Act." *Education Week* 5 (25) (March 5): 5, 13.

_____ . 1986b. "Florida Scraps Master-Teacher Program." *Education Week* 5 (39) (June 18): 1, 10.

Southern Regional Education Board. 1986. *SREB Recommendations to Improve Teacher Education.* Atlanta: Southern Regional Education Board.

State Capitals. 1986a. "Virginia Legislature Funds Education Package." *Education Week* 5 (27) (March 19): 6.

_____ . 1986b. "Georgia: New Funds for Education Reform." *Education Week* 5 (29) (April 9): 6.

_____ . 1986c. "Kentucky Education Reforms Win Full Funding." *Education Week* 5 (30) (April 16): 8.

_____ . 1986d. "Arizona: Salary Hike Voted, But Cap Remains." *Education Week* 5 (36) (May 28): 6.

TEA. 1985. *State Summary Table.* Unpublished table. Austin: Texas Education Agency.

Texas Legislature. 1985. *Supplement to the House Journal, Sixty-Ninth Legislature, Regular Session, Text of Conference Report House Bill no. 20.* Austin: Texas Legislature.

Twentieth-Century Fund. 1983. *Making the Grade.* New York: Twentieth-Century Fund.

Wise, A. E. 1986. "A Case for Trusting Teachers to Regulate Their Profession." *Education Week* 6 (5) (October 8): 24.

3 THE SUPPLY OF U.S. TEACHERS
Quality for the Twenty-First Century

James N. Fox

As it prepares to enter the twenty-first century, the United States is striving to remain competitive in the world economy. The success of this quest depends, in large part, on the initiative and creativity of U.S. workers. And teachers play an important role in this quest. Teachers today can prepare the workers of tomorrow by developing and nurturing the creativity and initiative of the United States' most precious resource—its children.

The teaching profession today stands at a crossroads. The Carnegie Forum (1986: 31) has estimated that, conservatively, between 1986 and 1992 we will need to hire 1.3 million teachers—over half of the current stock of 2.3 million teachers. This presents both an opportunity and a challenge. The opportunity is to rethink the skills, knowledge, and personal characteristics that we want teachers to possess; the challenge is to develop the teaching profession to the point where it will attract and retain sufficient numbers of teachers with these capabilities.

This chapter analyzes the factors that undergird the current debate about teacher shortages and discusses the difficulties met in defining the demand for teachers, the complexities of the supply side of the

The views expressed in this chapter are the author's and do not necessarily reflect the positions or policies of the Office of Research or the U.S. Department of Education. No official support or endorsement of the U.S. Department of Education is intended or should be inferred.

equation, and the importance of considering the quality of teachers as well as numbers, per se. The chapter points out that forecasting techniques work best under stable circumstances and that the market for U.S. teachers is currently anything but stable. Even if the projection models dealt adequately with the technical issues regarding teacher supply and demand, under current conditions they are likely to generate imprecise estimates. Finally, the chapter offers a strategy for policymakers to use in order to raise the quality of the teachers they employ: "Backward linking"—asking a set of systematically related questions—can help assure that the characteristics of teachers best fit the particular circumstances in which they will work.

IS THERE A TEACHER SHORTAGE?

Gerald (1985: 79) estimates that between 1988 and 1992 schools of education will produce less than 75 percent of the teachers needed to staff U.S. schools. On the other hand, Feistritzer (1986: 1) concludes, "Contrary to predictions, there seems to be no problem finding enough qualified teachers to meet demand." The Carnegie Forum (1986: 27) tells us, "Unless teaching as a career changes, in the years to come there will be a growing gap between teacher supply and demand, according to quite conservative projections." But Hecker (1986: 17) concludes that no shortage of teachers currently exists and "indications . . . are that no shortage of teachers will develop" between now and 1995.

How can well-intentioned analysts differ so markedly in their views of teacher supply and demand? The problem with projecting teacher shortages stems from three sources: the elusiveness of demand, the complexity of supply, and differing views of teacher quality.

Elusive Demand

How many teachers do we need? During the 1983–84 school year, the average number of pupils per classroom teacher (by state) ranged from a low of 14.4 in Wyoming to a high of 24.2 in Utah (Grant and Snyder 1986: 45). The range in these numbers demonstrates that uniform agreement regarding the appropriate pupil-teacher ratio simply does not exist. Differences in the pupil-teacher ratio reflect differences in class size and in the number of ancillary teachers.

Differences in class size result, in part, from the existence of small schools. But these differences also reflect explicit policy decisions. And these policy decisions impact directly on the demand for teachers. Assume, for the sake of illustration, that all states, in the interest of raising "quality," choose to reduce class size to 14.4, the average pupil-teacher ratio in Wyoming. Under this assumption, the demand for teachers would increase by almost 30 percent. Similarly, if, in the interest of "efficiency," all states choose pupil-teacher ratios similar to Utah's, then the demand for teachers would decline by a little more than 20 percent.

The bottom line is that class size and the number of supplementary teachers are policy decisions that significantly influence the demand for teachers. Models of teacher demand must include not only demographic factors such as the number and ages of children and their geographic distribution; the models also must include projections of policy decisions regarding class size and the numbers of supporting teachers. Projecting demographic trends is a technical task that is fairly straightforward; projecting policy decisions lies at the opposite end of the methodological spectrum.

Complex Supply

Most professionals enter their careers in a fairly lockstep manner. For example, an individual wishing to become a physician, an attorney, or some other professional attends college and graduate school and then enters some type of induction program such as serving an internship and residency or clerking for a judge or serving as a junior partner in an established law firm.

The training and career patterns in teaching are not as straightforward as those in many other professions. In the first place, unlike members of many other professions, a substantial number of teachers drop out between training and work. An analysis by Vance and Schlechty (1982: 23) of 1972 high school graduates suggests that more than 20 percent of those who majored in education or received a teaching certificate did not become teachers.

In the second place, unlike other professions, teaching does not hold its entrants well. Vance and Schlechty (1982: 23) note that in a national sample of teachers, 15 percent leave the profession during the first few years of teaching, and another 45 percent expected to leave by the time they reached age 30. The National Governors' Association Report (1986: 37) paints an even grimmer picture. It suggests that 40 percent of all teachers quit within the first two years of teaching. Analysts disagree about the overall attrition rate from teaching, as well. Some say 6 percent of all teachers resign each year; others argue that the correct number is 9 percent (Rodman 1987: 7).

Trained teachers who do not immediately enter the profession, as well as those who teach but leave, create a so-called reserve pool of teachers. This pool supplies a large number of entrants to the profession at any given point in time. The National Education Association (1981: 9) reports that in 1981, more than one-third of the vacancies for teachers were filled by individuals who were not recent college graduates. In the mid-1980s a number of states reported that close to 50 percent of their teacher vacancies are filled by individuals who have not recently graduated from college (Papageorgiou 1987). Of course, a number of these teachers are transferring from other districts, but many of them are also entering from the reserve pool.

Thus, the supply of teachers is not easy to project. Even if we know how many individuals are majoring in education, we must estimate how many of them will actually teach. And then we need to know how many of those who enter teaching will remain in the profession. Finally, and perhaps most problematic, we must estimate how members of the teacher reserve pool will respond to various market forces.

Quality Considerations

The above discussion of supply and demand deals with quantity alone. Quality is another important dimension of the teacher workforce. Several studies have examined the quality of the teacher workforce, focusing primarily on the academic ability of teachers (Koerner 1963; Weaver 1981; Vance and Schlechty 1982; Sykes 1983b; Fox 1984). The consistent conclusion of this work is that teachers tend to score lower on tests of academic ability than do members of other professions.

Another lens to apply to assess the quality of teachers is the degree to which they hold certificates in the field in which they teach. Certification is limited as a measure of quality because certification requirements vary widely from state to state (Goertz 1986). None-theless, an examination of certification provides a broad measure of quality, particularly for high school teachers.

A recent national survey of teachers indicates that in 1984, 11 per-cent of high school teachers taught primarily outside their area of state certification and 15 percent had less than a college minor in the field where they most frequently taught (Carroll 1985: 2, 17).

Recent education reforms are likely to exacerbate this problem. The majority of the states have recently specified that high school students must take an additional year of mathematics, science, Eng-lish, and social studies (Goertz 1986: 13). These requirements are likely to lead to even more teachers teaching out of field. For exam-ple, Bell (1984: 3) estimates that each additional required year of study in either science or math will generate a nationwide demand for an additional 34,000 high school teachers.

Clearly, policymakers must be concerned about both the quality and quantity of U.S. teachers. But even if the technical details re-garding the supply of and the demand for teachers could be over-come, difficulties would remain. Forecasting techniques work best under stable conditions; projections are most likely to be accurate when the future mirrors the past. This situation, in turn, occurs most often in the absence of major disruptions. Forecasting the supply of and the demand for teachers therefore remains unreliable because the market for teachers is currently anything but stable.

METAMORPHOSIS OF THE MARKET FOR TEACHERS

The current market for teachers is in a state of substantial agitation. Teachers are being assigned new responsibilities; they are being asked to teach in new areas; and they are entering the profession through new avenues.

New Roles and Responsibilities

Nybeg and Farber (1986: 4) point out that

> Public-school teachers have almost no authority over the design and admin-istration of [schools] . . . . Criteria for determining class composition and size, scheduling, curriculum and test content; the training, evaluation, and promo-

tion of faculty; delegating workloads; planning and allocation of "space" . . . , and so on—all this is controlled by legislatures and by lay boards and their administrators.

But the distribution of authority is changing. A number of recent major reports unanimously emphasize the need to provide more autonomy to teachers in order to upgrade the quality of the profession. The Holmes group (1986: 30) calls for teachers who are "empowered to make principled judgments and decisions on their students' behalf." The Carnegie Forum (1986: 58) is more expansive:

> Within the context of a limited set of clear goals for students set by state and local policymakers, teachers, working together, must be free to exercise their professional judgement as to the best way to achieve these goals. This means the ability to make—or at least to strongly influence—decisions concerning such things as the materials and instructional methods to be used, the staffing structure to be employed, the organization of the school day, the assignment of students, the consultants to be used, and the allocation of resources available to the schools.

The National Governors' Association (1986: 38), drawing on the work of the California Commission (1985: 36), adds its endorsement of this principle:

> Teachers will have to be involved in decisions about discipline, school goals, their own continuing education, curriculum, and schoolwide problem solving.

These principles are being implemented. A coalition of high schools has joined Brown University to build on the ideas advanced in Theodore Sizer's *Horace's Compromise.* An important thrust of this group is to provide more autonomy to teachers (Carnegie Forum 1986: 59). One school in the North Branch School District (forty-five miles north of Minneapolis–St. Paul) illustrates the degree to which autonomy can be extended. Jim Walker, the district superintendent, has placed two teachers in control of planning, budgeting, and delivering instructional services to ninety fourth graders (cited in Carnegie Forum 1986: 90).

These reforms illustrate the increasing autonomy of teachers, in general. Another dimension of this movement calls for differentiated staffing: assigning different tasks with varying levels of responsibility to different teachers.

Traditionally, schools are made up of side-by-side classrooms, where each teacher is required to undertake a variety of activities ranging from diagnosing students' needs and prescribing the appropriate instructional strategy to assuring that students do not litter in the lunchroom. As a result of teaching's range of responsibilities, some praise the profession by emphasizing the success of the teacher/student relationship at its best; others argue that teaching amounts to little more than glorified babysitting. In truth, elements of both characterize the working lives of teachers. The Carnegie Forum 1986: 40) estimates that up to 50 percent of a teacher's time is spent on noninstructional activities.

Differentiated staffing assigns different tasks with varying levels of responsibility to different individuals. For example, the Holmes Group (1986: 9–10) recommends three different levels of responsibility. Career professionals would serve in a manner similar to clinical professors in the field of medicine, using "their pedagogical expertise to improve other teachers' work, as well as to help children." (This is similar to the responsibilities of the lead teacher proposed by the Carnegie Forum 1986: 58–60). Professional teachers would make up the majority of the workforce and would be capable of operating independently. Typically, they would be responsible for learning activities in their particular classrooms. Finally, instructors would be supported and supervised by career professionals. The instructors might be bright college graduates or entrants from other professions who might wish to teach for a limited period of time.

The idea of differentiated staffing is not simply languishing in commission reports. It is taking hold in real schools. Some teachers evaluate their peers; some are serving as mentors; and some help translate research into practice.

Peer Evaluation. Increasingly, teachers are being asked to evaluate other teachers. Wise and others (1984) studied school districts with highly developed teacher evaluation procedures. They found that all of these districts deliberately "involved expert teachers in the evaluation process." Teachers also perform the evaluations under the Tennessee Career Ladder Program (Furtwengler 1985: 55). Evaluators are drawn from the ranks of experienced teachers and are screened and trained. They then work full-time for the state. The demands placed on teachers who serve as evaluators are different from the demands placed on the typical classroom teacher, so that the capabilities needed to succeed as a peer evaluator may not be identical to those needed to succeed as a classroom teacher.

Mentors.   Another new role for teachers is to help other teachers. Under California's Mentor Teacher Program, authorized in 1983, each district-designated mentor receives a stipend of $4,000, and the district receives $2,000 per mentor to cover implementation costs. "Mentors are appointed for one-, two-, or three-year terms to work in a staff development capacity with new teachers, other career teachers, and 'teacher trainees' (persons entering the profession either right out of undergraduate schools or mid-career without formal teacher training experience)" (Wagner 1985: 24). Unlike teachers serving as evaluators for the Tennessee Career Ladder Program, California's mentors must continue to teach at least 60 percent of the time. Toledo's Intern-Intervention Program (Waters and Wyatt 1985: 365–67) and the Charlotte-Mecklenburg Career Development Plan (Haynes and Mitchell 1985: 12) assign similar duties to mentor teachers.

Gray and Gray (1985: 39) have found that beginning teachers report needing help from mentors with such tasks as "discipline and classroom management, curriculum and lesson planning, and school routines. Most of all, they feel a need for moral support, guidance, and feedback." Mentors who most successfully provide this kind of help are "people oriented and secure, and take a personal interest in their protegés' careers."

Gray and Gray (1985: 41) map out the evolution of the successful mentor/protegé relationship where the mentor starts out as directive and successively weans the protegé, until the novice finally becomes slef-sufficient. For example, in terms of leadership, the mentor (M) starts out by telling the protegé (P) what to do; during the next phase, M sells P on what to do; next, M invites P's participation; then M delegates to P and supports; and finally, P is self-directed.

Research Linkers.   Another emerging role for teachers is to serve as research linkers. These individuals serve as the bridge between the research and practitioner communities; they translate research findings into practical advice that can be readily applied by practicing teachers. Selected teachers prepare research syntheses and design and conduct training activities that focus on how the research findings could be applied in actual instructional settings. To date, "research translations" have been developed to deal with classroom management, teacher feedback and praise, direct instruction/interactive teaching, time-on-task, cooperative team grouping, student learning styles, student coaching, critical thinking, and adult learning (Rauth 1986: 28).

This program grew out of a grant to the AFT from the National Institute of Education to conduct a pilot program. Known as the Educational Research and Dissemination Program, this pilot tested the concept in New York City, Washington, D.C., and San Francisco. From those initial sites, the program has grown to cover 130 sites by 1986. How has it been received? Participants in training sessions conducted by research linkers have responded positively (Rauth 1986: 29):

> This is the most useful inservice I've had in my twenty plus years of teaching. Keep it up.
>
> As a result of this training, I can see a tremendous improvement in both student achievement and behavior just from using ideas learned from the various researchers.

Again, the most capable research translators may not possess the same skills, talents, and interests as the most successful classroom teachers.

Teaching in New Areas

In addition to taking on new roles and responsibilities, teachers are being asked to teach in new curricular areas. Sykes (1983a: 101) argues that as students enter an increasingly complex society they will need a more sophisticated education. This societal development, in turn, requires teachers who are "masters of the disciplines they are to impart, and of a pedagogy that aspires to more than drill and memorization of facts." Sykes's view reflects a growing call for more teaching of higher order thinking skills.

Sternberg (1987: 255) suggests that teachers of thinking skills should be trained in liberal arts, psychology, and philosophy. He also emphasizes that all teachers in the school should be aware of what is being taught so they can reinforce the approach. Other teachers, he argues," can undermine thinking-skills training if they think or teach in a way that counters the spirit of inquiry fostered in a thinking-skills curriculum."

Chipman and Segal (1985: 3) argue that little explicit instruction in thinking and learning skills takes place in U.S. schools. And the results of this are readily apparent. The National Assessment of Educational Progress (NAEP) recently surveyed a national sample of young adults (ages 21 to 25). They found that less than 10 percent could perform such higher-order tasks as using text information to describe orally the distinctions between two types of employee fringe benefit plans; only one in five individuals could perform such tasks as accurately using a bus schedule; and only 10 percent could perform such tasks as filling out an order form, calculating the costs for a number of items, and totaling the cost (Kirsch and Jungeblut 1986: 14, 26, 34). Another NAEP report, based on a 1984 assessment of a national sample of students in grades four, eight, and eleven, found that about 80 percent of students have "difficulty organizing their thoughts coherently in writing." The report attributes this to a "pervasive lack" of emphasis on higher-order skills throughout the school curriculum (NAEP 1986: 11).

What exactly do we mean by *higher-order thinking skills?* Olson (1984: 33) presents a helpful typology of thinking skills. Level I is knowledge. Based on recall, this level requires remembering previously learned material. The next level is comprehension. This involves translation—grasping the meaning of the material. Level III, application, involves generalizing or using the learned material in new and concrete situations. The next level is analysis, which involves breaking down the material into its component parts so that it can be understood more easily. Level V is synthesis. This involves composition, or putting material together to form a new whole. And level VI is evaluation, which involves judging the value of material for a given purpose.

Increasingly, school systems are beginning to recognize the importance of teaching higher-order thinking skills. For example, the California Board of Education recently rejected all mathematics textbooks proposed for kindergarten through eighth grade because the books overemphasized memorization and math drills and inadequately helped students develop logical thinking skills (Fallon 1986: 11; *Education Week* 1986: 4). (California is a major influence on textbooks manufacturing nationwide because its purchases account for 11 percent of the total textbook market.)

The New York Times has noted a program designed to increase the teaching of higher-order thinking in several urban school districts. Under this program, sponsored by the College Board and administered by the University/Urban Schools National Task Force, English and math courses for selected high school students would be infused with the teaching of reasoning skills. Participating school districts include New York, Chicago, San Francisco, Detroit, Minneapolis, and Memphis (Maeroff 1983).

Academicians increasingly offer guidance in this field. Witness, for example, the publication of such works as *Educational Leadership: When Teachers Tackle Thinking Skills* (1984), *Thinking and Learning Skills: Relating Instruction to Research* (Segal, Chipman, and Glaser 1985), *Thinking with the Whole Brain: An Integrative Teaching/Learning Model* (Cooke and Haipt 1986), and *Teaching Thinking Skills: Theory and Practice* (Baron and Sternberg 1987).

A recent article in *Newsweek* suggests that the United States needs to develop a workforce with keen problemsolving skills in order to keep its economy competitive in the worldwide marketplace. The article mentions recent technological advances that present increasing opportunities for ingenious problemsolvers to help companies remain competitive (Rogers 1987: 36-37).

The need for higher-order thinking has been eloquently summarized by Sternberg (1986: 19):

> As technology advances and the complexity of science and society increases, the importance of high-level thinking can only increase as well. Thinking-skills programs make explicit what has been implicit all along: that learning without thinking is mindless, whereas thinking without learning is empty.

New Channels

New programs are evolving to bring these new teachers into our nation's schools. Probably the best known of these is New Jersey's alternate route program. Under this plan, an individual with thirty credits in a subject field can qualify to teach by passing the subject matter Special Area Exam of the National Teachers Exam. Once a candidate accepts a teaching position, it becomes the responsibility of the school district to provide a total of 200 clock hours of professional training in three areas: curriculum, including methods and materials of teaching; student development and learning, including the psychological foundations of teaching; and the classroom and the school, which includes many of the interactive dimensions of teaching such as questioning, feedback, time management, and pacing instruction. During the first year the alternate route teacher is supervised and evaluated by a team consisting of an experienced teacher/

mentor, the building principal, a curriculum supervisor, and a college faculty member or school district employee with the appropriate background and training (Galluzzo and Ritter 1986).

California and Texas have enacted similar programs, and a number of Southeastern states (Virginia, Tennessee, Kentucky, Georgia and Florida) are in varying stages of developing alternative route plans based, in large part, on recommendations advanced by the Southern Regional Education Board (Culver, Eicher, and Sacks 1986: 21–22).

Haberman (1986) argues that alternative certification programs are essentially the same as the emergency certification programs that have been available to virtually all states for years. Both routes permit individuals without teacher preparation to serve in schools. Emergency certification is widely employed. Haberman (1986: 14) notes, for example, that Texas in 1985 issued 5,892 emergency certificates, compared to about 5,630 teachers who entered teaching that year through regular teacher preparation programs.

However, proponents of alternative route programs might argue that these programs differ substantially from merely granting an emergency certificate. Candidates for alternative route programs are carefully screened, and, once chosen, their induction programs are specifically designed to provide them with effective on-the-job training, constant support and guidance, and helpful formative evaluations. Recipients of emergency certificates are seldom treated as well.

Clearly, the marketplace for teachers is changing. In light of all this, what should policymakers do?

"BACKWARD LINKING" FOR TEACHER QUALITY

The tools available to forecast teacher supply and demand are rather blunt. Even if they were sharpened, they operate in a environment that renders them less than precise. Rather than attempting to generate finely tuned estimates of teacher supply and demand, policymakers in this field might better concentrate their energy on attempting to develop policies that lead to upgrading the quality of teachers in U.S. schools. Described below is a process to help guide policymakers in this effort.

Typically, policymakers focus explicitly on the policy tools available to them. As a result, for example, they might debate the explicit merits and limitations of a college loan forgiveness program designed to encourage individuals to enter teaching as a career. As an alternative to this approach, policymakers might consider a process called "backward linking," which is an adaptation of Elmore's (1979: 602–605) "backward mapping." Backward linking is a series of systematically linked questions designed to help assure that policies that are adopted are most likely to produce their intended effects.

When policymakers use a backward-linking approach, discussion of policy tools becomes the last link in the chain, not the first. For example, regarding policies to improve teacher quality, one series of questions might be:

1. What knowledge and skills do we wish children to learn?
2. What teacher behaviors are most likely to result in the desired learning?
3. What skills, knowledge, and other characteristics should teachers possess in order to engage in the required teaching behaviors?
4. What recruitment and training activities are most likely to produce teachers with the required characteristics?
5. What policies are most likely to activate and support the desired chain of events?

Each of these is discussed in more detail below.

What Should Children Learn?

A major aspect of recent education reforms has been to raise high school graduation requirements. Goertz (1986: 13) reports that forty-one states recently raised course work standards for high school graduation. Course work requirements in these states have been raised for *all* students. This illustrates the fact that policies tend to be painted with a broad brush. Does it make sense to implement the recommendations of the National Commission on Excellence in Education (1983: 24) and require *all* high school students to take four years of English, three years of mathematics, three years of science, and three years of social studies in order to graduate? Reasonable people will disagree about this issue. But debates about course requirements could be usefully focused by addressing such underlying questions as, "What is the *purpose* of high school?"; "Is the purpose the same for all students?"; "What is given up when we require more study in certain areas?"; "Will more students drop out if school appears less relevant to many youngsters?"

The Commission's call for increased graduation requirements was motivated, in large part, by the imperative to keep the United States competitive in the world economy (NCEE 1983: 6–7). That competitiveness depends to a large degree on maintaining a substantial stock of intelligent, highly skilled, well-trained, and highly motivated individuals in such fields as science, engineering, and commerce. But is U.S. economic competitiveness increased when *every* student in the United States is required to meet the graduation requirements advanced by NCEE? Is there a segment of the population that might be better served by developing, for example, certain occupational skills?

The National Commission on Excellence in Education points out that high curricular standards must do more than help build a competitive economy. "For our country to function, citizens must be able to reach some common understandings on complex issues, often on short notice and on the basis of conflicting or incomplete evidence" (NCEE 1983: 7). But is this ability to reach a consensus on difficult issues developed by requiring students to take more English, mathematics, social studies, and science courses? Or is it better developed by learning the types of higher-order thinking skills that are discussed earlier in this chapter?

Teaching Behaviors

Brophy and Good (1986) conducted a comprehensive review of research regarding the relationship between teacher behavior and student achievement. They conclude that appropriate teaching behavior can lead to higher student achievement. They argue that the way that teachers present information is important. For example, presentations should be well structured and clear, and general rules and key concepts should be repeated and reviewed. The difficulty of material should be regulated so that students are challenged but not frustrated. In addition, classrooms should be well managed so that students spend the maximum amount of time engaged in academic learning. Brophy and Good caution that such guidelines are not pat prescriptions; teachers should understand general concepts and "adapt them to the particular contexts within which they teach" (Brophy and Good 1986: 370).

The above research is based on traditional approaches to education. Recent studies on the human intellect open intriguing new vistas for progressive educators. For example, the work of Ornstein and Thompson (1984) strongly suggests that we are currently tapping but a small portion of our intellectual potential. An increasing number of forward-looking teachers are joining a grass-roots movement to build educational programs that are designed to expand the learning capabilities of students. These intriguing programs incorporate such principles as attenuating stress, building students' self-confidence, tapping the full capacity of the mind, and other procedures to expand students' capabilities to learn (McCarthy 1980; Williams 1983; Neve 1985; Mitchell and Conn 1985; Cooke and Haipt 1986; Neve, Hart, and Thomas 1986; Schuster and Gritton 1986).

Teacher Capabilities and Training

Lanier and Little (1986: 546) point out that professors of education have not agreed on "a common body of knowledge that all school teachers should possess before taking their first full-time job." They point out that teacher education, available in almost three-quarters of all four-year colleges and universities in the nation, "conveys in its broad outlines the appearance of standardization." However, in fact, as they demonstrate, tremendous variation exists across programs. Conant (1963: 125) found that required semester hours for elementary school teachers ranged from twenty-six to fifty-nine. Lortie (1975: 58) discovered that "it is difficult to get precise, reliable informaton on what proportion of . . . [those hours] is centered on pedagogy and related courses." Similarly, practice teaching requirements ranged from ninety clock hours to 300 clock hours (Conant 1963: 125). Arends (1983, cited in Lanier and Little 1986: 548) notes extensive variation regarding the continuing education of teachers, as well.

In light of the above, the National Center for Research on Teacher Education (n.d.), with funding from the U.S. Department of Education's Office of Research, has launched a five-year study of alternative types of teacher education programs, including both preservice and inservice programs. The work focuses on the ability of alternative training approaches to impact the knowledge, skills, and dispositions required to teach, particularly in the areas of writing and mathematics.

Recruitment and Retention

What type of recruitment strategies will upgrade the quality of the U.S. teaching workforce? Often how a question is phrased can constrain or broaden the range of possible solutions. An anecdote about a contractor for the Defense Department illustrates this point. A contractor was handed an assignment to determine the optimal location for missile silos. The contractor took the liberty of redefining the assignment as designing an optimal defense system. This new question gave rise to the triad of the Strategic Air Command, the Polaris submarines, as well as land-based missiles.

Similarly, the question, "How can we recruit and retain a talented teacher workforce?" will generate a different set of answers than a slightly rephrased question. Specifically, focusing on retaining all teachers closes out some potentially powerful options. For example, under current traditional paths for entering teaching, prospective candidates must choose between preparing for a teaching career or preparing for other endeavors that are probably more lucrative and prestigious. But if we drop the requirement that all teachers should be retained, then bright, talented individuals could serve in the schools for a limited period of time and then go on to pursue their lifetime careers. These individuals, whom we might call *instructors*, could major in a field that would prepare them for their lifelong careers. They could receive intensive teacher training over the summer prior to entering teaching. Once in the schools, the instructors could work under the close guidance of mentors, whom we might call *professional educators*. The relationship between instructors and professional educators in schools would be similar to the relationship between nurses and physicians in hospitals. The instructors would tend to the day-to-day learning needs of the students. The professional educators would provide overall guidance and would be available to deal with problematic situations as they arose. A cost analysis has demonstrated that such a plan could pay the entire cost of college for instructors, could pay professional educators *twice* the average teacher's salary, and would impose *no increase* in cost to the nation's taxpayers (Fox 1984: 233).

SUMMARY

Is there a teacher shortage? Experts disagree because (1) the demand for teachers is an elusive concept, (2) teachers enter the market in a complex manner, and (3) little agreement exists regarding the issue of teacher quality. But even if these technical problems could be solved, predictions of teacher shortages would probably remain off the mark. Forecasting techniques work best under stable conditions. The current market for teachers is anything but stable: Teachers are taking on new responsibilities, being asked to teach in new areas, and entering the profession through new channels.

Nonetheless, more than 1 million teachers must be hired over the next few years. This presents both a challenge and an opportunity to policymakers who will help determine what type of teachers serve in U.S. schools. When deciding what types of strategies to employ in order to attract quality teachers, policymakers might wish to be guided by a technique called backward linking. This consists of asking a series of systematically linked questions where the policy strategy becomes the final link in the chain rather than the initial focus of attention.

If the United States is to remain competitive in the world economy of the twenty-first century, it must maintain a creative and diligent workforce. The workers of tomorrow are being trained in schools today. It is possible to simultaneously upgrade the attractiveness of the teaching profession, increase the skill of those who serve in that field, and improve the quality of education our children receive.

REFERENCES

Arends, R. 1983. "Teachers as Learners: A Descriptive Study of Professional Development Activities." Paper presented at the annual meeting of the American Educational Research Association, Montreal.

Baron, Joan Boykoff, and Robert J. Sternberg, eds. 1987. *Teaching Thinking Skills: Theory and Practice*. New York: W. H. Freeman.

Bell, T. H. 1984. "Keynote Address." In *Teacher Shortage in Science and Mathematics: Myths, Realities, and Research*, edited by John L. Taylor, pp. 3–7, Washington, D.C.: National Institute of Education.

Brophy, Jere, and Thomas L. Good. 1986. "Teacher Behavior and Student Achievement." In *Handbook of Research on Teaching*, edited by Merlin C. Wittrock, pp. 328–75. New York: Macmillan.

California Commission on the Teaching Profession. 1985. *Who Will Teach Our Children? A Strategy for Improving California Schools*. Sacramento, Calif.: The Commission.

Carnegie Forum on Education and the Economy. 1986. *A Nation Prepared: Teachers for the 21st Century.* Report of the Task Force on Teaching as a Profession. Washington, D.C.: The Forum.

Carroll, C. Dennis. 1985. "Background Characteristics of High School Teachers." High School and beyond Tabulation. Washington, D.C.: U.S. Department of Education, National Center for Education Statistics.

Chipman, Susan F., and Judith W. Segal. 1985. "Higher Cognitive Goals for Education: An Introduction." In *Teaching and Learning Skill*, edited by Judith W. Segal, Susan F. Chipman, and Robert Glaser, pp. 1–19, Hillsdale, N.J.: Lawrence Erlbaum.

Conant, James B. 1963. *The Education of American Teachers.* New York: McGraw-Hill.

Cooke, Jane Kita, and Mildred Haipt. 1986. *Thinking with the Whole Brain: An Integrative Teaching/Learning Model.* Washington, D.C.: National Education Association.

Culver, Victor I., B. Keith Eicher, and Annabel L. Sacks. 1986. "Confronting the Teacher Shortage: Are Alternative Certification Programs the Answer?" *Action in Teacher Education* 8 (2) (Summer): 19–24.

Education Week. 1986. 6 (7) (October 22): 4.

Educational Leadership: When Teachers Tackle Thinking Skills. 1984. 42 (3) (November).

Elmore, Richard F. 1979. "Backyward Mapping: Implementation Research and Policy Decisions." *Political Science Quarterly* 94 (4) (Winter): 601–16.

Fallon, Michael. 1986. "California Board Expected to Reject Math Textbooks." *Education Week* 6 (7) (October 15): 11.

Feistritzer, Emily. 1986. "Teacher Crisis: Myth or Reality?" Washington, D.C.: National Center for Education Information.

Fox, James N. 1984. "Restructuring the Teacher Work Force to Attract the Best and the Brightest." *Journal of Education Finance* 10 (2) (Fall): 214–37.

Furtwengler, Carol. 1985. "Tennessee's Career Ladder Plan: They Said It Couldn't Be Done." *Educational Leadership* 43 (3) (November): 50–56.

Galluzzo, Gary L., and Donald E. Ritter. 1986. "Identifying Standards for Evaluating Alternate Route Programs." *Action in Teacher Education* 8 (2) (Summer): 59–66.

Gerald, Debra E. 1985. *Projections of Education Statistics to 1992–93: Methodological Report with Detailed Projection Tables.* Washington, D.C.: National Center for Education Statistics.

Goertz, Margaret E. 1986. *State Education Standards: A 50-State Survey.* Research Report. Princeton, N.J.: Educational Testing Service.

Grant, W. Vance, and Thomas D. Snyder. 1986. *Digest of Education Statistics 1985–8*, Washington, D.C.: U.S. Department of Education, Center for Statistics.

Gray, William A., and Marilynne M. Gray. 1985. "Synthesis of Research on Mentoring Beginning Teachers." *Educational Leadership* 43 (3) (November): 37–43.

Haberman, Martin. 1986. "Alternative Teacher Certification Programs." *Action in Teacher Education* 8 (2) (Summer): 13–18.

Haynes, Robert C., and Kay F. Mitchell. 1985. "Teacher Career Development in Charlotte-Mecklenburg." *Educational Leadership* 43 (3) (November): 11–13.

The Holmes Group. 1986. *Tomorrow's Teachers: A Report of the Holmes Group.* East Lansing, Mich. Holmes Group.

Hecker, Daniel. 1986. "Teachers' Job Outlook: Is Chicken Little Wrong Again?" *Occupational Outlook Quarterly* 30 (4) (Winter): 12–17.

Kirsch, Irwin S., and Ann Jungeblut. 1986. *Literacy: Profiles of America's Young Adults.* Princeton, N.J.: National Assessment of Educational Progress, Educational Testing Service.

Koerner, James D. 1963. *The Miseducation of American Teachers.* Boston: Houghton Mifflin.

Lanier, Judith E., and Judith W. Little. 1986. "Research on Teacher Education." In *Handbook of Research on Teaching*, edited by Merlin C. Wittrock, pp. 527–69. New York: Macmillan.

Lortie, Dan C. 1975. *Schoolteacher: A Sociological Study.* Chicago: University of Chicago Press.

Maeroff, Gene L. 1983. "Teaching to Think; A New Emphasis." *The New York Times*, Education Supplement, January 9.

McCarthy, Bernice. 1980. *The 4MAT System: Teaching to Learning Styles with Right/Left Mode Techniques.* Barrington, Ill.: EXCEL.

Mitchell, William, and Charles P. Conn. 1985. *The Power of Positive Students.* New York: William Morrow.

National Assessment of Educational Progress. 1986. "The Writing Report Card: Writing Achievement in American Schools." Princeton, N.J.: National Assessment of Educational Progress, Educational Testing Service.

National Center for Research on Teacher Education. No date. East Lansing, Mich.: Michigan State University.

National Commission on Excellence in Eduation. 1983. *A Nation at Risk: The Imperative for Educational Reform.* Washington, D.C.: U.S. Government Printing Office.

National Education Association. 1981. "Teacher Supply and Demand in the Publis Schools." NEA Research Note. Washington, D.C.: NEA.

National Governors' Association. 1986. *1991 Report on Education: Time for Results.* Washington, D.C.: NGA.

Neve, Charmaine Della. 1985. "Brain-Compatible Learning Succeeds." *Educational Leadership* 32 (2) (October): 83–85.

Neve, Charmaine Della, Leslie A. Hart, and Edgar C. Thomas. 1986. "Huge Learning Jumps Show Potency of Brain-Based Instruction." *Phi Detla Kappan* 68 2 (October): 143–48.

Nyberg, David, and Paul Farber. 1986. "Authority in Education." *Teachers College Record* 88 (1) (Fall): 4–14.

Olson, Carol Booth. 1984. "Fostering Critical Thinking Skills through Writing." *Educational Leadership* 42 (3) (November): 28–39.

Ornstein, Robert, and Richard F. Thompson. 1984. *The Amazing Brain*. Boston: Houghton Mifflin.

Papageorgiou, Mary. 1987. Personal communication.

Rauth, Marilyn. 1986. "Putting Research to Work: AFT Program Delivers Latest Findings to Teachers." *American Educator* 10 (4) (Winter): 26–31, 45.

Rodman, Blake. 1987. "Teacher Shortage Is Unlikely, Labor Bureau Report Claims." *Education Week* 6 (16) (January 14): 7.

Rogers, Michael. 1987. "Silicon Valley's Newest Wizards: High-Tech-Design Teams That Deliver at High Speed." *Newsweek* 109 (1) (January 5): 36–37.

Schuster, Donald H., and Charles Gritton. 1986. *SALT, Suggestive Accelerative Learning Techniques*. New York: Gordon and Breach.

Segal, Judith W., Susan F. Chipman, and Robert Glaser, eds. 1985. *Thinking and Learning Skills: Relating Instruction to Research*. Hillsdale, N.J.: Lawrence Erlbaum.

Sternberg, Robert J. 1986. "In Defense of 'Critical Thinking' Programs." *Education Week* 6 (6) (October 15): 19.

Sternberg, Robert J. 1987. "Questions and Answers about the Nature and Teaching of Thinking Skills." In *Teaching Thinking Skills: Theory and Practice*, edited by Joan Boykoff Baron and Robert J. Sternberg, pp. 251–60. New York: W. H. Freeman.

Sykes, Gary. 1983a. "Public Policy and the Problem of Teacher Quality: The Need for Screens and Magnets." In *Handbook of Teaching and Policy*, edited by Lee S. Shulman and Gary Sykes, pp. 97–125. New York: Longman.

Sykes, Gary. 1983b. "Teacher Preparation and the Teacher Workforce: Problems and Prospects for the 80's." *American Education* 19 (2) (March): 23–30.

Vance, Victor S., and Phillip C. Schlechty. 1982. "The Distribution of Academic Ability in the Teaching Force: Policy Implications." *Phi Delta Kappan* 64 (1) (September): 22–27.

Wagner, Laura A. 1985. "Ambiguities and Possibilities in California's Mentor Teacher Program." *Educational Leadership* 43 (3) (November): 23–29.

Waters, Cheryl M., and Terry L. Wyatt. 1985. "Toledo's Internship: The Teachers' Role in Excellence." *Phi Delta Kappan* 66 (5) (January): 365–67.

Weaver, W. Timothy. 1981. "The Tragedy of the Commons: The Effects of Supply and Demand on the Educational Talent Pool." Paper presented at the Annual Meeting of the American Association of Colleges for Teachers Education, Detroit, Mich., February 19.

Williams, Linda Verlee. 1983. *Teaching fot the Two-Sided Mind*. New York: Simon and Schuster.

Wise, Arthur E., et al. 1984. *Teacher Evaluation: A Study of Effective Practices*. R-3139. Washington, D.C.: Rand Corporation.

4 TEACHERS' SALARIES
An International Perspective

Stephen B. Lawton

The impetus for this chapter was apparent differences in teacher markets between the United States and Canada and a modest hypothesis about these differences. Specifically, why is it that the United States is experiencing a shortage of teachers, particularly in mathematics and science, while Canada has a surplus of teachers and has experienced little difficulty in finding qualified teachers in all areas? My modest hypothesis is that in Canada teachers' salaries are competitive with other employment opportunities for university graduates, including positions requiring backgrounds in mathematics and science, and that in the United States this is not the case.[1]

Testing this hypothesis has not been as easy as stating it. Adequate data are difficult to acquire; salaries paid in one economy are hard to compare with those paid in another; and there is no clear reason that the comparison should include only two countries. Both the United States and Canada are in a global competition for jobs and trade. Perhaps some of our more successful competitors, such as West Germany or Japan, have discovered how to link salaries to effective teaching or, in other words, to the development of the human capital needed by their economies.

Ultimately, I decided to focus on the three questions addressed by Stephen Barro (1986) in his comparison of teachers' salaries in the

United States and Japan, expanded to include a number of other countries: [2]

1. How does the *level* of public school teachers' salaries (measured in teachers' purchasing power) compare among various countries?
2. How does the teachers' salary *structure* compare in various countries?
3. How well are teachers rewarded *relatively* in various countries—that is, compared with levels of income and output in each country and with the rewards available in nonteaching occupations?

SALARY LEVELS

To compare the levels of teachers' salaries in two or more countries, two items are necessary: data on salary levels and a method for expressing salaries in terms of a common unit of measure.

The primary source of salary data used here is the 1982 and 1985 editions of the Union Bank of Switzerland's (UBS) *Prices and Earnings around the Globe.* Salary data in these publications have at least two limitations. First, salary levels are reported only for the major city or cities in forty-three different countries and not for the nations as a whole. Second, only salaries for primary school teachers are given, and then only for a teacher "who has taught in the public school system (not in private schools) for about 10 years; about 35 years old, married, no children" (UBS 1985: Table 13, footnote 1). Such a teacher will be referred to as a typical teacher, although it is recognized that the characteristics of the modal or average teacher in a given nation may not fit the profile selected by UBS. In addition, alternative sources of data for the United States, Japan (Barro 1984), and Canada (Statistics Canada 1985) were used to validate UBS data for these three nations.

A common unit of measure is used for salaries given in *Prices and Earnings around the Globe:* U.S. dollars calculated using exchange rates. For a number of reasons, this approach to comparing salaries is not entirely suitable. Exchange rates may be quite volatile and rarely reflect the relative purchasing power of domestic currencies in domestic markets. Instead, salary conversions using purchasing power parities (PPPs) are preferred. The PPP for a given country is the amount of the national currency needed to purchase the same amount of goods and services (usually termed a *market basket*) that one U.S. dollar will purchase in the U.S. domestic market. Any nation's currency might be used as the base currency, of course, but it is usual for the U.S. dollar to be used for this purpose.

An article in the British journal *The Economist* ("Could Golden Arches Prop Up the Peso?" 1986) explains purchasing power parities in the following way, with the McDonald's Big Mac hamburger, which is sold in forty-one countries, as the market basket being purchased:

> In Washington, a Big Mac costs $1.60 (U.S.); in Tokyo, our Makundonarudo correspondent had to fork out 370 yen ($2.40). Dividing the yen price by the U.S. dollar price yields a Mac-PPP of $1 equals 231 yen; but on September 1 the dollar's actual exchange rate stood at 154 yen. The same method gives a Mac-PPP against the West German mark of 2.66 marks, compared with a current rate of 2.02 marks.

> Conclusion: on Mac-PPP grounds, the dollar looks undervalued against the yen and mark.

PPPs based on a broader basis than the Big Mac are available from the Organization for Economic Cooperation and Development OECD 1986) for twenty-two countries. Converting UBS salary levels using exchange rates to salary levels using PPPs involved two steps. First, the exchange rates used by UBS were applied in reverse in order to express salaries in terms of national currencies. Second, salaries in local currencies were divided by the appropriate PPPs. The results: salary levels expressed in terms of U.S. dollars using PPPs.[3]

By way of example, UBS reports the 1985 salary level for Canada (the average for Toronto and Montreal) is $24,950 (U.S.) (UBS 1985: Table 13). Dividing this figure by the 1985 exchange rate of $.72884 (U.S.) = $1.00 (Can.) (UBS 1985: Table 25) yields a salary level of $34,232 (Can.). OECD's reports a 1984 PPP for GDP for Canada, the latest available, of 1.13. Dividing the salary level expressed in Canadian dollars by 1.13 yields a salary level of $30,294 (U.S.) using PPPs. That is, in 1985 a teacher in the United States would have to be paid $30,294 (U.S.) in order to have the same purchasing power as the typical urban primary school teacher in Canada. In fact, UBS reports a comparable U.S. teacher was paid $24,600 (U.S.), indicating that in terms of relative purchasing power, the typical Canadian teacher was paid 1.23 times as much (or 23 percent more than) the typical U.S. teacher. It is worth noting that if exchange rates rather than PPPs are used to convert Canadian salaries, then they exceeded U.S. salaries by only 1.4 percent.

Table 4-1 summarizes the results of the analysis of 1982 and 1985 gross earnings of primary school teachers for the twenty-two countries for which salary and purchasing power parities were available.

In terms of purchasing power, the income of teachers in the twenty-two countries considered was 78 percent of that of U.S. teachers in 1985. This figure reflected a slight increase from 75 percent in 1982, implying that even during this period of reform in the United States the pay of teachers there declined relative to that in other developed nations. Of course, U.S. teachers were still paid well above average, in terms of purchasing power, as is true for most U.S. workers (a point returned to later).

Among the twenty-two nations highest salaries in terms of purchasing power were paid in Switzerland (134 percent of U.S. salaries in 1985), Canada (123 percent of U.S. salaries), Luxembourg (119 percent), and Australia (101 percent). Lowest salaries were paid in Turkey (29 percent of U.S. salaries), Portugal (49 percent), France (56 percent), and Austria (56 percent). Salaries in Japan were slightly lower than those in the U.S. in terms of purchasing power (93 percent), and those in Germany were still somewhat less (85 percent of U.S. levels).

Some other data are available that can be used to assess the accuracy of the salary data reported by the Union Bank of Switzerland on which the analysis in Table 4-1 is based. U.S. teachers' salaries are reported in Barro (1986) and Feistritzer (1983); Japanese teachers' salaries in Barro (1986); and Canadian teachers' salaries in Statistics Canada (1985).

Barro, referencing statistics produced by the National Education Association and published by the National Center for Education Statistics (NCES), gives a 1983-84 average salary of $21,452 for U.S. elementary teachers. The secondary teachers' average was $22,667, and the combined average was $22,019. Feistritzer (1983: 44-49), in the Carnegie Foundations report, *The Condition of Teaching*, gives an overall average salary of $20,531 for 1982-83, and she notes that among the forty-eight contiguous states state averages ranged from $14,285 in Mississippi to $25,100 in New York, a ratio of 1:1.76. (The average in Alaska was $33,953 and

Table 4-1. Gross Earnings of Primary Schoolteachers in U.S. Dollars Using Purchasing Power Parities for GDP, 1982 and 1985.

Country[b]	Salaries in U.S. Dollars		Ratio to U.S. Salary	
	1982	1985	1982	1985
United States	$23,000	$24,600	1.00	1.00
Canada	25,399	30,294	1.10	1.23
Japan	19,940	22,876	.87	.93
Austria	12,219	13,656	.53	.56
Belgium	17,367	17,991	.76	.73
Denmark	17,214	20,034	.75	.81
Finland	12,825	14,530	.56	.59
France	13,627	13,764	.59	.56
Germany	19,801	20,944	.86	.85
Greece	10,380	14,510	.45	.59
Ireland	16,622	20,143	.72	.82
Italy	11,725	16,126	.51	.66
Luxembourg	25,977	29,359	1.13	1.19
Netherlands	18,705	18,171	.81	.74
Norway	15,467	18,251	.67	.74
Portugal	NA	12,052	NA	.49
Spain	14,742	19,781	.64	.80
United Kingdom	15,345	18,220	.67	.74
Australia	19,697	24,809	.86	1.01
Sweden	17,578	18,753	.76	.76
Switzerland	28,882	33,070	1.26	1.34
Turkey	6,154	7,176	.25	.29
Average[c]	17,270	19,505	.75	.78

Sources: Salaries are from Union Bank of Switzerland (1982, 1985). PPPs for GDP for 1982 and 1984 (the latest available) are from OECD (1986).

a. See text for description of calculations and explanation of methodology.

b. Countries are listed in the order presented in OECD sources. For 1982 the U.S. figure is based on the unweighted average of salaries given for Chicago, Los Angeles, New York, and San Francisco; for 1985, for Chicago, Houston, Los Angeles, and New York. Canadian figures are based on the unweighted average of salaries given for Montreal and Toronto, and the Swiss figures on the unweighted average of salaries given for Geneva and Zurich. In other cases, salaries in one major city are used. Data for Australia, Sweden, Switzerland, and Turkey are listed separately since they are not normally included in OECD surveys.

c. Salary averages for 1982 and 1985 for the eighteen countries normally included in OECD surveys were $17,080 and $19,183. These averages are used in later tables for which data on all twenty-two countries listed in Table 4-1 were unavailable.

in Washington, D.C., $26,048.) On the average, 1982–83 salaries were 12 percent lower in terms of purchasing power than in 1972-73.

For Japan, Barro reports the average salary for elementary or lower secondary teachers in 1983–84 to be equivalent to $20,254 U.S. in terms of purchasing power including basic salary, bonuses, and allowances. The secondary average was $22,290 (U.S.), and the combined average, $20,775. According to his comparisons, Japanese elementary teachers' salaries in 1983–84 averaged 94 percent of U.S. teachers' salaries, while Japanese secondary teachers' salaries averaged 98 percent and the combined salaries 94 percent of U.S. teachers' salaries. However, adjusting the U.S. data to accord with the Japanese school year, he concludes that overall Japanese salaries were 97 percent of the U.S. average.

Statistics Canada (1985) reports that the average salary of Canadian elementary teachers (excluding those in Quebec and Alberta for which data were not available) for the 1983–84 school year was $33,580 (Can.), which is equivalent to $29,717 (U.S.) in terms of purchasing power. The average for secondary teachers was $37,840 (Can.), equivalent to $33,345 (U.S.). Averages for elementary teachers ranged from a low of $29,060 (Can.) ($25,717 (U.S.)) in Prince Edward Island to $34,550 (Can.) ($30,575 (U.S.)) in British Columbia, a ratio of 1:1.19. Average salaries for secondary teachers ranged from $30,350 (Can.) ($26,858 (U.S.)) in Prince Edward Island to $39,320 (Can.) ($34,796 (U.S.)) in Ontario, a ratio of 1:1.30. In terms of purchasing power, these averages reflect salaries that are equivalent to 139 percent of the U.S. 1983–84 average for elementary teachers, and 147 percent of the U.S. average for secondary teachers. Even using exchange rates (the appropriate approach when costing winter holidays in Florida), the Canadian elementary average salary equals $24,511 (U.S.), 114 percent of the U.S. average, and the secondary average equals $27,620 (U.S.), 122 percent of the U.S. average.

Comparing these data for the United States, Japan, and Canada with the data reported for the same three countries in Table 4–1 leads to the conclusion that the data from the Union Bank of Switzerland (on which Table 4–1 is based) reflect somewhat above-average salaries for the three nations, as would be expected given that these data are based on salaries in large urban centers. If this bias is reasonably constant from country to country, as seems to be the case with the three countries for which other data sources were available, then the ratios of teachers' salaries of a given country's average teachers' salary to the U.S. average would not be appreciably affected. For Japan, the ratio in question for elementary teachers was .93 for 1985 using UBS data (Table 4-1) and .94 for 1984 according to Barro's analysis (without adjustments for school year differences). For Canada, the ratio for 1985 based on UBS data was 1.23, as opposed to 1.30 for 1984 using a combination of Statistics Canada data and those reported by Barro. We can be quite confident, then, that the salary data and ratios reported in Table 4-1 are valid within a reasonable margin of error of perhaps plus or minus 10 percent. Such a level of uncertainty would not affect the pattern evident in Table 4-1.

SALARY STRUCTURES

A salary structure is the configuration of the varying levels of pay, including bonuses and allowances, received by members of an organization's workforce; this configuration reflects individual differences such as seniority, level of education, level of skill, level and type of assignment, location, family need (such as number of dependants), and the like. The following analysis emphasizes three countries (Canada, the United States, and Japan) and provides some data on sixteen others; data for the latter group are based on information from the World Confederation of Organizations of the Teaching Profession (1986). An earlier and somewhat more extensive analysis is provided by the International Labour Office (1978).

In the United States teacher pay is generally based on a salary schedule or grid that applies to all teachers employed in a given local school system (except Hawaii with its statewide system). These grids have two dimensions or axes—experience and training. Typically, there are between ten and fifteen experience "steps" and four training "categories." Additional payments normally are available only for undertaking extra responsibility such as coaching a team. Barro (1986: 16) indicates that the ratio of maximum to minimum salaries on grids is usually about two to one and suggests that typical starting and maximum salaries in 1983–84 were $13,764 and $28,147, respectively.

Salary structures for teachers in Canada are quite similar to those in the United States in that compensation is based on a two-dimensional grid. Experience steps usually number between eleven and thirteen, and there are usually four training categories for those with a bachelor's degree. However, there are also typically several lower, non-bachelor degree categories that apply to about 25 percent of all elementary teachers and almost 10 percent of all secondary teachers. Virtually all new teachers, though, must have earned a degree, except in Nova Scotia where the teacher training for elementary teachers remains separate from the university. A typical starting salary for a teacher with sixteen years of schooling including a minimum of four years of postsecondary education and a bachelor's degree was $22,100 (Can.) in 1984 (equivalent to $19,558 (U.S.) in purchasing power), and a typical maximum for a teacher with at least eighteen years of education was $40,250 (Can.) (equivalent to $35,619 (U.S.)), a ratio of 1:1.8 (Canadian Teachers' Federation, 1986).[4] If the typical minimum for those without a degree but with fifteen years of schooling is used, the ratio is 1:2.1.

In contrast to U.S. states (except Hawaii), most Canadian provinces have provincewide salary scales that are bargained at the provincial level or by joint local-provincial bodies. Locally negotiated salary grids apply only in British Columbia, Alberta, Manitoba, and Ontario. In Ontario a school board may have as many as three separate salary schedules—one for elementary men teachers, one for elementary women teachers, and one for secondary teachers. In practice, though, the grids rarely differ by more than a few hundred dollars, and the two elementary teachers' organizations usually conduct joint negotiations.

Unlike Canadian and U.S. teachers, Japanese teachers are paid along a one-dimensional scale, supplemented by an annual bonus equal to about five month's wages and various special allowances. The basic grid for national schools in Japan (the national guide) and thirty-nine steps in 1984. Additional training is reflected by a person's being advanced several steps along the grid. The ratio of the maximum salary to the minimum for a teacher with a bachelor's degree was 1:2.9 for elementary and lower secondary teachers and 1:3 for upper secondary teachers, who are paid a somewhat higher maximum. For 1984 annualized salary equivalents ranged from $9,013 (U.S.) to $31,414 (U.S.), including typical bonuses and allowances (Barro 1986: 11–12).

The 1986 edition of the report by the World Confederation of Organizations of the Teaching Profession, "Study on Teachers' Work-

Table 4-2. Ratios of Maximum to Minimum Salaries by Level of Instruction for Teachers in North America, Japan, and Europe.

Country	Elementary	Secondary	Secondary Maximum/ Elementary Minimum	Years to Maximum
United States	1:2.0	1:2.0	1:2.0	15
Canada	1:2.1	1:1.8	1:2.1	13
Japan	1:3.3	1:3.1	1:3.4	39
Austria	1:2.2	1:2.5	1:3.1	38
Denmark	1:1.3	1:1.5	1:1.7	18
England and Wales	1.2.3	1:2.3	1:2.3	13
Finland	1:1.6	1:1.6	1:1.9	20
France	1:1.5	1:2.2	1:2.7	30
Federal Republic of Germany	1:1.8	1:1.8	1:2.0	30
Gilbraltar	1:2.3	1:2.3	1:2.3	13
Ireland	1:1.6	1:1.6	1:1.6	14
Italy	1:1.4	1:1.5	1:1.6	40
Luxembourg	1:2.0	1:1.8	1:2.8	24
Malta	1:1.8	1:1.9	1:2.5	11
Netherlands	1:2.0	1:2.6	1:2.9	22
Norway	1:1.3	1:1.5	1:1.6	24
Scotland	1:1.5	1:1.6	1:1.6	12
Spain	1:1.4	1:1.4	1:1.6	42
Sweden	1:1.4	1:1.4	1:1.6	16
Average	1:1.8	1:1.9	1:2.2	23

Sources: Barro (1986); Canadian Teachers' Federation (1986); World Confederation of Organizations of the Teaching Profession (1986).

ing Conditions in Europe," provides some information on salary structures in sixteen European countries. In most of these nations, educational requirements are more extensive for secondary school teachers than for elementary school teachers, and secondary teachers are paid higher salaries. The ratios between the maximum to minimum salaries, both within level (that is, elementary or secondary) and between levels are reported in Table 4-2.

Three conclusions can be made from the table. First, the United States and, for all practical purposes, Canadian practice of a single pay scale for both elementary and secondary teachers tends to be the exception, rather than the rule. Indeed, this practice holds only in the case of the United Kingdom and its present or former colonies. All other countries pay their secondary teachers significantly more than their elementary teachers, as is evident from the higher ratios of secondary maxima to elementary minima. Second, flat pay scales with fifteen steps or fewer are also limited to countries with British connections; other nations prefer to have scales with twenty, thirty, or more steps. Finally, there is great variation in the ratio of maximum to minimum salary levels; these range from a low of 1:1.6 in nations such as Ireland, Norway, Scotland, and Sweden to 1:3.4 in Japan and 1:3.1 in Austria.

RELATIVE LEVELS OF SALARIES

This chapter has examined how well teachers are paid in one country compared with those in other countries and how teachers at different levels are paid in comparison with one another within certain nations. This section discusses how well teachers are paid relative to others in their countries. A number of ways are used to carry out this task: (1) Teachers' incomes are related to their nation's per capita gross domestic product; (2) they are related to their nation's per capita private consumption; (3) they are related to salaries paid to workers in other fields within their nation; and (4) they are related to their nation's average industrial wage. For convenience, the third and fourth analyses are reported together.

In Table 4-3 the salaries of typical teachers (where, again, *typical* refers to the demographic profile of a teacher used in the UBS data to remove the effect on salaries of different teacher characteristics) are expressed as a percentage of gross domestic product per capita

Table 4-3. Primary Schoolteachers' Salaries as a Percentage of Gross
Domestic Product per Head in U.S. Dollars Using PPPs, 1982 and 1985.

Country	GDP per Head		Salary as Percentage of GDP per Head	
	1982	1984[a]	1982	1985
United States	$13,107	$15,356	175%	160%
Canada	13,219	15,198	192	199
Japan	10,509	12,235	190	187
Austria	10,043	11,345	122	120
Belgium	11,082	12,150	157	148
Denmark	11,680	13,422	147	149
Finland	10,772	12,217	119	119
France	11,550	12,643	118	109
Germany	11,742	13,265	169	158
Greece	5,715	6,300	182	230
Ireland	7,019	7,795	237	258
Italy	9,140	10,044	128	161
Luxembourg	12,114	14,385	214	204
Netherlands	10,622	11,710	176	155
Norway	13,250	15,367	117	119
Portugal	4,796	5,021	NA	240
Spain	7,419	8,279	199	239
United Kingdom	9,753	11,068	157	165
Average	10,195	11,544	165	173

Sources: Salary data from Table 4-1. GDP per head in U.S. dollars using current PPPs
for 1982 and 1984 are from OECD (1986).
   a. Latest data available. Comparable data for Australia, Sweden, Switzerland, and
Turkey not available.

with both variables being measured in terms of their purchasing
power. These percentages indicate the portion of the national wealth
paid to "typical" teachers—in effect, their share of the national pie.
In 1985 teachers' salaries average 173 percent of GDP per capita,
but they ranged from a low of 109 percent in France to a high of
258 percent in Ireland. U.S. teachers' standing was somewhat below
average at 160 percent, an apparent reversal from 1982 when, at
175 percent, they stood somewhat above the average of 165 percent.
Both Canada, at 199 percent, and Japan, at 187 percent, ranked

above the United States in terms of the share of the national wealth paid to their average teacher, while Germany and the United Kingdom paid shares similar to those in the United States. It is notable that a number of the less wealthy nations including Greece, Ireland, Portugal, and Spain paid over 230 percent of GDP per capita to their teachers.

Also indicated in Table 4–3 are the per capita GDPs for the various countries expressed in terms of U.S. dollars using PPPs. To some extent, the data shed somewhat different light on the usual assumption that nations like Germany and Japan are outperforming the United States and Canada. In fact, only Luxembourg and Norway produced wealth at a rate comparable to the two North American nations.

Table 4–4 presents another approach to looking at teachers' share of their national pie by calculating typical salaries as a percentage of per capita private consumption (in U.S. dollars using PPPs). Unlike GDP, which reflects the total wealth that a nation produces regardless of how it is used—to pay foreign debts, to save, to purchase collective goods and services, or to spend privately—private consumption measures only what people in a nation actually spent on themselves. The United States spends relatively more of its national wealth on private consumption than do other nations of similar wealth, probably because it provides less in the way of government services and has a lower rate of savings per capita. For example, medical care in Canada and Roman Catholic schools in five Canadian provinces are government financed rather than privately financed, whereas in the United States expenditures on both would be reflected in the statistics on private consumption. In addition, the rate of saving is higher in both Japan, at about 17 percent of income, and in Canada, at about 12 percent of income, than in the United States, where it has averaged about 4 percent of income in recent years.

Teachers' salaries as a percentage of per capita private consumption range from a low of 172 percent in France to a high of 464 percent in Ireland; the average is 297 percent. United States teachers' pay, by this index, is even poorer than that based on GDP per head. Ranked tenth of eighteen in Table 4–3, its standing falls to fourteenth place in Table 4–4. The standings of Canadian and Japanese teachers, though, differ little; they stand sixth and seventh in Table 4–3 and fourth and seventh in Table 4–4. In least wealthy nations

Table 4-4. Primary Schoolteachers' Salaries as a Percentage of Private Consumption per Head in U.S. Dollars Using PPPs, 1982 and 1985.

Country	Private Consumption per Head		Salary as Percentage of Private Consumption per Head	
	1982	1984[a]	1982	1985
United States	$8,743	$10,214	263%	241%
Canada	7,488	8,484	339	357
Japan	5,957	6,744	335	339
Austria	5,720	6,490	214	210
Belgium	7,099	7,637	245	236
Denmark	6,064	6,842	284	293
Finland	5,554	6,287	231	231
France	7,373	8,009	185	172
Germany	6,561	7,274	302	288
Greece	3,754	4,089	277	355
Ireland	4,180	4,338	398	464
Italy	5,724	6,251	205	258
Luxembourg	7,763	8,540	335	345
Netherlands	6,773	7,270	276	250
Norway	5,994	6,624	258	276
Portugal	3,002	3,076	NA	392
Spain	5,110	5,456	288	362
United Kingdom	5,733	6,535	268	279
Average	6,033	6,675	277	297

Sources: Salary data from Table 4-1. Personal consumption per head in U.S. dollars using current PPPs for 1982 and 1984 are from OECD (1986).

a. Latest data available. Comparable data for Australia, Sweden, Switzerland, and Turkey not available.

of those considered—namely, Ireland, Portugal, and Spain—teachers have the best pay relative to national levels of consumption.

The third approach to assessing the relative pay of teachers within the nations surveyed involves comparing pay levels of teachers with those in other occupations, and the fourth approach involves comparisons with average industrial wages. Table 4-5, using data from the Union Bank of Switzerland and the International Labour Office

Table 4–5. Salaries in Other Occupations Relative to Teachers' Salaries in OECD Countries, 1985. [a]

Country	Sales	Average Wage	Construction	Bus Driver	Toolmaker	Electrical Engineer	Manager
United States	52	73	95	97	120	146	204
Canada	46	60	83	78	85	124	159
Japan	59	69	69	104	94	130	248
Austria	63	82	89	119	125	225	226
Belgium	70	69	91	101	95	158	155
Denmark	79	70	92	93	108	142	195
Finland	64	62	97	98	98	154	224
France	61	78	57	119	113	309	305
Germany	45	68	66	98	95	137	180
Greece	55	55	71	112	104	136	180
Ireland	60	65	53	65	81	132	170
Italy	88	83	75	106	94	174	159
Luxembourg	37	58	41	80	79	141	158
Netherlands	70	73	80	98	97	152	231
Norway	68	81	124	105	101	138	132
Portugal	50	NA	50	78	73	155	175
Spain	46	51	48	64	83	174	127
United Kingdom	53	74	76	81	94	159	138
Average	59	69	75	94	97	160	187

Sources: Union Bank of Switzerland (1985) and International Labour Office (1985).

a. Teachers' salary in each country = 100; salaries for other occupations are expressed as a percentage of the teachers' salary in that country (see Table 4-1). Position descriptions are as follows: salesclerk employed in ladies' wear department of a large department store; received some training but not especially in selling with several years of selling experience (about age 20 to 24, single); average industrial wage, annualized pay based on five-day week, forty-eight-week year, using data on hourly wages and hours worked per week or month; construction worker, unskilled or semi-skilled laborer (about age 25, single); bus driver employed by municipal system, about ten years driving experience (about age 35, married, two children); toolmakers/lathe operators, skilled mechanic with vocational training and about ten years experience with a large company in the metal working industry (about age 35, married, two children); electrical engineer employed by an industrial firm in the machinery or electrical equipment industry, electric power company, or similar; completed university studies (college, technical institution or institute of higher technical education) with at least five years of practical experience (about age 35, married, no children); technical department manager of a production department (more than 100 employees) in a sizable company of the metal working industry; completed professional training with many years of experience in the field (about age 40, married, no children).

(1985), expresses the annual pay of those persons in six different occupations and uses the average industrial wage in each of eighteen nations as a percentage of primary teachers' salaries in those countries. For example, sales staffs in major U.S. cities are paid an annual wage equal to about 52 percent of the typical elementary school teacher; the average industrial wage equals 73 percent of such a teacher's salary, while electrical engineers are paid 46 percent more than (or 146 percent of the pay for) this teacher (Table 4–5).

The relatively low pay of U.S. teachers relative to those in other jobs, a matter that has been commented on by a number of writers (such as Feistritzer 1983; Hawley 1986), is evident in the table. Their salaries average 37 percent more than the average industrial worker; are essentially equal to those of construction workers and bus drivers; and are well below those of toolmakers, electrical engineers, and managers. Relative to other nations, only in the case of electrical engineers is the pay differential relative to teachers' salaries less than average, and even this fact is due to the effect on the average differential paid electrical engineers by the exceedingly high differential for France.[5] Excluding France, the average would be 152 percent.

In Canada pay for other occupations expressed as a percentage of teachers' salaries is considerably lower than the United States, and a similar pattern pertains in Japan, with the exception of drivers and managers. Indeed, bus drivers seem to do well in a number of nations, earning as much or more than teachers in Japan, Austria, Belgium, France, Greece, Italy, and Norway. Managers fare particularly well relative to teachers in France, Japan, the Netherlands, Finland, and the United States.

Hawley (1986: 713) notes "that teacher salaries would have to be increased by about 40 percent in order to make teaching competitive on strictly economic dimensions with other occupations and professions that attract reasonably bright college graduates." The data in Table 4–5 tend to confirm such an assessment and suggest that an increase on the order of 25 percent would be necessary to provide U.S. teachers pay appropriate to international norms for the position of teachers in the overall occupational structure.

DISCUSSION AND CONCLUSION

The initial puzzlement that gave rise to the chapter concerned apparent differences in the U.S. and Canadian labor markets for teachers, and it was hypothesized that the differences were due to different salary levels in the two nations. A review of the evidence presented above supports this hypothesis. According to all measures used—purchasing power, salary relative to per capita gross domestic product and per capita private consumption, and salaries of other occupations as a percentage of typical teacher salaries—Canadian teachers are paid considerably better than U.S. teachers. The salary differences—on the order of 23 percent in terms of purchasing power and 50 percent in terms of salaries as a percentage of per capita private consumption—would seem adequate to account, in economic terms, for Canadian university graduates even with skills in areas of high demand and low supply, such as mathematics and science, deciding to choose teaching as a career.

The problem of the study was broadened to consider other countries, including Japan and Germany, in the hope that some insight might be gained into how other nations, successful competitors on the economic front, provide for their teachers. Generally speaking, Japan rewards its teachers more highly than does the United States but not as well as does Canada. Only Luxembourg and Switzerland seem to provide teachers with higher salaries (at least for the nations considered), although a number of less wealthy European nations, led by Ireland, provide high salaries relative to the wealth of their nations.

This international perspective of teachers' salaries, of course, has its limitations. First, no account has been taken of different working conditions of teachers—such as class size, length of school year, and types of responsibilities. Second, a single data series, provided by the Union Bank of Switzerland, has provided most of the salary data. What cross-checking was carried out suggested the data were reasonably reliable, but remuneration policies can be quite subtle and complex, as Barro (1986) and the International Labour Office (1978) make clear for Japan. Third, the method used by the Union Bank of Switzerland to measure typical salaries may underestimate modal salaries in nations such as Austria, France, and Japan where salary scales have thirty or more steps and a high ratio of maximum to minimum salaries. Finally, except for the simple economic hypothesis that gave rise to the research, no theoretical framework has been advanced in order to make sense out of the descriptive data presented.

Expanding on this last point, it is clear that there is a need for a theory of teacher supply and demand that would take into account a number of factors: the structure of national economies, supply of university (and otherwise trained) individuals, and national traditions. That the highest salaries, relative to per capita private consumptions, are paid in nations such as Ireland, Spain, Portugal, and Greece that are in the process of transforming themselves from agrarian to modern economies, is probably not an accident. The high wages paid in construction and in most other areas in Norway is no doubt related to its share of the North Sea energy boom of the late 1970s and early 1980s.

Explaining the differences in teachers' salaries between the United States and Canada may be a good place to begin to build on the work of Barro (1986), the International Labour Office (1978), and the World Confederation of Organizations of the Teaching Profession (1986); this explanation would help to refine our understanding of why teachers are paid what they are. These two nations share many common values and political structures (Lawton 1979), and their economies are closely linked. Yet Canada already does in practice what analysts such as Levin (1985) and Hawley (1986) deem impossible: It pays all teachers substantially higher salaries than the United States does. Instead, these authors focus on paying salary differentials for teachers in areas where supply is low (such as mathematics and physics); they tend as well to overlook the extent of joint production in education, wherein the quality of education a child receives is not divisible into the individual "value added" contributions made by each teacher but is the sum of their collective efforts. Rewarding one group of teachers by paying higher salaries without having a negative effect on the attitudes, motivations, and efforts of other teachers, and thereby lessening the overall quality of education, would seem to be difficult, at best.

The lesson to be learned from the international data is that levels of pay that attract well-qualified people to teaching, even in areas of relatively short supply, are possible. Sights should not be set too low. At the same time, it is necessary to understand the social, political, and economic contexts that make such levels of pay possible if useful plans to alter teacher pay levels are to be made. My only concern, I must admit, in suggesting such an agenda is that Canadians might learn from Americans how to pay their teachers less, rather than Americans learn how to pay their teachers more.

NOTES

1. In general, there is an oversupply of teachers in Canada. Evidence of an adequate supply of mathematics and science (including physics and chemistry) teachers is provided by the lack of writings on the topic. A 1978 Canadian Teachers' Federation report on teaching opportunities did not mention a need for math and science teachers, and a major review of science education in Canada. (Connelly, Crocker, and Kass 1985: 228) devotes just one page to the topic. A December 1986 telephone survey of six major centers across Canada revealed that persons responsible for hiring teachers perceived a tight but adequate supply of science and mathematics teachers except in the Metropolitan Toronto area, where rapid growth and an economic boom have created at least a temporary shortage. Of more general concern was the tight or inadequate supply of French immersion teachers at all levels.

   On the U.S. situation, see Guthrie and Zusman (1982), Blosser (1984), Olstad and Beal (1984), Shugart (1983), Shymansky and Aldridge (1982), and Hawley (1986). For a formal development of the economics of labor markets including the relationships between supply, demand, and price, see Rumberger (1985) and Levin (1985).

2. Although the work on this chapter was underway at the time Barro's paper became available, the author acknowledges his indebtedness to Barro for the definition of the problem, development of methodology, and direction to important sources. Also acknowledged is the assistance of N. M. Goble, Secretary General, and Thomas Rehula, Acting Coordinator Teachers' Rights Programmes, World Confederation of Organizations of the Teaching Profession, who provided much of the salary information analyzed in the chapter.

3. OECD reports two types of PPPs, one based on gross domestic products and one based on a market basket of privately consumed goods and services. The former was used in these analysis because, as the more general, it includes goods and services—including public education—that are publicly consumed. In most cases, PPPs for private consumption are within a few percentage points of PPPs for GDP, and using the former would not significantly alter the overall conclusions of this study.

4. The typical minima and maximum were calculated by finding the unweighted average of minima and maxima for provinces with provincial scales combined with equivalent figures for major city boards in provinces with local negotiations—that is, Vancouver (British Columbia), Calgary (Alberta), Winnipeg (Manitoba), and Carleton Board of Education (Ontario).

5. The very low salaries reported for primary teachers in Austria and France may reflect, in part, the effect of these nations' salary scales that, with over

thirty steps and a maximum to minimum ratio on the order of 1:3.0 (see Table 4–2), pay relatively low salaries at the start of a career but better salaries late in the career or, in the case of France, after merit advances along the scale. Because the UBS data series specifies the characteristics of the typical teacher (about age 35 with ten years of experience), it may tend to underestimate typical salaries if staff are more senior or have been advanced due to merit in France.

REFERENCES

Barro, Stephen M. 1986. *A Comparison of Teachers' Salaries in Japan and the United States.* Report prepared for the National Center for Education Statistics (NCES) under U.S. Department of Education Contract 300–84–0265. Washington, D.C.: SMB Economic Research. Mimeo.

Blosser, Patricia E. 1984. "What Research Says: Science Teacher Supply and Demand." *School Science and Mathematics* 84 (3) (March 1984): 244–49.

Canadian Teachers' Federation. 1978. *Teaching in Canada.* Ottawa: CTF.

Canadian Teachers' Federation. 1986. "Summary of Major Teacher Salary Scales in Canada, 1970–71 to 1985–86." Economic Service Bulletin 1986–5. Ottawa: CTF.

Connelly, F. Michael, Robert K. Crocker, and Heidi Kass. 1985. *Science Education in Canada, Vol. 1: Policies, Practices and Perceptions.* Informal Series/60. Toronto: Ontario Institute for Studies in Education.

"Could Golden Arches Prop Up the Peso?" 1986. Reprinted from *The Economist. The Globe and Mail*, September 18.

Feistritzer, C. Emily. 1983. *The Condition of Teaching: A State by State Analysis.* Princeton, N.J.: Carnegie Foundation for the Advancement of Teaching.

Guthrie, James W., and Ami Zusman. 1982. "Teacher Supply and Demand in Mathematics and Science." *Phi Delta Kappan* 64 (1) (September 1982): 28–33.

Hawley, Willis D. 1986. "Toward a Comprehensive Strategy for Addressing the Teacher Shortage." *Phi Delta Kappa* 67 (10) (June 1986): 712–18.

International Labour Office. 1978. *Teachers' Pay.* Geneva: ILO.

_____. 1985. *Year Book of Labour Statistics.* 45th Issue. Geneva: ILO.

Lawton, Stephen B. 1979. "Political Values and Educational Finance in Canada and the United States." *Journal of Education Finance* 5 (1) (Summer 1979): 1–18.

Levin, Henry M. 1985. "Solving the Shortage of Mathematics and Science Teachers." *Educational Evaluation and Policy Analysis* 7 (4) (1985): 371–82.

Olstad, Roger G., and Jack L. Beal. 1984. "The Science and Mathematics Teacher Shortage: A Study of Recent Graduates." *Science Education* 68 (4) (July 1984): 397–402.

Organization for Economic Cooperation and Development. 1986. *National Accounts, Vol. I: Main Aggregates*. Paris: OECD.

Rumberger, Russell. 1985. "The Shortage of Mathematics and Science Teachers: A Review of the Evidence." *Educational Evaluation and Policy Analysis* 7 (4) (Winter): 355–69.

Shugart, Sanford C. 1983. "The Context of the Physical Science and Mathematics Teacher Shortage." *High School Journal* 66 (4) (April/May): 245–50.

Shymansky, James A., and Bill G. Aldridge. 1982. "The Teacher Crisis in Secondary School Science and Mathematics." *Educational Leadership* 40 (2) (November): 61–66.

Statistics Canada. 1985. *Education in Canada: A Statistical Review for 1983–84*. Ottawa: Minister of Supply and Services Canada. Catalogue 81–229.

Union Bank of Switzerland. 1982. *Prices and Earnings around the Globe*. UBS Publications on Business, Banking and Monetary Topics, Vol. 81. Zurich: Union Bank of Switzerland, Economic Research Department.

_____. 1985. *Prices and Earnings around the Globe*. UBS Publications on Business, Banking and Monetary Topics, Vol. 97. Zurich: Union Bank of Switzerland, Economic Research Department.

World Confederation of Organizations of the Teaching Profession. 1986. *Study of Teachers' Working Conditions in Europe*. Morges, Switzerland: WCOTP.

5 RESTRUCTURING TEACHER COMPENSATION SYSTEMS
An Analysis of Three Incentive Strategies

Betty Malen, Michael J. Murphy, and Ann Weaver Hart

This chapter examines policies that seek to improve teacher quality by restructuring the compensation system. Assuming that compensation systems operate not only to reimburse workers but also to induce change, policymakers are attempting to revamp the manner in which teacher salaries are distributed. Three incentive strategies are embedded in policies recently enacted or currently under consideration in state legislatures: (1) merit pay, (2) expanded jobs, and (3) redesigned jobs. In this chapter, we analyze each strategy—its central features, its initial effects, and its potential for achieving desired outcomes—and then highlight implications for those who are investing scarce resources in the reform of teacher salary systems.

Empirical research on the effects of merit pay, job expansion, and job redesign strategies in school settings is limited but instructive. Studies in Utah[1] augmented by studies conducted in other states provide the primary data for this chapter. When coupled with related literature, the available field research can address an important, if not an "urgent priority," (Kirst 1985: 6), the assessment of education

Portions of this chapter are contained in an occasional policy paper, "Career Ladder Reform in Utah: Evidence of Impact, Recommendations for Action" (Malen, Murphy, and Hart 1987). The policy paper was sponsored by the Graduate School of Education, University of Utah, Salt Lake City, Utah, January 1987.

We are indebted to John Bennion, Roald Campbell, Sue Geary, Don Kauchak, and Ken Peterson for their critical reviews of earlier versions of this chapter.

reforms. Because many states cannot afford "to fully fund all of the various schemes to improve the teaching profession," legislatures need to decide which components of the teacher-related interventions warrant continuation, extension, or termination (Kirst 1985: 4). Because the relationship between policies and outcomes is never "pure, single and uncontaminated," systematic assessments of policy effects cannot provide definitive answers (Patton 1986: 151). But they can offer reasonable estimates of impact and general directions for investment.

PERSPECTIVE

Assessing Initival Effects

Broad policy goals guide this assessment of initial effects. The merit pay, job expansion, and job redesign strategies have common objectives. All attempt to fundamentally alter the distribution of economic rewards in ways that improve teaching and strengthen retention. We analyze, then, whether economic rewards are redistributed, whether teaching is influenced, and whether retention is likely to be affected.

Salary and status serve as indexes of the extent to which economic rewards are fundamentally altered. We focus on salary and status because the strategies aim to create salary differentials and assume that status gains will accompany these salary variations.

Changes in work patterns and the perceived influence of these new patterns on the teachers' desire and ability to improve are used to gauge impact on teaching. We also report side effects—unanticipated or unintended consequences that are viewed as impediments to the goal of improved teaching. These indicators are admittedly imprecise. They are, however, a useful first step. As Rosenholtz argues, "it makes sense to measure the effects of current reform efforts in terms of the perceptions of teachers involved, since only those factors that are perceived by teachers can affect their subsequent attitudes and behaviors" (Rosenholtz forthcoming: 3).

Satisfaction with work is a fairly strong measure of the likelihood that individuals will remain in their jobs (*Work in America* 1973: xvii; Bluedorn 1982) and is a reasonable measure of the likelihood that teachers will remain in teaching (Kottkamp et al. 1986: 561). We use this concept to estimate retention effects.

Assessing the Potential of the Strategies

Our discussion of the potential of merit pay, job expansion, and job redesign strategies to achieve desired outcomes is grounded in the notion of congruence. A dominant theme in pay incentive literature is that the "key to pay system effectiveness is in finding or creating a correct fit between the pay system and the rest of the organization" (Lawler 1981: 178; Patten 1977: 153). Because the pay system is only one of many elements operating to shape attitudes and behaviors in organizations, it must be aligned with the work environment and consistent with, or potent enough to modify, the dominant views and values of the individuals to be affected. If the pay system is not credibly or persuasively aligned, its effect will be neutralized or negated by the numerous forces that interact to influence the performance and satisfaction of the people in the organization.

To be congruent with and hence effective in a particular context, the literature on pay incentives indicates that the compensation strategy must fit the major characteristics of the workplace. It must fit the nature of the work, the types of tasks to be accomplished; the culture of the organization, its norms, traditions, and informal networks; and the constraints imposed by the formal arrangements and work conditions. In addition, the compensation strategy must offer dependable rewards that are salient to the individuals for whom the pay system is designed (Lawler 1981: 159). When applied to school settings, this perspective suggests that to operate effectively, the pay system must accommodate complex work, engrained autonomy/ equality/civility norms, the vulnerability precipitated by existing work conditions, and the teachers' need for dependable intrinsic as well as extrinsic rewards.

Complex Work

Teaching can be characterized as complex work for several reasons. First, teaching is adaptive. It requires individuals to continuously adjust to new and unpredictable circumstances. Although some aspects of teaching can be handled through preplanned routines, other aspects emphasize "responding to conditions arising on the job, exercising proper judgment regarding what is needed, and maintaining intellectual and technical flexibility" (Mitchell and Kerchner 1983: 215). Second, teaching requires individuals to use a variety of skills. Teachers are often expected, for example, to foster social as well as academic development, instruct single individuals and large groups, orchestrate remediation as well as enrichment, weave creative experiences into controlled environments, and balance these various classroom responsibilities with other school/community service obligations. Third, teaching is interdependent. The accomplishment of work is contingent on others. Accomplishment is influenced, for instance, by the interests, abilities, circumstances, and responses of students and the actions of other teachers.

Autonomy/Equality/Civility Norms

In most schools, administrators and teachers subscribe to "a set of understandings," a set of norms that guide and govern work relationships (Lortie 1964: 275). Three norms are particularly apparent in schools: "(1) the teacher should be free from the interference of other adults while teaching, (2) teachers should be considered and treated as equals, and (3) teachers should act in a nonintervening but friendly manner toward one another" (Lortie 1964: 275). These rules interact and reinforce one another to create what Lortie (1964: 275) terms an "autonomy-equality pattern" and what we would describe as an autonomy/equality/civility pattern.[2] Educators believe policies and practices that compromise these norms infringe on the "private domain" (Lortie 1964: 275) of teachers, constitute unfair treatment, and jeopardize personal relationships. Educators are therefore prone to resist, counter, or adjust requirements so that disruption is minimized, cherished values are protected, and camaraderie is preserved.

Vulnerability

Teachers face stress-producing work conditions. They experience multiple, ambiguous, and often contradictory demands; chronic resource shortages; intense client interactions; incessant pressures to make consequential service delivery decisions on the basis of incomplete information; and intermittent challenges to their emotional and physical safety (Lipsky 1980). Moreover, teachers face these conditions in isolation (Lortie 1975; Rosenholtz 1984). Much of the teachers' work is carried out in self-contained classrooms that insulate them from both the support and scrutiny of colleagues.

These conditions and arrangements do more than constrain capacity to accomplish tasks. They contribute to an atmosphere of vulnerability. The discrepancy between what most professionals want to do and what they are able to do, given the uncertainties and adversities of the workplace, is a major source of anxiety (Duke 1984). Most teachers are painfully aware that service delivery falls short of the ideal (Duke 1984). At any time, any teacher could lose hold of the situation; at any time, any teacher could be criticized for short-changing a student; at any time, even the most talented, dedicated teacher could face failure (McLaughlin 1986: 422). Work arrangements and conditions, then, precipitate and perpetuate "a general lack of confidence, a pervasive feeling of vulnerability, a fear of being 'found out' (Lieberman and Miller 1984: 13). Policies that accentuate those fears evoke resistance. Teachers "shy away from situations where conclusions about a lack of professional adequacy may either be publicly or privately drawn" (Rosenholtz forthcoming: 32). Teachers, like other human beings, act to shield themselves from threatening forces.

Salient, Dependable Extrinsic, and Intrinsic Rewards

People can be motivated by both extrinsic and intrinsic rewards. Extrinsic rewards are "primarily external and material such as pay and promotion" (Johnson 1986: 57). Intrinsic rewards are "primarily internal and intangible such as pride in work or achieving a sense of efficacy" (Johnson 1986: 57). Because "most individuals must receive both the intrinsic and extrinsic rewards they desire and feel they deserve," a strategy affecting both is potentially more potent than a strategy manipulating one or the other (Lawler 1981). A rich body of literature demonstrates, however, that "teachers are more powerfully affected by intrinsic rewards—particularly their sense of responsibility for student learning and their enjoyment of warm social relationships—than by extrinsic rewards [pay differentials, social status, or public recognition] delivered after their work has been observed and evaluated by others" (D. Mitchell 1986: 17). Because intrinsic rewards are more salient, a compensation strategy that supports opportunities for teachers to derive intrinsic as well as extrinsic rewards is likely to be more compelling than a strategy that offers only material gains. Whatever reward is offered, recipients must view the reward as stable and dependable. Unless recipients can count on the reward, there is little reason to adjust behavior (Vroom 1964).

MERIT PAY STRATEGY

Central Features

Merit pay relates salary to qualitative differences in the performance of similar work—in this instance, classroom teaching (Lieberman 1985: 104). The aim is to directly link salary increments to performance criteria such as the use of certain prescribed teaching behaviors or the results of various student achievement measures (Murnane and Cohen 1985: 1). This strategy emphasizes extrinsic rewards. The payoff is largely material, a salary benefit, accompanied by increased status through public recognition of superior performance (Lawler 1981). The focus is individual. Although the expectation is that when systems "reward the best" they will "inspire the rest" to either excel or exit (Cohen and Murnane 1985: 42), compensation is tied to the individual teacher's performance. There are, of course, merit pay plans based on group performance, but they are not widely used in school settings (Hatry and Greiner 1985; Stern 1986). Since most states are concentrating on the individual teacher as the unit for distribution, we confine our analysis to this form of merit pay.

Merit pay is a major component of most career ladder policies (Bray et al. 1985: 28–34; Lortie 1986: 572; Stern 1986: 305). In Utah, for example, there is a legislative requirement to disperse at least 10 percent of state career ladder funds solely on the basis of classroom teaching performance. Although Florida named its new policy a career ladder, it remains essentially a merit pay plan.[3] Advancement on Tennessee's career ladder is based primarily on classroom teaching evaluations. Additional responsibilities may be part of the upper level, but the emphasis is clearly merit pay (Tennessee Department of Education 1985).

Initial Effects

Merit Pay and Distribution of Salary—Status Benefits. The merit pay strategy does not effectively alter the distribution of salary and status benefits in school systems. In most instances, financial rewards are not fundamentally restructured. Status gains are either denied by pressures for secrecy or offset by social sanction.

Salary. There are three indications that merit stipends are relatively blunt, routinely circumvented, or intensely resisted devices for redistributing salaries. First, merit pay is typically used to supplement rather than supplant the basic salary schedule. Payments come in addition to, not in lieu of, the contracted wage. Unless the stipend is exceptionally large, the major portion of the employee's compensation is still the basic salary (Hatry and Greiner 1985: 14). Further, eligibility requirements reinforce the seniority and training components of existing salary arrangements. In most states, teachers must be in the system for several years and complete additional hours of training before they can apply for a merit award (Bray et al. 1985: 28–34; Education Commission of the States 1985; Erlandson and Wilcox 1985; Malen and Murphy 1985; Utah State Office of Education 1985: 14). When the merit pay strategy rests in part on allocation criteria nested in traditional salary schedules, it operates to reinforce more than restructure the distribution of monetary rewards.

Second, merit stipends are likely to be dispersed broadly, to all or nearly all who apply.[4] In Utah only a small percentage of applicants were denied merit awards (Malen and Hart forthcoming). Applicants were denied primarily on technical-procedural grounds; individuals had not "followed all the guidelines" for submitting information. This rather inclusive and relatively routine dispersement of rewards is not unique to Utah. A prominent feature of merit pay distribution in other settings is to "quietly award merit pay to almost all teachers" (Murnane 1986: 5–6). Merit pay becomes, in effect, a uniform salary increase for all, or nearly all teachers.

Third, where regulations that prohibit broad distribution are introduced, they are usually challenged, relaxed, or repealed. Attempts to restrict distribution ignite teacher resistance. The political pressure prompts policymakers to either drop merit pay altogether or hone compromised policies that ease rules and expand coverage.

Utah's legislation does not impose quotas,[5] but other states, notably Tennessee and Florida, have tried to do so. In these states, teachers fought the caps in legislative and judicial arenas. Their intense resistance resulted in an elimination or a revision of the quota system (Snider 1986: 1; Rodman 1985: 6; Handler and Carlson 1984, 1985). The effect in Tennessee was a dramatic increase in the proportion of teachers eligible for awards (Handler and Carlson 1985: 15) and an anticipated increase in the number of teachers applying for and receiving awards.[6] The effect in Florida was an explicit agreement to extend coverage (from 3 percent to 28 percent of the teaching force), expand coverage further when the legislature appropriates the agreed on funding, or repeal the program if the state funding commitment is not honored (Snider 1986: 20).

Status. When merit awards are given, procedural and social pressures within schools interact to keep recipients and rewards secret. Although individuals might derive some benefits from the private knowledge that their efforts were deemed worthy of additional money, the prestige or status benefits embedded in public recognition are not attained. When outside regulatory agencies insist on public disclosure, public recognition benefits are offset by peer sanctions.

In Utah, for example, procedures to keep merit awards a private matter included selection committee decisions to mail checks to recipients in the summer when, as one member explained, "it's more difficult to find out who got what." Privacy pressures were also apparent in shared agreements to keep names of recipients confidential, "to be discreet," "to keep our mouths shut." These tendencies are not unique to Utah. Attempts to keep merit awards "inconspicuous" to "practice secrecy" (Murnane 1986: 5), regarding the size and the recipient of merit bonuses are evident in other locations as well (Cohen and Murnane 1985: 7, 8). When secrecy operates, it is difficult to see the pay-for-performance connection, and it is unlikely that money, or any of its status spinoffs, can serve as motivators for members of the organization (Lawler 1981: 102; Nadler and Lawler 1977: 32).

Where public disclosure occurs, the teacher response is often to discredit those selected. Thus, any status and recognition benefits are offset by the criticism and derision of other teachers. Where teachers learned the names of merit designees in Utah, the recipients were subjected to "heavy teasing" and "a continuous onslaught of ribbing." Colleagues accused individuals of "brown nosing" and "bragging." They discounted recipients by noting that some of the best teachers did not apply and by exchanging stories of how teachers on remediation one year were granted merit awards the next. In states where award winners were widely publicized, even more intense reactions surfaced. On one survey in Tennessee, 97 percent of the respondents, including those selected, reported that the most deserving teachers were not promoted (Rosenholtz forthcoming: 46). In some cases, promoted individuals were subjected to "collective faculty ostracism" (Rosenholtz forthcoming: 46). If attempts to provide status and recognition beget ridicule and denigration, it is hard for meritorious teachers to experience a net gain in prestige.

In sum, the merit pay strategy operates as a relatively weak vehicle for reallocating salary and a potentially counterproductive means for conferring status. The current experience echoes previous experiments. Although merit pay policies have been enacted, removed, revived, and retried for decades, few endure (Hatry and Greiner 1985: 111-12; Cohen and Murnane 1985: 3-6). The strategy does not appear to be a viable approach to the redistribution of economic rewards in school settings (Johnson 1984: 176-80).

Merit Pay and Effect on Teaching. The merit pay strategy can change work patterns. Although it can stimulate educators to use their time differently, it does not cause them to perform more effectively. Merit stipends have little influence on either the teachers' desire or ability to improve. Further, merit pay produces side effects that impede improvement.

Change in Work Patterns. In Utah the merit pay strategy directed attention to classroom observation and evaluation activities. Both principals and teachers consistently reported that the time devoted to teacher appraisal increased substantially as a result of the merit pay policy. Most informants applauded the new emphasis on supervision and evaluation (Nelson 1986: 15), but they consistently reminded us that instruction could be discussed, teachers could be supervised, feedback could be provided, and inept teachers could be remediated or removed without a merit pay policy.

Influence on Desire and Ability to Improve. Although merit pay was an impetus for increased supervision, the stipend was not viewed as either an essential component of the supervision process or a strong catalyst for improved teacher performance. The effect of increased supervision on teaching was related more to the quality of the evaluation process than the prospect of a monetary gain. Where supervisors were perceived to be knowledgeable, where feedback was seen as pertinent, and where conferences and conversations were handled with tact and candor, teachers found classroom visitations and conferences "helpful," "worthwhile," "really useful." Where these conditions were not met, evaluation was referred to as "a joke," "a sham," "a punishment." Teachers maintained that the "information," "insight," "concrete suggestions," and "personal support" acquired from credible and trusted supervisors improved their work. The money was peripheral. The bonus itself did not strengthen either their desire or their ability to be better teachers. As one teacher summarized: "Fine if I receive it, fine if I don't. I will feel bad because I don't get an extra thousand dollars but that's not going to change the way I go about my routine, my preparation, my teaching." In Utah, as in other states, "neither reward recipients nor fellow teachers felt that program [merit pay] motivated them to work harder" let alone perform better (Pine 1983: 1; Miller and Say 1982).

Perhaps it is too early to expect or detect a link between merit pay and improved teaching. Yet in describing the effect of merit pay plans that have been in operation for at least five years, Cohen and Murnane (1985: 28) note that "no one told us that merit pay itself improved teachers' classroom work. Several teachers said that the plans . . . affected instruction, but it was the evaluation, as much or more than the raises, to which they pointed. And even these teachers saw only marginal changes. Nearly all the teachers regarded merit pay simply as recognition for good teaching," not a cause of good teaching. In short, the strategy "does not appear to have strong effects on the way teachers teach" (Murnane and Cohen 1985: 29).

It is certainly possible that teachers are not aware of or deem it inappropriate to acknowledge the impact of merit payments on classroom performance. But as Cohen and Murnane argue, "when so many teachers made the same point, all quite independently" (1985: 28), it is difficult to discount their judgment. Moreover, the empirical research on merit pay reiterates a rich body of literature that concludes that teachers are "more motivated by the content and process of their work than the opportunity for extra compensation" (Johnson 1984: 183; see also Lortie 1975; Kottkamp et al. 1986). It is not surprising, then, that teachers responded to the quality of the interactions about their work, not the possibility of a merit stipend for their work.

Side Effects that Impede Improvement.   Even though informants appreciated the time devoted to credible and constructive feedback, they expressed frustration with the time consumed by other requirements of the merit pay strategy. Many informants stated that they were "overloaded" and "exhausted" by committee meeting demands. Others noted that preparation of dossiers was a "hassle" that either "takes time away from students" or "gives you one more thing to do at home." Principals and teachers alike reported that it was necessary to "reassure," "assuage," and "nurture" people more because the merit pay evoked "anxiety," "tension," "strain." Informants in Utah were distressed by the cost/benefit calculation inherent in the merit pay strategy. They argued that the gain—increased attention to instruction—could occur without the "complications," "distractions," and "pressures" that accrue when "money gets attached" to the supervision process. These sentiments are consistent with research findings in other states. Although educators in Tennessee, for example, reacted quite positively to aspects of clinical supervision (Handler 1986: 8), they maintained that dossier requirements and strained relationships drew energy away from instructional preparation and impeded instructional improvement (Rosenholtz forthcoming: 46).

Merit Pay and Satisfaction.   Teacher satisfaction with the merit pay strategy is related primarily to the ability to convert merit pay plans into uniform salary increases for all or nearly all teachers. Where teachers can transform the plans, merit pay is viewed by both recipients and nonrecipients alike as an irritant that they can live with because it serves the instrumental aim of acquiring additional appropriations for public schools. The merit pay strategy does not, in these instances, significantly affect work satisfaction or career plans. Where teachers are less able to transform the plans, the strategy evokes widespread and intense dissatisfaction from both recipients and nonrecipients. Merit pay is seen as an insult, an injustice. In these instances, the strategy may operate to reduce commitment to the teaching profession and alter career plans.

Palatable When Converted to Broad-Based Increments. In Utah merit pay is palatable. Although teachers resent having to "prove their worth" and "brag about themselves" in order to "get a few dollars" and although they label the process "demeaning" and "belittling," they do participate. In fact, most districts are funneling more money into the merit pay provision than is legislatively required (Utah State Office of Education 1985: 33). Our data suggest that growing numbers of teachers are considering applying for merit stipends. Teachers "go along with" merit pay because they have adapted the central features. They have converted a strategy characterized by selective rewards to a program characterized by broad-based increments. Further, they have recognized the political utility of the strategy.

Because nearly all who apply receive stipends, differentiation has been limited, and risk has been reduced. Teachers are "less concerned because they understand how the process is going to go." Because funds are uniformly dispersed, it is more acceptable to "claim your share." As one summarized, "everybody can get the money that way." Because merit pay does not carry the additional work responsibilities required by the job expansion and job redesign strategies, as informants bluntly stated, "It's easier."

Most informants viewed merit pay as a "useful tool" to garner public support for higher tax rates and increased education appropriations (Malen 1986: 17), a "game to play" given the limited state funds for education, "a hoop we have to jump" to get a modest salary increment. Like educators in other settings, educators in Utah accept merit pay strategy because it can be converted to salary gains for nearly all teachers and, for the time being at least, it can serve as a symbolically salient rubric for elevating and legitimating education expenditures (Murnane and Cohen 1985: 30).

Under these conditions, merit pay is viewed as inconsequential. It does not appear to significantly influence work satisfaction or career plans. Our informants provided no evidence that the strategy was either holding them in or driving them out of the profession.

Counterproductive When Not Converted to Broad-Based Increments. Where merit bonuses are more selectively awarded, the strategy evokes widespread and intense dissatisfaction. In Tennessee, for example, 90 percent of the teachers surveyed reported that merit pay had a negative impact on morale; 60 percent conceded a decline in their commitment to the teaching profession (Rosenholtz forthcoming: 46). These sentiments may change as teachers secure broader coverage. Given the breadth of negative responses at this time, the merit pay strategy may be offending teachers who are performing reasonably well. If teachers act on their attitudes, an incentive for retention may become a stimulus for defection.

Potential of Merit Pay Strategy

Judged by legislative action and poll data, the merit pay strategy is appealing to many policymakers and some educators.[7] When applied in school settings, however, merit pay does not operate as a robust incentive. It does not effectively redistribute salary and status benefits, substantively alter teaching, or noticeably enhance satisfaction. Unless its essential features are diluted, the strategy elicits more negative than positive responses from those that it seeks to motivate.

There are a number of reasons why this strategy is incapable of permeating school settings and precipitating desired outcomes. The strategy is not congruent with either the nature of teacher work or the norms of the workplace. The strategy intensifies the vulnerability of teachers and offers in exchange rewards of low salience and dependability.

Merit Pay and Complex Work.   In order to tie pay to performance in ways that are convincing and motivating, an inclusive definition of effective performance must be developed, stable measures must be available, individual contributions must be decipherable, and most of the factors affecting performance must be under the individual's control (Lawler 1981: 86); Hatry and Greiner 1985: 29; Stern 1986: 294). These requirements are relatively easy to meet in some contexts. Where worker performance can be simply gauged by counting and inspecting a single, tangible end product or can be reliably estimated by intermittently monitoring adherence to prescribed routines, the merit pay strategy can be installed and sustained with modest effort and investment (Murnane 1985; Wallace and Fay 1982). The strategy makes sense to employees because there is a fairly clear logic—an obvious, direct, and constant relationship—between their work and their pay.

In complex work settings, however, the fit between work and compensation is not self-evident. Employees must be convinced that the criteria used to distribute performance payments account for the adaptive, diverse, and interdependent character of their work. Most educators do not believe that existing evaluation systems meet this standard. The distrust of evaluation systems creates dilemmas that prompt most complex organizations—private corporations as well as school systems—to reject the merit pay strategy.

Distrust of Locally Developed, State-Mandated, Technically So-phisticated Evaluation Systems. Educators "feel very strongly that the means for selecting meritorious teachers are not objective and that such systems create artificial distinctions" (Harris & Associates 1986: 5). Although teachers recognize that evaluation systems can give them feedback on certain aspects of their classroom activities (Nelson 1986: 16, 17), they do not see them as global indicators of the substantive quality of their work, let alone as fair measures of the financial worth of their work.

Utah relied on locally developed evaluation systems. Even though districts acquired assistance from experts, involved teachers, and devoted considerable time and energy to the design of their evaluation systems, educators were unable to rely on them as a means for distributing performance payments. Informants maintained that dossiers could reflect "packaging" as well as performance. Informants reported that classroom observers could spot the extremes, but, like educators elsewhere, they concluded that "precise . . . defensible discriminations" could not be made (Hoogeveen and Gutkin 1986: 375). Informants believed that teachers could "fake it" on the days they were being observed and that evaluations could be "distorted."

Further, principals recognized the importance of being "positive," "encouraging," and "nurturing" in their appraisals. Several shared the view that if teachers were given high scores, they would "work hard to live up to them." Others expressed concern about "the principal in the building down the street ranking everybody a ten" and a desire for their faculty to be well represented in the pool of award winners. Whether any of these forces—the desire to be positive, a sense of pride in the reputation of the school, an obligation to compensate for the "inflated" ratings submitted by their counterparts in other schools—actually prompted supervisors to bias assessments cannot be ascertained from the data. What can be said is that educators were suspicious of the process. They were not convinced that their evaluation systems could accurately differentiate the performance of teachers or effectively detect the bias of evaluators. They were reluctant to rely on either the teacher's portfolio or the supervisor's assessment as a means for "legitimate," "justifiable," and sizable pay differentials. Because selection committees were unable to defend acquired data and unwilling to garner counter data (to "prove a colleague undeserving"), the propensity to distribute money to all who applied was pronounced.

Research in other settings indicates that educators do not trust state-articulated and -mandated evaluation systems either. Texas adopted a seventy-one-item appraisal system and required extensive written justification for ratings. Here the logistical load is enough to "encourage dissension and hedged ratings" (Phillips 1986: 5). A survey of Florida educators documents a low level of confidence in that state's evaluation approach. Even though the methods were judged to be technically defensible given the current knowledge on effective teaching, the vast majority of respondents maintained that the evaluations do not identify excellent teachers and may even designate poor teachers as master teachers (Mgt. of America, Inc., 1985: 6–4). The recommendation to employ outside evaluators is seen as costly but necessary to establish some credibility (Mgt. of America, Inc., 1985: 2–6). Ironically, Tennessee used outside evaluators and invested heavily in promoting that option as objective and fair. The state spent $5.1 million dollars to administer a $3.8 million program (Olson 1986: 25). Still, respondents in Tennessee studies maintained that evaluation procedures "better measured teacher's cunning and endurance than their effectiveness" and that "a significant number of mediocre teachers" could reach the highest career-ladder levels (Rosenholtz forthcoming: 40). Teacher portfolios were also suspect because "these could be fabricated without the dimmest glimmer of relevance to one's actual classroom performance" (Rosenholtz forthcoming: 42).

Perhaps with technical improvements or different tactics, teachers will learn to trust the evaluation system.[8] We are not, however, optimistic. Trust in the evaluation system does not appear to be a function of the approach taken. Educators did not trust locally developed, collaborative methods or state-standardized, mandated approaches. Nor does trust appear to be a function of technical knowledge, per se. Even where experts have been involved in designing and endorsing the evaluation system, and major investments have been made in developing elaborate, comprehensive appraisal processes, educators still do not trust the evaluations. The tension appears to be much more fundamental.

Teaching is a multifaceted, interdependent, and unpredictable process (Johnson 1986). Thus, educators tend to reject the *notion* that their work can be reduced to and thereby assessed on a few measurable goals, a cluster of prescribed behaviors, or a series of calculations that purportedly account for their individual contribution to a collective enterprise. Because the nature of work done by most educators is inconsistent with the assumptions about work embedded in the merit pay strategy, it will be difficult to develop an evaluation system that accurately and fairly captures the complexity, diversity, and nuance of teaching. Educators will be inclined to do what was predicted a decade ago, "come up with new technical objections" as fast as current objections get set aside (Garms and Guttenburg 1970: 51). Performance appraisal is likely to remain a contentious and expensive issue.

Dilemma for Policymakers. Policymakers can manage the evaluation issue by allowing educators to transform merit pay into uniform salary increases for nearly all teachers or by investing resources in tighter regulation. Both options are troublesome. The first option denies the integrity of a merit pay policy. The second option directs scarce resources to legitimating activities—to fairly cumbersome and costly oversight functions that have had little if any effect on the perceived credibility of evaluation processes.[9]

Limited Use of Strategy in Corporate and School Settings. Because it is difficult to establish credible, manageable, and economical performance appraisal in complex work settings, most corporations have chosen alternative compensation schemes. Contrary to popular beliefs, in many organizations performance has a "minimal impact on total compensation. Much more important is seniority" (Lawler 1981: 40). Examinations of private-sector salary patterns reveal that even in businesses and corporations that claim to rely on performance appraisals as the major means of dispensing salary increases, "pay is not closely related to performance" (Hamner 1977: 291). Compensation is "more closely correlated with such impartial factors as level of education, experience, and number of subordinates than with the quality of the work performed" (Bornfriend 1985: 185; Patten 1977; Lawler 1981: 40). A prominent pattern in private business is to manage salary increases so that the "variance between the best and the worst performer is so small as to be insignificant" (Lawler 1981: 40) and to "practice secrecy" regarding the size and the recipient of any performance bonus (Lawler 1981: 102; Nadler and Lawler 1977: 32). Because the performance pay concept docs not fit complex work settings, most public and private school systems, like most corporations, opt not to structure their compensation systems on merit pay principles (Murnane and Cohen 1985: 19; Lawler 1981: 40).

Merit Pay and Autonomy/Equality/Civility Norms. Merit pay challenges a long-standing commitment to autonomy/equality/civility in the workplace. It is viewed as disruptive and destructive. Because merit pay is not strong enough to reshape norms, educators adjust it to fit the established patterns.

When confronted with merit pay, teachers in Utah anticipated "hurt feelings," "flack," "jealousies," "friction," and "backbiting." Principals shared those concerns. They did not want to spur teachers "to go out and rally allies for their particular cause. We could end up with very divided staffs." Educators tried to contain the "potential for enormous resentment" by "giving something to everybody." As one principal summarized: "The discrimination was not very great between teachers. . . . People could come away feeling good. . . . If we continue on that basis we'll be O.K." Apparently their instincts were well founded. In the few instances where teachers were denied merit awards, committee members "took a lot of flack." There was, as one poignantly stated "a great deal of pain." Given the pain, educators chose to abide by the norms whenever possible.

The norms, traditions, and values of the workplace influence how any change is managed. Evidence from government and corporate as well as school settings indicates that when a compensation strategy is not congruent with the culture of the organization, "the merit pay plan will be managed in ways that make it ineffective (Lawler 1981: 177). Employees will adjust the new system so that it does not conflict with the accepted codes of conduct or infringe on the deeply engrained norms of the organization.

Merit Pay and Vulnerability. The merit pay strategy is resisted because it exacerbates the vulnerability of educators. Merit pay threatens to expose a teacher's inadequacies while providing few remedies. Neither the conditions of the workplace nor the ability of individuals to cope with those conditions is addressed. The strategy simply seeks to reward those who are performing well. It does not bolster the capacity of those who may not be performing well.

In Utah vulnerability prompted teachers to shield themselves from a strategy that could erode confidence, threaten personal relationships, or otherwise disrupt an already volatile work environment. They were not willing to "judge" their peers or "set themselves apart." They were much more prone to "band together so the system doesn't tear you apart." Like employees in other organizations, teachers need to protect their self-esteem and their personal support network (Rosenholtz forthcoming: 32). And teachers in Utah protected both by converting merit pay into a system of salary increments for nearly all teachers.

Merit Pay and Salient, Dependable Rewards. The merit pay strategy relies on a narrow band of incentives—a salary supplement and presumably status benefits. Although these rewards have a role to play, like people in other organizations teachers "seek simultaneously many kinds of satisfactions, not just those with economic roots" (Hackman and Oldham 1980: 37). Because the merit pay strategy is confined to a single set of rewards and to what teachers define as the least salient set of rewards, it is not compelling to most teachers. Because the reward offered is not particularly attractive and is consistently viewed as tentative, it is not very potent.

In sum, the merit pay strategy is not congruent with school settings on any of the critical dimensions. Because merit pay violates both the logic and the values of the workplace, intensifies vulnerability, and offers in return rewards of low salience and dependability, the strategy fails to serve as a source of inspiration and improvement.

JOB EXPANSION STRATEGY

Central Features

The job expansion strategy relates salary to the willingness of individuals to take on additional work. Although jobs can be expanded in a variety of ways, salary is often linked to ad hoc projects that teachers initiate or bid then complete during an extended work day or an extended work year. Typically, classroom teaching assignments are not reduced. Projects are appendages to and not substitutes for classroom teaching assignments. We confine our analysis to this version of job expansion because it is the model most often used in school settings (Murphy and Hart 1985: 11).

The project model seeks to capitalize on the creativity of teachers by providing opportunities for them to pursue their special interests. It also seeks to enhance system capacity by channeling resources to previously unaddressed problems. The project model blends extrinsic and intrinsic rewards. Although extra pay is offered and peer recognition is possible, the opportunity to diversify and enrich one's work with new and potentially stimulating tasks is available as well. The focus is individual. Although projects may be defined by the organization, to stimulate entrepreneurship projects are typically kept open-ended and loosely structured so that teachers can pursue their unique interests. Projects may involve small teams, but most do not. When projects are part of a career ladder, the individual focus is further reinforced by the need to award advancements to individuals rather than groups.

The job expansion strategy is not new. For decades, districts have hired teachers to do extra work—to teach summer school, write curriculum, tutor students, manage extracurricular programs, and handle a variety of tasks (Duke 1984: 30–33). This familiar practice is now incorporated in career-ladder policies and other teacher-incentive legislation. Job expansion is widely used in Utah (Malen and Murphy 1985; Malen and Hart forthcoming). It is apparent in the extended contract/special project options in Tennessee, South Carolina, and New Jersey, and in the pilot teacher-incentive programs in several other states (Tennessee State Department of Education 1985; Waters et al. 1986; Education Commission of the States 1985).

Initial Effects

Job Expansion and Distribution of Salary–Status Benefits. The job expansion strategy does not substantially alter the distribution of salary and status benefits. Financial rewards are not fundamentally restructured. Status rewards are rarely conferred.

Salary. There are two indications that the job expansion strategy does not operate to redistribute salary. First, money is usually disbursed as a temporary supplement to the teachers' basic salary. Typically the supplement is small, adding $500 to $1,500 or the equivalent of five to fifteen paid days to the teachers' earnings. When the payment is linked to a project, the stipend ends when the project ends. Salary gains are often short-term and episodic (Malen and Murphy 1985: 274).

Second, projects tend to be broadly distributed. In Utah, for example, teachers organized to either take turns, rotate projects on an annual basis, or allocate funds to virtually all proposals submitted during the year (Malen and Hart forthcoming). In some schools teachers made explicit "You take it this year, and I will take it next year" compacts with each other. Administrators and selection committee members often agree that when there were "two equal" project proposals the award would go to the teacher who had not had a project the previous year. In other schools, teachers organized to parcel funds to virtually all applicants. Both administrators and teachers seemed willing to accept dilution in grant amounts to secure a general distribution of benefits (Malen and Hart forthcoming). The tendency to distribute project monies broadly is not unique to Utah. Many teachers sought and most secured project supplements in South Carolina's pilot program (Waters et al. 1986: 3). Approximately two-thirds of all eligible teachers received special project/ extended contract stipends in Tennessee (*Tennessee Education* 1986: 1).

Status. Two patterns indicate that the job expansion strategy has little effect on status. First, projects are usually not systematically evaluated or widely disseminated. Even though broad distribution of project awards minimizes the special recognition dimension of status, it is possible to acquire some distinction if quality projects are identified and highlighted. But selection committees in Utah were reluctant to evaluate projects. Both the equality norm and the idiosyncratic nature of the projects themselves made discrimination difficult. Informants believed that to "be fair," it was important to "give everybody a chance." They also found it hard to establish criteria and judge proposals that were driven primarily by individual interests and aspirations and only loosely linked to district goals and priorities. In Utah and other settings the strategy spawned projects "as varied as the teachers who planned and implemented them" (*Tennessee Education* 1986: 1). In Utah and other settings selection committees found it difficult to assess such diverse proposals (Waters et al. 1986: 3). Moreover, few projects were widely disseminated. Teachers were reluctant to "brag" about their work. A few projects were featured in the media, and some were disseminated in the schools. Most were not widely publicized.

An exception to this pattern was found in districts that combined the project model with redefined teacher roles and responsibilities (a strategy that we term *job redesign*, analyzed in the next section). When projects were part of a job redesign effort, they were more widely disseminated. In these instances project teachers acquired some recognition because they presented and demonstrated their work. Although they were teased and "ribbed," peers often applauded the work and expressed respect for project teachers. They said, for example, "I was surprised to learn there were so many talented teachers in this school."

Second, projects often support work already underway or extend conventional activities. In Utah teachers used projects to prepare materials, organize supplies, develop curriculum, finance hall supervision, direct plays, sponsor student recognition programs, and inventory equipment. Informants maintained that teachers invest a great deal of their "own time" doing school work. They "volunteer" their services so that important school functions can be accomplished. Given this perspective, some teachers used the project outlet to support what they were already doing and to shore up existing services. Because these projects supported activities already underway or extended conventional work, status was not appreciably affected.

There were exceptions to this pattern. Some teachers developed projects that added new dimensions to their work (Malen and Hart forthcoming). They expanded programs, wrote curriculum, investigated alternative instructional strategies, and shared results with their peers. When teachers perceived that individuals had put forth substantial effort and produced a quality project that benefited them, they reported "new respect" for project teachers. Increased status was observed in these instances.

In sum, the job expansion strategy by itself does not operate to significantly adjust the distribution of salary and status benefits in school settings. The salary supplements tend to be short-term, broadly distributed stipends. Because there is little change in the salary received or the tasks performed, status is virtually unaffected, unless the project model is used in conjunction with job redesign.

Job Expansion and Impact on Teaching.   The job expansion strategy can change work patterns. In some cases, the changes have a positive influence on the teachers' desire and ability to improve. In other cases, there is little impact. Job expansion also produces side effects that interfere with improvement.

Change in Work Patterns.   The job expansion strategy changes work quantitatively and episodically. Teachers in Utah applied for minigrants to do work "above and beyond" their classroom duties with the understanding that projects would be executed within a specified time and documented usually in a final report. Where projects were rotated, an "on-off" affect resulted, with some teachers "on" project work and others "off" at any given time. Where projects were parceled out to all who applied, teachers had some additional time, money, and organizational support to complete their work. Assessments of the extent to which the job expansion strategy operated to improve teacher performance varied considerably.

Influence on Desire and Ability to Improve. In some cases projects enhanced the desire and the ability of teachers to improve. Teachers who completed projects said, "I learned a great deal" and the project "helped my teaching." Other teachers also reported benefits. Projects generated instructional resources, new techniques, curriculum units, and other support services. Informants maintained that these projects were "really useful." They helped teachers become "more progressive" and "better equipped to face instructional challenges." Informants found assistance with computers, the teaching of writing, and the development of critical thinking skills particularly valuable. Informants also praised enrichment activities, discipline plans, and positive reinforcement programs for students. They concluded that these projects "made this school a better place to teach." In other cases, projects had little influence on the teachers' desire and ability to improve. Projects were not completed; they were of low quality; they were not shared. Consequently, they had little impact. They were, as informants candidly stated, "a waste."

Side Effects that Impede Improvement. In certain instances informants contended that projects interfered with teaching by creating overload for and by precipitating tension among teachers. Informants reported that job expansion was "overextending" project teachers, taking time and energy away from classroom instruction. The projects "got to be too much." Where teachers were trying to complete projects during the school year, the sense of overload was especially pronounced. As one put it, "I can't do my career ladder project between 7 AM and 9 AM and still be at my best when the kids come for class." Another summarized, "I'm doing a worse job because I have too many things to do." Informants contended that the strategy was taxing other teachers as well. When projects involved students, some teachers needed time during the school day to carry out the project. In these instances, other teachers "picked up the slack." Their class sizes were increased; class composition was changed. Teachers reported increased discipline problems and increased demands on their time and energy. The words of one teacher capture the concern: "I'm working harder; [she's] making extra money; and all the other students are suffering."

Informants also observed that the strategy was divisive. Because some teachers were receiving extra pay for extra work, other teachers were less eager to "contribute" and "cooperate." Informants said, for instance, "Why should I do that? I'm not getting paid for it." "Let them do that. They're getting paid." Whether these sentiments actually prompted teachers to cut back on their "volunteer" work could not be ascertained from the data. But the tendency to define duties and activities outside the classroom as fee-for-service arrangements may precipitate unintended consequences in the workplace. Teachers may become less "cooperative"—less willing to absorb tasks essential for school functioning. The net effect could be an extension of a trend begun with collective bargaining (McDonnell and Pascal 1977)—a further bifurcation of teachers jobs, with compensation systems based on classroom teaching assignments and all other functions managed by fee-for-service contracts.

Job Expansion and Satisfaction. Although teachers in Utah were not as enthusiastic as the superintendents surveyed in Tennessee (*Tennessee Education* 1986: 1), they voiced general support for the job expansion strategy (Nelson 1986: 19). Participants tend to be more positive than nonparticipants. Both groups have mixed reactions.

Sources of Satisfaction and Dissatisfaction for Participants. Most participants appreciated the salary supplement. When projects formalized current activities, participants noted that the extra money makes "the extra work teachers already do a little more tolerable." When projects extended the teachers' activities, most did not view the money as sufficient, given the amount of work done. They stated they would "scale down" their project proposals next year. Even though the supplements were not judged to be sufficient, teachers liked the opportunity to "moonlight in school." Individuals who wanted to augment their income had some chance to do so. They could unify their work once more. As one put it, "I'm doing two jobs but at least they are in the same place and they do relate." Another added: "It is the best job for moonlighting that I know of. . . . It offers you another change to still deal with your specific field and your expertise."

Most participants enjoyed their projects. Because "there probably isn't a teacher alive who doesn't have a pet notion or two about how to improve classroom learning" (*NEA Today* 1986: 14), even modest amounts of time, money, and organizational support for a pet project can have broad appeal. Further, the organizational support may communicate a note of district approval—a validation of the individual's ideas and efforts (McDonnell 1983: 27–28; Kanter 1983).

When projects created additional work, participant satisfaction was tempered by a sense of overload—by the dissonance created when projects diverted energy from their "immediate job," classroom teaching. As Duke (1984: 32) points out, "All too often, . . . job expansion leads to the overtaxing of already strained teacher energies. Many of our informants concurred. Again, they stated that they would "scale down" their proposals for next year. Participant satisfaction was further tempered by the peer tensions previously described and by suspicions of legislative intent. Most were not convinced that the legislature would provide sufficient or stable funds.

Sources of Satisfaction and Dissatisfaction for Nonparticipants. Nonparticipants were positive when projects helped them or improved the school. They spoke highly, for example, of curriculum projects forwarded to them, instructional materials that they could copy and use, and discipline projects that addressed schoolwide behavior problems.

Nonparticipants were upset, however, when projects were not completed or shared. They condemned the "waste." Projects were, in their judgment "self-serving" and "gold-bricking." Nonparticipants were also upset when attempts to circulate projects in formalized ways "intruded" on their time. Informants did not see why they should be required to "sit for hours" through meetings that had little or no salience for them "just so they can get their money." Although informants recognized that the individual contractors could be gaining financially and growing personally because of a project and although they appreciated some of the presentations, they were discontent when presentations were "imposed" on other teachers.

Informants resented the expectation that teachers should do more work. Some were unwilling to "jump through hoops for $1000." Others stated, "Teachers are expected to do more all the time. . . . I can't work any harder." Even though projects were set up as voluntary, teacher-initiated options, teachers felt pressured to apply. Several informants were concerned that if they did not "do a career ladder project" they might be viewed as less committed and less dedicated than their peers. Many feared the strategy was a "ploy" by the legislature to "get teachers to work harder and then come in and say: 'see, you can do more if you have to, now do it without the money.'"

In light of these mixed reactions, it is not surprising that teachers said the opportunity to do special projects would not significantly influence their career plans. Informants identified some attractive features of the strategy—the opportunity to pursue interests, the chance to develop ideas that might improve their teaching, the support for "above and beyond" effort and "extra" work. But the short-term nature of special projects and the widespread suspicion of legislative intent meant that most were not willing to build their careers on such an unstable, unpredictable program.

Potential of the Job Expansion Strategy

Although job expansion does not substantially alter the distribution of salary and status benefits, it does provide salary increments and occasional status gains. Job expansion does not systematically improve teaching or significantly affect satisfaction, but projects can, in certain cases, enhance teaching and engender satisfaction. By itself, the project approach has limited ability to induce major changes in teacher performance and retention for several reasons. The strategy is only partially congruent with the nature of teacher work. It is constrained by the autonomy/equality/civility norms and the vulnerability of educators. It is restricted in its capacity to provide salient, dependable rewards. However, under certain conditions, the job expansion strategy has some potential.

Job Expansion and Complex Work. The job expansion strategy fits the adaptive and varied character of complex work. Projects can be tailored to the individual needs and interests of teachers, and they can be applied to virtually any aspect of the teachers' job. But the strategy is difficult to align with the interdependent dimension of teacher work. Interdependent work requires interaction, coordination, and integration as well as invention, spontaneity, and flexibility. Managing the job expansion strategy so that it fosters both individual creativity and institutional achievement is not an easy task. If projects are too structured and too controlled, the entrepreneurial appeal can be lost. Yet if projects are too disparate and too detached from the central operations of the organization, then "good ideas" may be lost. However valuable a project is to an individual, if that project remains an isolated activity, "then it is likely" writes Kanter (1983: 299), that the gain "will never take hold, fade into disuse, or produce a lower level of benefits than it potentially could.

In the settings we studied, projects were, for the most part, individually designed, sporadically diffused, and loosely coupled to organizational priorities. The project model was not prompting teachers to develop connections with one another. A few teachers collaborated on projects; most did not. Some projects were disseminated; most were not. Although research in school and corporate settings indicates that the special project model can operate to foster collaboration and integration in organizations (McDonnell 1983: 27–28; Kanter 1983), we did not see the model enhancing those processes in most of the schools we studied.

Job Expansion and Autonomy/Equality/Civility Norms.   Job expansion, as currently deployed, complements the norms of schools. Autonomy is retained through voluntary participation and personal projects. Equality is protected through the broad distribution of project awards and the limited use of comparative assessment and formal dissemination. Civility is maintained because private work, elusive criteria, and casual exchange make projects unobtrusive.

Although job expansion is congruent with these norms, it is constrained by them. Teachers were reluctant to regulate the quality of projects. They did not want the application process to become competitive or cumbersome. Teachers were also reluctant to systematically disseminate project results. Participants did not want to "show off" or "elevate themselves." Nonparticipants resented being required to attend inservice sessions when projects were not of interest to them. In most of the settings that we studied, the norms of the workplace operated to limit quality control, coordination, and systematic dissemination.

Job Expansion and Vulnerability.   Job expansion in its current form is not threatening. Projects are typically low profile. Teacher performance is not exposed. Essentially, the teacher is left alone. Job expansion does increase the number of tasks that a teacher is expected to do, but it offers individuals resources, notably time and money, to carry out the work. The strategy does not fundamentally alter work conditions, nor does it directly address the isolated work arrangements. But for those who can design stimulating projects and balance the sense of overload, some opportunity to develop new insights, new ways to approach both the classroom activities, and the "above and beyond" duties is provided. Attempts to impose quality controls and publicize project results would create stress for teachers, but as it presently operates the job expansion strategy is not threatening.

Job Expansion and Salient, Dependable Rewards. Job expansion seeks to blend extrinsic and intrinsic rewards. Extrinsic rewards were more pronounced in our data than intrinsic rewards. Teachers identified the extra money and the chance to earn it by "moonlighting in school" as a major benefit of the job expansion strategy. Although most teachers enjoyed their projects and some said they "learned a lot," the idiosyncratic, ad hoc nature of the projects limited intrinsic rewards. Individually initiated projects necessarily reflect existing vision and capacity. Like teachers elsewhere, teachers in Utah differed markedly in their ability to design and carry out quality projects (Waters et al. 1986: 3). Some "very impressive" projects were completed. But as one principal bluntly stated: "The problem is we have got some 'dingbats' out there submitting all sorts of stuff for money."

If projects are not well conceived, the opportunity for personal growth is restricted. Moreover, if projects are not well integrated, the chance of promoting professional growth throughout the system is minimal. The short-term character of projects makes it difficult to secure and sustain continuity. Because teachers are often permitted to initiate activities, to "do more" (Cusick 1983; Powell et al. 1985), unless the new activity is fundamentally different the intrinsic value of that opportunity is reduced. In the schools we studied, teachers tended to use projects to support what they were already doing or to extend conventional activities. Consequently, the gratification derived from enriched work, professional interaction, and new skill development was limited.

In sum, the job expansion strategy is partially congruent with complex work. Because the strategy is hard to align with the interdependent dimension of teaching and susceptible to the constraints imposed by the autonomy/equality/civility norms, it is restricted in its ability to induce systemwide improvements. In its current form, the strategy is neither threatening nor compelling. Teachers receive an extrinsic reward. But the more salient intrinsic rewards are elusive. Given the short-term nature of projects and tentative funding prospects, both sets of rewards tend to be undependable. Thus, job expansion has limited potential to achieve desired outcomes.

Throughout this analysis we have noted that the impact of the job expansion strategy varied across sites. Some schools were able to utilize the job expansion strategy more effectively than others. Their ability to capitalize on this strategy appeared to be related to the credibility of the person doing the project, the strength of existing work relationships, and the capacity to cope with the demands of the job expansion strategy.

Credibility of Project Teacher. When individual credibility was high— that is, when teachers believed that the individual doing the project was capable and conscientious—they were more receptive to the product and more receptive to the job expansion strategy. They were more willing to listen and share ideas informally, more willing to attend workshops, inservice sessions and otherwise participate in dissemination activities.

Strength of Existing Work Relationships. In schools where teachers and administrators respected one another and exchanged ideas informally, projects tended to reflect broad needs of the school and circulate throughout the school. Further, in settings where the project model was linked to job redesign, formal structures for disseminating projects were available. Conversely, where teacher/administrator relationships were strained, projects reflected individual interests and remained isolated and invisible. No formal or informal network for dissemination existed. Some teachers did not know what projects were underway. Most teachers were unaffected.

Capacity to Cope with Demands. At times, the extra work requirements were viewed as "overloads." When administrators continuously articulated, clarified, and reiterated purposes and goals, the sense of overload was still present, but it was not paralyzing. When teachers were provided support (clerical assistance, principal reinforcement, peer appreciation), they responded more positively to the projects. When teachers were "on their own," the stress overshadowed the benefits of projects.

JOB REDESIGN STRATEGY

Central Features

The job redesign strategy relates salary to redefined work roles and extended work schedules.[10] Salary is linked to new positions that carry formal staff development, peer supervision, curriculum-instructional improvement, and broad decisionmaking responsibilities, as well as classroom teaching assignments. Often the classroom teaching load is reduced so that promoted teachers can carry out their new responsibilities. These new positions alter traditional authority relationships because functions previously and exclusively assumed by principals and district specialists are now assigned to and shared with teacher leaders. Salary is also linked to extended schedules. Teachers assuming the new positions extend their work year to ten or eleven months. Nonpromoted teachers also extend their work schedules. Additional days are built in to the school calendar to provide time for reflection, interaction, and renewal and time to consume the services provided by promoted teachers.

The job redesign strategy seeks to bolster the capacity of the school system to perform its critical functions through arrangements that develop, diffuse, and more fully utilize the talents of teachers. In addition, it aims to create attractive advancement opportunities for teachers. The strategy utilizes extrinsic and intrinsic rewards. Salary and status benefits are offered, and opportunities to diversify work, exert leadership, and develop abilities are available as well (Murphy and Hart 1985: 11; McKelvey and Sekaran 1977). Both work schedules and authority relationships are restructured so that teachers can orchestrate and participate in activities that enhance professional competence and confidence. The primary focus is institutional. Positions are created, jobs are defined, and plans for managing the system are developed. A parallel individual emphasis is, however, an integral component of this approach. Job redesign seeks to make work more fulfilling by altering the job itself and by providing continuous professional development options. It rests on the ability to change both the jobs and the people (Hackman and Oldham 1980: 71–98) in ways that foster individual growth, purposive interaction, and institutional engagement.

The job redesign strategy is not as widespread as the merit pay and job expansion approaches, but it is evident in state policies that include mentor teacher positions and career ladder statutes permitting or requiring teachers to assume additional responsibilities on promotion to the new levels (Bray et al. 1985: 28–34; Education Commission of the States 1985). In Utah job redesign is included as one of several options for the dispersement of career ladder funds (Malen and Murphy 1985: 273). Two districts in the state have selected this strategy as the major component of their career ladder programs (Malen and Hart forthcoming). Job redesign is permitted at the top level of Tennessee's career ladder (Tennessee State Department of Education 1985). Upper-level teachers in Florida's revised career ladder policy may be required to "undertake additional instructional leadership responsibilities" (Florida Statutes ch. 86–157: 7). California's optional mentor teacher program, Charlotte-Mecklenburg's mentor teacher-staff development plan, and New Mexico's new "support teams requirement" reflect incremental moves toward job redesign (Wagner 1985; Hanes and Mitchell 1985; Viadero 1986: 8). When compared to the comprehensive restructuring of teacher roles and relationships called for by the Holmes Group (1986) and the Carnegie Forum (1986), current attempts to use the job redesign strategy are relatively modest ventures. Nonetheless, these attempts provide a basis for gauging the viability of this strategy in school settings.

Initial Effects

Job Redesign and Distribution of Salary—Status Benefits.   The job redesign strategy produces noticeable and substantial variations in salary and status. Pressures to broaden salary dispersements are present, and social sanctions are applied to teachers in new roles. However, the evidence suggests that the central features of the strategy can withstand these forces.

Salary.   In Utah, while all teachers were compensated for additional contract days, salary differentiation was still significant. Earnings of teachers promoted to top positions increased by as much as $6,000. Earnings for teachers in the intermediate levels increased by $1,500 to $3,000. Even though new positions were created, pressure to dispense money in an egalitarian fashion was strong (Malen and

Hart forthcoming). During the first year of implementation teachers insisted that new posts should be short-term assignments, filled for only a year or two and then reopened. Teachers recommended that jobs be rotated so "everybody could have a chance." The pressure to convert new positions to annual or biannual rotations appears to be subsiding, however, as teachers recognize the importance of continuity in roles and the benefits that all can accrue from the reservoir of resources made available through these new arrangements. Further, support for larger salary variations is developing, as teachers see that individuals in the new roles "work their tails off" and "deserve even more money than they get."

Status. Status distinctions were also noticeable and substantial. Many teachers interpreted the promotions as signs of recognition. They stated, for example, that being a career ladder teacher meant "You are one of the best." "You are at the top of your profession." Status distinctions did evoke social sanctions. Both teachers and principals reported that promoted teachers were accused of being "administrative stoolies," "pets," "lackies." They were "harassed," "shunned," "ridiculed," "dumped on," "dragged through the coals." Like the merit pay strategy, job redesign evoked "a great deal of pain."

Some promoted teachers coped with that pain by withdrawing from peers, concentrating on less visible tasks, or resigning. As one explained, "We all have to wortk together; the last thing I want is to be seen as different from other teachers." Others responded by denigrating the value of their new roles. Teachers told peers, for instance, that they had accepted the new positions not because the work was appealing or important but because they were "really strapped financially this year." As time went on, however, some promoted teachers found solace and support from teachers who expressed appreciation for the assistance received and respect for the efforts expended. Although these reassurances were often delivered in private, the positive feedback helped individuals endure harsh public criticisms. While social sanction persisted, social support grew. In other settings as well as in Utah, it was possible for some promoted teachers to gain stature (Wagner 1985).

In sum, the job redesign strategy affects the "position, prestige, and pocketbook" of teachers. The redistribution of economic and status rewards is threatened by pressures for uniform allocation of salary through short-term or rotated positions and by social sanctions. But the evidence suggests that the central features of this strategy need not be subsumed by these forces.

Job Redesign and Impact on Teaching.   The job redesign strategy can alter work patterns. It does prompt educators to use their time differently. Under certain conditions, the strategy influences both the teachers' desire and ability to improve. Job redesign does, however, produce side effects that impede improvement.

Change in Work Patterns.   In Utah the job redesign strategy directed attention and resources to instructional planning, classroom supervision, mentorship, curriculum, and staff development activities. The strategy created a "talent pool"—a "resource base" to carry out and coordinate tasks in each of these areas. There was "somebody to go to besides the principal" and a structure that "gets people connected to each other to work together on problems." Assessments of the extent to which these changes operated to improve teaching varied considerably across schools.

Influence on Desire and Ability to Improve.   In virtually all instances Utah teachers claimed that the additional work days—that is, the extended contract time granted them—aided planning, preparation, and professional interaction (Nelson 1986: 14, 26). In some schools, the additional days merged with inservice sessions, workshops, ongoing classroom observations, and collegial consultation to "help teachers teach better." Most informants in these schools reported that they were more aware of their teaching styles, more receptive to discussions of alternative teaching techniques, better informed about principles of lesson design, and better equipped with what they termed a "repertoire of skills" for handling discipline and instruction. The new arrangements resulted in "all kinds of new and creative lesson ideas—in opportunities to "take our strengths and enlarge on them and get help in our weak areas." A structure that enabled teachers to "share," "see the talents of others," "get interacting with each other," and "work together to tackle problems" was created. The technical assistance and collegial support offered by promoted teachers generated "increased enthusiasm about our jobs and ourselves" and provided "materials and skills that we could really use in the classroom." In other instances, teachers reported "no benefit at all." They were frustrated and discouraged. They viewed teacher leader activities as "Mickey Mouse busy work," as "extra work that doesn't help teaching."

Side Effects that Impede Improvement. Promoted teachers reported that their new responsibilities detracted from their classroom duties. Students were, in their estimation, "shortchanged." Even though teaching loads were reduced, teacher leaders perceived that they lacked the time and energy "to do both jobs [new responsibilities and regular teaching duties] well." Teacher leaders contended that "something has to give and it's often your own classes." Nonpromoted teachers maintained that the activities constrained them by "pushing everybody to the same mold," "freezing us," "making us hesitant, afraid of failing."

At times, informants experienced more personal tension than collegial cooperation. They reported that the new arrangements were "pitting teachers against teachers," "forcing teachers to fight for the bone they tossed us." Others added, "It's a morale buster. . . . It's divided us, created hostility." "It's become dog eat dog . . . and there's no greater educational awareness, just diminished support for each other." The result, they argued, was that teachers were "less willing to do what they had always done" and less able to do what they had always done. They were "exhausted," "stretched too thin." They wanted relief. As several put it, "Just let me teach."

Job Redesign and Satisfaction.   Like teachers elsewhere, teachers in Utah are, at this point, ambivalent and reserved in their response to the job redesign strategy (Harris and Associates 1986: 24). Some aspects are satisfying; other aspects are disconcerting. Both promoted and nonpromoted teachers are in the process of balancing and weighing these competing sentiments.

Sources of Satisfaction and Dissatisfaction for Promoted Teachers. Promoted teachers valued the additional money. They also reported meaningful growth as a result of their experience in new roles. As one captured it: "For the first time in my life I feel like a professional." Informants attributed this effect to the training they received in classroom observation techniques and effective teaching behaviors, presence in the inner circle of the school's information and decisionmaking network, the opportunity to train and counsel other teachers, and the chance to see first hand what was happening beyond as well as behind their classroom doors. The activities were gratifying. As one observer put it "The more they [teacher leaders] did the more they enjoyed doing it just for the enjoyment of doing it." These positive responses of promoted teachers are consistent with a broad body of literature suggesting that jobs characterized by variety, expanded decisionmaking authority, and ongoing opportunities to develop special skills and talents can be significant sources of work satisfaction (Kahn 1973: 34; see also Herrick 1973; Seashore and Barnowe 1972; Hackman and Oldham 1980).

But the enthusiasm of promoted teachers was tempered by the confusion surrounding program goals and the ambiguity of their new roles—what informants described as "the lack of direction," "the uncertainty of exactly what's expected," "the lack of clarity about who is supposed to initiate what." Like other mentor/master teachers, our informants were "quietly perplexed about how to proceed (Little 1985: 34) and frequently frustrated by the absence of goal and role consensus. Their enthusiasm was further tempered by the sanctions of peers, the sense of overload, and the dissonant choices they confronted as they tried to fulfill their new duties and their classroom obligations. Most promoted teachers were struggling to balance the benefit/burden equation, to decide if their new positions were "really worth the effort."

Those calculations were complicated by the widespread perception that the legislature would not fund the career ladder at appropriate levels for extended periods of time. The words of one capture the prevailing view: "The legislature is always doing something. It is not going to last. They are not going to keep the money coming. It will all be gone in a year or two. Why go through all the hassle?" Most promoted teachers were not ready to let the new positions affect their career plans. They were not willing to "hang their hats" on such tentative, "tenuous" advancement opportunities.

Sources of Satisfaction and Dissatisfaction for Nonpromoted Teachers. Virtually all treasured the "built in time" for reflection, preparation, and interaction (Nelson 1986: 13). The extra days allowed teachers to "breathe again," "get revived," "keep up the creative energy," "get in touch with other teachers," "add zest and new ideas to lessons." In most schools, informants reported that the demonstration of instructional techniques, the curriculum materials, the opportunities to work with teacher leaders in the classroom or during inservice sessions "broadened horizons" and fostered "mutual respect. . . . People saw each other in a new light." The staff development activities and collegial interactions were often "refreshing," "exciting," "really helpful." Teachers added, "I wish they [promoted teachers] could come in much, much more." "I deeply appreciated having a teacher supervisor; . . . in the past I felt so alone." Many praised the "greater awareness," "personal growth," "new skills," and "genuine support" they acquired.

Clearly, the new arrangements addressed salient aspects of teacher satisfaction: the availability of ideas, the refinement of skills, the increased opportunities for collegial interaction and individual reflection. The new arrangements also affected teacher perceptions of their own efficacy. Many indicated that they were more cognizant of their teaching and more confident in their classrooms: "We feel more positive about ourselves." "We give ourselves credit now for what we do well." "We're more gutsy, more sure of ourselves."

These findings parallel themes from research conducted in other states. Apparently where teachers are permitted and encouraged to become a network of resources for one another, they do secure valuable assistance from individuals in mentor/master teacher positions and from individuals who without formal title or designation respond to requests for help and support (Hanes and Mitchell 1985: 13; Kottkamp et al. 1986: 563; Academy for Educational Development 1985: 35). The opportunities to associate with and learn from colleagues, the opportunities to prepare, accrue "an enriched store of usable knowledge," master skills, and acquire confidence have very strong appeal (Lortie 1986: 575; Kottkamp et al. 1986: 565; Harris and Associates 1986: 42). These opportunities enable teachers to experience the most potent reward of all—"the satisfaction of reaching larger numbers of students more deeply" (Lortie 1986: 575).

Support for the job redesign was not universal. Some nonpromoted teachers resented the role and status differentiation. Some stated they would like to see the program eliminated. Even where positive sentiments were recorded, they were muted by the ambiguity of goals and roles, a pervasive sense of overload, and the incidents of social sanction previously described. The positive sentiments were also diminished by unresolved fairness issues and assessments of legislative intent.

Teachers were struggling with two major issues: fair compensation for positions and fair allocation of positions. Widespread concern surfaced that the most capable teachers would not apply for or remain in the new roles because the salary was not commensurate with the expectations and the social pressure was too painful. Although subsiding, tension between access to and continuity in new positions was still present. Teachers were torn by the desire to "give all teachers a chance" through short-term, rotated assignments and the desire to grant those selected for career ladder positions some tenure. While these workplace issues were disconcering, other legislative issues were even more unsettling.

Informants were generally suspicious of legislative intent. The career ladder policy was interpreted by some as a way to avoid paying all teachers a "decent" salary. The career ladder reform was referred to as a "gimmick to pacify teachers"; a way "to placate teachers for not giving them money across the board"; a vehicle for minimizing "the real issues . . . class size, books, materials, liveable salaries." Given these concerns, it was difficult for teachers to trust the job redesign strategy, let alone permit that strategy to shape their career plans. In Utah the state context may do as much to determine the fate and effect of redesigned jobs on teachers as the central components of the strategy.

Potential of Job Redesign Strategy

While there are persuasive indications that the job redesign strategy can redistribute salary and status benefits, improve teaching, and provide satisfying experiences to teachers, experience with job redesign in schools is rather limited. The strategy is not widely used. It has not been tried as often or studied as extensively as merit pay or special project approaches. Even where job redesign is being attempted, the positive effects are by no means guaranteed. Job redesign entails a fundamental restructuring of the organization. As such, it is an ambitious, arduous strategy. Job redesign rests on the ability to create individually appealing and institutionally appropriate arrangements. For that reason, it is an intricate, involved strategy.

While the job redesign strategy is challenging, the available evidence suggests that it is also promising. Job redesign is congruent with complex work and capable of reshaping engrained norms. Although the strategy initially intensifies the vulnerability of educators, it addresses vulnerability in constructive ways and creates conditions conducive to the realization of meaningful rewards.

Job Redesign and Complex Work. Job redesign recognizes that in order to make appropriate adaptive judgments, manage the variety of tasks embedded in teaching, and coordinate the efforts of inter-dependent individuals, educators need ongoing opportunities to acquire knowledge, hone skills, and share information. Because the job redesign strategy seeks to bolster the capacity of teachers to accomplish work through arrangements that systematically promote professional development and collegial interaction, it fits the complex character of work in schools.

Even though this strategy is consistent with the nature of teacher work, it is extremely difficult to install and sustain. Job redesign calls for and relies on a carefully crafted realignment of institutional functions. Beyond the conceptual demands of diagnosing existing arrangements and redefining organizational roles and responsibilities (S. Mitchell 1986), it raises critical implementation issues and imposes immense energy drains. While the Utah experience with job redesign is modest when compared with the comprehensive recommendations for redesigning jobs in recent task force publications (Holmes 1986; Carnegie 1986), it illustrates some of the difficulties associated with this strategy.[11]

Administrators and teachers in Utah were struggling. They were, for example, wrestling with the ambiguity of goals and roles. Informants were not convinced that expectations for positions were realistic, let alone commensurate with the compensation. People were trying to figure out how to connect the new positions and activities with both the immediate concerns of individual teachers and the broad goals of the school. People were trying to cope with the trauma of major change. These and other issues meant that educators were at least as exhausted by the pressures as they were enthused by the prospects of job redesign. Even where administrators and teachers were exerting strong leadership, informants feared they would "burn-out" before the model was in place. Their anxieties were intensified by bleak funding prospects and widespread suspicion of legislative intent.

Whenever an organization engages in major change, confusion, disruption, and strain result. Job redesign in school settings is no exception. It taxes leadership, stamina, and resolve. Although the strategy is congruent with the nature of work, we reiterate that it is still very difficult to install and sustain and it is highly susceptible to funding fluctuations.

Job Redesign and the Autonomy/Equality/Civility Norms. The job redesign model challenges the norms of the work place. The classroom is no longer a private domain; teachers are not equal in rank and stature; their interactions go beyond friendly exchanges. Job redesign confronts the autonomy/equality/civility norms, but it also operates, in some instances, to reshape these norms.

Job redesign changes behavior.[12] It requires teachers to talk with each other and work with each other on professional development issues and school wide problems. As teachers experience new patterns of behavior, some begin to see that autonomy is not synonymous with privacy, that differentiated roles can foster collective benefits, and that professional consultation is as appropriate as friendly conversation. The job redesign strategy can stimulate, in subtle but significant ways, changes in teacher attitudes and orientations. The process is slow and uneven. Clusters of teachers continue to adhere to the traditional patterns. But clusters of teachers also start to modify those patterns as they alter their behavior and experience the benefits of those new behaviors.

Job Redesign and Vulnerability. Because job redesign exposes "how teachers teach, how they think about their teaching and how they plan for teaching to the scrutiny of peers" (Little 1985: 34), the strategy intensifies the vulnerability of educators. It "places teachers' self esteem and professional respect on the line" (Little 1985: 34). But the strategy also accommodates vulnerability by developing capacity and reducing isolation. While teaching weaknesses are more visible, they can become less prevalent as teachers acquire additional knowledge and skill and less traumatic as teachers acquire confidence and receive support and assistance from their colleagues. Job redesign does not change the stressful work conditions per se. But it can alter the isolated arrangements and enhance the capacity of teachers to cope with those work conditions.

Job Redesign and Salient, Dependable Rewards. Job redesign combines extrinsic and intrinsic rewards. Because teachers are most responsive to intrinsic rewards, the job redesign strategy is particularly compelling. It provides opportunities for teachers to participate in activities that increase the likelihood they will derive intrinsic rewards. Teachers can experience personal and professional growth, develop collegial relationships, and acquire a stronger sense of efficacy (Ashton and Webb 1986). These experiences can be gratifying (Kasten 1984: 11; Bredeson, Fruth, and Kastern 1983). Moreover, they contribute to the likelihood that teachers can acquire the strongest reward of all, successful interactions with students. The job redesign strategy holds promise because it uses the compensation system to create conditions and support arrangements that make intrinsic rewards more probable. When effectively deployed and sustained, extrinsic benefits merge with the more salient intrinsic benefits to form a potent constellation of rewards.

In sum, job redesign is credibly aligned with the complex nature of teacher work and appears capable of reshaping autonomy/equality/civility norms. Initially, the strategy increases the vulnerability of the workplace, but it offers in exchange the prospect of securing meaningful rewards.

Our data reveal that some schools were able to capitalize on the benefits of the job redesign strategy more effectively than others. The ability to secure positive results was related to the credibility of the person in the position, the strength of existing work relationships, and the capacity to cope with the demands of the job redesign strategy itself.

Credibility of Promoted Teachers. Where promoted teachers had expertise and interpersonal skill, where they exhibited initiative—"really grabbed ahold [sic]" "didn't wait for somebody to tell them what to do"—and where they concentrated on activities that were highly visible and immediately useful to teachers, the new arrangements were well received. In these situations, informants respected the promoted teachers, appreciated the investment they were making on behalf of the school, and praised their assistance: "They can show you how to do things." They made my job easier." "They're making this school better." When promoted teachers could establish credibility by demonstrating that their work could bolster the capacity of classroom teachers and thereby alleviate some of the strains experienced by teachers, the job redesign strategy acquired support.

In Utah, as in other settings, teacher leader credibility was "hard-won" and individually conferred (Little 1985: 34). The person had to validate the position by assisting colleagues in specific and sensitive ways. A rich blend of personal initiative, expertise, diplomacy, and responsiveness, qualities that correspond to the characteristics of successful mentors in other contexts, enabled teacher leaders to be effective in their roles (Gray and Gray 1985).

Strength of Existing Work Relationships.   Where administrators and teachers had a constructive working relationship in place, where the professionals had some previous and positive experience with collaborative projects and collective problemsolving structures, the job redesign strategy was viewed more positively. These schools were in a position to "ride out the disruption" created by any major change. Although there was tension and stress, these schools were better equipped to absorb the strain and embrace the new roles and responsibilities. As informants put it, the school "weathered the storm well." Conversely, in schools where the principal-faculty relationships were already strained, the job redesign strategy did not take hold. Informants acknowledged that the principal/faculty conflicts were so intense, the distrust was so pronounced, they were "not about to try anything new." They "fought the career ladder" and "didn't really give it a chance."

Existing relationships often condition how change is received (Schein 1984; McDonnell 1983; Moos 1979; Berman and McLaughlin 1978). Apparently existing relationships make the workplace more or less conducive, more or less "hospitable," more or less able to deal with the "shock waves that reverberate throughout the organization" whenever a job redesign effort is made as well (Hackman 1977: 266).

Capacity to Cope with the Demands.   In all settings, the energy required to define new roles, select individuals for those positions, develop, coordinate, and evaluate their activities was "exhausting." Teachers and administrators overestimated the amount of work promoted teachers could realistically accomplish, and they underestimated the implementation toll.[13] Informants were concerned that the demands of getting the new arrangements in place would "eat us alive." Many were not sure that they could "keep up this pace." In some schools this energy drain was recognized and accommodated. Principals were willing to continuously articulate purposes, adjust their priorities, and provide support for those involved. Promoted teachers established support networks, and both principals and teacher leaders concentrated on ways to insightfully link new activities to teacher needs so that intrinsically rewarding experiences could be generated and meaningful returns on the energy invested could be realized. Where these types of human resource adjustments were not made, the energy drain inherent in installation overshadowed the potential benefits of the job redesign strategy.

SUMMARY AND IMPLICATIONS

Policies that seek to improve teacher quality by restructuring compensation systems are among the most prominent and costly interventions recently enacted or presently under consideration by state legislatures. Although these policies are commonly termed career ladders, they actually incorporate or emphasize quite different incentive strategies. While we examined only three alternatives and relied heavily on the perceived impact of these alternatives on the current teacher corp, our analysis suggests factors that warrant attention in the selection of teacher compensation strategies and directions for funding the diverse approaches embedded in current policies.

In determining an approach to teacher compensation reform congruence requirements warrant attention. We noted at the outset that a dominant theme in pay incentives literature is that the pay system must be congruent with the major characteristics of the organization in order to be effective. Our analysis of pay incentives in school settings illustrates that premise.

An incentive strategy such as merit pay that is not aligned with schools on any of the critical dimensions simply does not take hold. It breaks down in installation. Central features are diluted; impact is negated. Selective salary stipends become broad-based increments that have little if any positive impact on the teachers' desire and ability to improve or on the teachers' decision to remain in the profession. The more congruent strategies—job expansion and job redesign—do take hold in some instances. Central features may be modified, but they are not abandoned. Impact is evident. Although special projects tend to be broadly distributed and often support conventional activity, at times they can enhance teaching and satisfaction. The most congruent strategy, job redesign, produces the greatest impact. Salary differentiation is attained. In most of the schools we studied, the redefined roles and relationships affected the teachers' desire and ability to improve and addressed salient dimensions of work satisfaction.

While the concept of congruence is important, it is not sufficient to account for our findings. Throughout our analysis of both the job expansion and the job redesign strategies, we reported divergent responses. The strategies were more or less successful in different settings. The divergent reactions appear to be related to the credibility of the person doing the expanded project or assuming the new role, the strength of existing work relationships, and the capacity to cope with the demands of the strategies. Our analysis suggests, then, that organizational conditions or what we term *organizational prerequisites* moderate the impact of incentive strategies in school settings. Our findings are summarized in Figure 5-1 below. The relative importance of the different factors is speculative at best. Yet the figure highlights factors that shaped teacher responses to compensation strategies, and it identifies barriers that congruent compensation strategies may need to overcome if they are to be effective in schools.

In order to permeate school settings, the teacher compensation strategy must be at least partially congruent with complex work and consistent with or strong enough to modify autonomy/equality/civility norms. The strategy must recognize vulnerability and offer salient, dependable, intrinsic as well as extrinsic rewards. Once a congruent strategy is devised, however, a second set of barriers interacts to condition the impact of that strategy on teachers and work. Individual credibility, the strength of existing work relationships, and the provision of human resource support to cope with the de-

Figure 5-1. Barriers to Effectiveness.

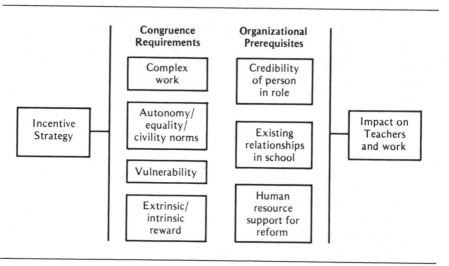

mands of these strategies conditioned the impact of both the job expansion and job redesign efforts. Our analysis indicates that unless these barriers are skillfully and continuously addressed, the potential benefits of a congruent strategy may not be realized.

When the three prominent incentive strategies embedded in current policies are assessed from this perspective, several funding implications surface. First, investment in merit pay is not a judicious use of scarce resources. Merit pay does not operate as a robust incentive in schools. Merit pay provides salary supplements to teachers and directs attention to evaluation and supervision, but these outcomes could be attained through direct investment in salaries and evaluation systems or through job redesign. Although merit pay may serve an important political purpose, garnering public support for education appropriations, we trust that policymakers seek substantive improvements from as well as symbolic justifications for education investments. The merit pay strategy is unable to produce substantive gains because it does not meet any of the congruence requirements. Its incongruence creates a no-win situation. Educators fight merit pay. They quietly transform it into broad-based salary increments or quickly challenge it in legislative and judicial arenas. Policymakers can fight back, but they are left with only two troublesome options. They can distribute merit bonuses to nearly all teachers, an option that denies the integrity of merit pay, or they can tighten controls, an option that shifts scarce resources from capacity building activities to costly and cumbersome oversight activities that have little positive impact. The harder policymakers try to force the fit, the more intense the resistance, and the more expensive the enforcement. Conflict escalates. Scarce resources are consumed by regulation and litigation. Because more compatible incentive strategies are available, policymakers need not limit themselves to the merit pay strategy.

Second, the job redesign strategy is a more prudent investment. Because this strategy can accommodate the major characteristics of the school setting, it is a more potent incentive for improving performance and retention than either the job enlargement or the merit pay approach. Although this strategy meets all the congruence requirements, its impact is conditioned by the organizational prerequisites identified in our data. Job redesign is neither quick nor easy. But when effectively deployed, it can be a powerful strategy for affecting teacher quality. Because job redesign makes fundamental changes in the structure of schools, it is highly susceptible to funding fluctuations. Therefore, a decision to invest in this approach should be viewed as a long-range commitment.

Finally, the job expansion strategy is a defensible investment, particularly when used in conjunction with job redesign. The strategy fits some features of school settings well. It allows individual teachers to engage in projects of interest to them and of import to the organization. But the strategy is often only loosely coupled to organizational purposes. Moreover, it is constrained by the norms and the vulnerability of the workplace and restricted in its capacity to offer salient rewards. Therefore, we do not recommend that systems rely on this approach as the primary means for improving performance and retention. If organizational prerequisites are addressed, job expansion can be a complementary component of the broader, more congruent job redesign strategy.

NOTES

1. Utah data include district career ladder plans (Utah State Office of Education 1985), a state office of education survey of teacher opinions regarding career ladder operations (Nelson 1986), fourteen in-depth studies of career ladder implementation processes in ten districts (Career Ladder Research Group 1984; Hart 1986a, 1986b, 1986c; Hart, Kauchak, and Stevens 1986; Kauchak and Peterson 1986; Hart and Murphy 1986; Malen and Hart forthcoming), and twenty-five additional, informal interviews with administrators, teachers, and career ladder planning committee members. Informal interviews were conducted during February and March of 1987.

2. We add the term *civility* to more explicitly acknowledge the third dimension of Lortie's set of norms. We recognize that Bird and Little (1986) also use the term *civility* to describe school norms. Their referent is broader than we intend here because it describes norms that guide student, teacher, and administrator interactions.

3. In telephone interviews with state officials conducted on September 19, 1986, informants termed Florida's new policy a "renaming of merit pay"—a change made to acquire teacher union cooperation. See also Florida Statutes (Ch. 86–157) and Snider (1986: 1, 20).

4. Some proponents of merit pay argue that broad distribution of benefits is desirable because the vast majority of teachers are deserving. Merit pay simply recognizes nearly all teachers for their good performance. However, most advocates of merit pay contend that broad, near universal coverage dilutes the impact of select, special recognition. As legislators in Utah

explain, their purpose is to reward the "exceptional," "superior," "really outstanding" teachers (Malen 1986).

5.   Several districts in Utah placed limits on the number of merit awards that could be given out. Only a handful of districts limit merit pay eligibility to less than 50 percent of their teachers. Most permit between 70 and 100 percent of their teachers to apply (Utah State Office of Education 1985).

6.   Under the original proposal, approximately 35 percent of the state's teachers would have been eligible for benefits. The caps were revised so that all teachers, except those at the beginning apprentice level (less than 3 years of experience) would be eligible for a $1,000 supplement and 87 percent of all teachers with three or more years of experience would be eligible to apply for the advancement to the higher pay brackets (Handler and Carlson 1984: 15). Telephone interviews with proximate observers, conducted on September 25, 1986, and December 2, 1986, and informal interviews with teacher association members, conducted on November 14, 1986, indicate that the number of teachers applying has increased significantly. These informants project that the "pass rate" to upper levels will "shoot up." Several anticipate a pass rate as high as 75 percent.

7.   A recent national survey concludes that merit pay is attractive to policymakers, but "teachers who are familiar with 'merit pay' systems are strongly opposed to them. . . . Seventy-two percent of American teachers are familiar with such systems, and 71 percent are opposed to the systems, while just 26 percent are in favor" (Harris and Associates 1986: 5).

8.   For a more extensive discussion of evaluation issues, see Wise and Darling-Hammond (1984–85), and Wise, et al. (1984).

9.   With others, Elmore (1980: 25) argues that "when it becomes necessary to rely mainly on control, regulation, and compliance to achieve results, the game is essentially lost. . . . Regulation increases complexity and invites subversion, it diverts attention from accomplishing the task to understanding and manipulating the rules."

10.   This strategy resembles the job differentiation movement of the late 1960s and early 1970s (*Differentiated Staffing* 1971; see also Garms and Guttenberg 1970; Freiberg 1984–85; English 1984–85). Because the job differentiation movement was packaged with a number of innovations, notably team teaching, individualized instruction, modular scheduling, open architectural arrangements, and the like, we use the term *job redesign* to describe the current attempt to realign work roles. The strategy has surfaced in the Carnegie Commission Report, the Holmes Group Report, and in calls for the diagnosis and development of career growth opportunities for teachers (Bacharach, Conley, and Shedd 1986).

11.   Others discuss these issues more thoroughly. See, for examples, Hackman and Oldham 1980; Berg, Freedman, and Freeman 1976; Roberts and Glick 1981.

12.   Hackman argues that in job redesign "the strategy is to change the behavior itself, and to change it so that the employee gradually acquires a positive attitude about his [sic] work, the organization, and himself [sic]" (1977: 272).

13.   Such miscalculations were probably inevitable because the timeline for designing and implementing career ladder programs in Utah was extremely tight. The time-consuming process of gathering information, diagnosing work conditions, defining new roles, and developing the network of support for the new arrangements was short-circuited. Educators had approximately six months to define and implement their career ladder plans, an ambitious schedule for the complex task of redefining teacher work (Malen and Hart forthcoming).

REFERENCES

Academy for Educational Development. 1985. *Teacher Development in Schools. A Report to the Ford Foundation.* New York: Academy for Educational Development.

Ashton, P. T., and R. B. Webb. 1986. *Making a Difference: Teachers' Sense of Efficacy and Student Achievement.* New York: Longman.

Bacharach, S. B., and S. C. Conley. 1986. "Education Reform: A Managerial Agenda." *Phi Delta Kappan* 67 (May): 641–45.

Bacharach, S. B., S. Conley, and J. Shedd. 1986. "Beyond Career Ladders' Structuring Teacher Career Development Systems." *Teachers College Record* 87 (Summer): 563–74.

Berg, E. Freedman, and M. Freeman. 1976. *Managers and Work Reform: A Limited Engagement.* New York: Free Press.

Berman, P., and M. W. McLaughlin. 1978. *Federal Programs Supporting Educational Change. Vol. VIII, Implementing and Sustaining Innovations.* Santa Monica, Calif.: Rand Corporation.

Bird, T., and J. W. Little. 1986. "How Schools Organize the Teaching Occupation." *Elementary School Journal* 86 (March): 493–511.

Bluedorn, A. C. 1982. "A Unified Model of Turnover from Organizations." *Human Relations* 35: 135–53.

Bornfriend, A. J. 1985. "Career Ladders and the Debureaucratization of Education." In *Merit, Money and Teachers' Careers*, edited by H. C. Johnson, Jr., pp. 183–96. New York: University Press of America.

Bray, J. L., P. Flakus-Mosqueda, R. M. Palaich, and J. S. Wilkins. 1985. *New Directions for State Teacher Policies.* Denver, Colo.: Education Commission of the States.

Bredeson, P. V., M. J. Fruth, and K. L. Kastern. 1983. "Organizational Incentives and Secondary School Teaching." *Journal of Research and Development in Education* 16 (November): 52–58.

Carnegie Forum on Education and the Economy. 1986. *A Nation Prepared: Teachers for the 21st Century.* Washington, D.C.: Carnegie Forum on Education and the Economy.

Cohen, D. K., and R. J. Murnane. 1985. *The Merits of Merit Pay.* Palo Alto, Calif.: Institute for Research on Educational Finance and Governance.

Cusick, P. A. 1983. *The Egalitarian Ideal and the American High School: Studies of Three Schools.* New York: Longman.

Differentiated Staffing. 1971. A Cooperative Project of the Central New York Regional Office for Educational Planning, Syracuse, N.Y., and Board of Cooperative Educational Services, Nassau Regional Office for Educational Planning, Jericho, N.Y.

Duke, D. L. 1984. *Teaching—The Imperiled Profession.* Albany, N.Y.: State University of New York Press.

Education Commission of the States. 1985. *Executive Summary-Career Ladder Survey.* Denver, Colo.: Education Commission of the States.

Elmore, R. F. 1980. *Complexity and Control: What Legislators and Administrators Can Do About Implementing Public Policy.* Washington, D.C.: National Institute of Education.

English, F. W. 1984-85. "We Need the Ghostbusters! A Response to Jerome Freiberg." *Educational Leadership* 42 (December/January): 22-27.

Erlandson, D., and J. Wilcox. 1985. "The Teacher Career Ladder in Texas." *School Organization* 5: 365-70.

Freiberg, H. J. 1984-85. "Master Teacher Programs: Lessons from the Past." *Educational Leadership* 42 (December/January): 16-21.

Garms, W. I., and R. Guttenberg. 1970. *The Sources and Nature of Resistance to Incentive Systems in Education.* Final Report on an Investigation under HEW Contract.

Gray, W. A., and M. M. Gray. 1985. "Synthesis of Research on Mentoring Teachers." *Educational Leadership* 43 (November): 37-43.

Hackman, J. R. 1977. "Is Job Enrichment Just a Fad?" In *Perspectives on Behavior in Organizations*, edited by J. R. Hackman, E. E. Lawler III, and L. W. Porter, pp. 263-73. New York: McGraw-Hill.

Hackman, J. R., and G. R. Oldham. 1980. *Work Redesign.* Reading, Mass.: Addison-Wesley.

Hamner, W. C. 1977. "How to Ruin Motivation with Pay." In *Perspectives on Behavior in Organizations*, edited by J. R. Hackman, E. E. Lawler III, and L. W. Porter, pp. 287-96. New York: McGraw-Hill.

Handler, J. R. 1986. *Shaping Tennessee's Career Ladder Program.* Paper prepared for the annual meeting of the American Education Research Association, San Francisco, Calif.

Handler, J. R., and D. L. Carlson. 1984. *Shaping Tennessee's Career Ladder Program. Part I, Improving Teacher Quality through Incentives Project.* Knoxville, Tenn.: University of Tennessee.

_____ . 1985. *Shaping Tennessee's Career Ladder Program. Part II, Improving Teacher Quality through Incentives Project.* Knoxville, Tenn.: University of Tennessee.

Hanes, R. C., and K. Mitchell. 1985. "Teacher Career Development in Charlotte-Mecklenburg." *Educational Leadership* 43 (November): 11-13.

Harris, L. and Associates. 1986. *The Metropolitan Life Survey of the American Teacher 1986: Restructuring the Teaching Profession.*

Hart, A. W. 1985. *Formal Teacher Supervision by Teachers in a Career Ladder.* Paper prepared for the annual meeting of the American Educational Research Association, Chicago, Ill.

_____ . 1986a. *Career Ladder Effects on Teacher Attitudes about Tasks, Careers, Authority, and Supervision.* Paper prepared for the annual meeting of the American Educational Research Association, San Francisco.

_____ . 1986b. *Career Ladders in Utah: The Site Perspective.* Paper prepared for the annual meeting of the American Educational Research Association, San Francisco.

_____ . 1986c. *Redesigning a Career: Two Comparative Case Studies.* Paper prepared for the annual meeting of the American Educational Research Association, San Francisco.

Hart, A. W., D. Kauchak, and D. Stevens. 1986. *Teacher Career Ladder Effects on the Work of the Principal.* Paper prepared for the annual meeting of the American Education Research Association, San Francisco.

Hart, A. W., and M. J. Murphy. 1986. *Career Ladder Implementation.* A report prepared for the Salt Lake City School District, Salt Lake City.

Hatry, H. P., and J. M. Greiner. 1985. *Issues and Case Studies in Teacher Incentive Plans.* Washington, D.C.: Urban Institute Press.

Herrick, N. Q. 1973. "Government Approaches to the Humanization of Work." *Monthly Labor Review* (April): 52-54.

Holmes Group. 1986. *Tomorrow's Teachers.* East Lansing, Mich.: Holmes Group.

Hoogeveen, K., and T. B. Gutkin. 1986. "Collegial Ratings among School Personnel: An Empirical Examination of the Merit Pay Concept." *American Educational Research Journal* 23 (Fall): 375-81.

Johnson, S. M. 1984. "Merit Pay for Teachers: A Poor Prescription for Reform." *Harvard Educational Review* 54: 175-85.

_____ . 1986. "Incentives for Teachers: What Motivates, What Matters." *Educational Administration Quarterly* 22 (Summer): 54-79.

Kahn, R. L. 1973. "The Work Module." *Psychology Today* (January): 35-39, 94-94.

Kanter, R. M. 1983. *The Change Masters: Innovation and Entrepreneurship in the American Corporation.* New York: Simon and Schuster.

Kasten, K. L. 1984. "The Efficacy of Institutionally Dispensed Rewards in Elementary School Teacher." *Journal of Research and Development in Education* 17 (November): 1-13.

Kauchak, D., and K. Peterson. 1986. *Career Ladders in Utah: Four District Case Studies.* Paper prepared for the annual meeting of the American Educational Research Association, San Francisco.

Kirst, M. 1985. *Sustaining State Education Reform Momentum: The Linkage between Assessment and Financial Support.* Palo Alto, Calif.: Stanford Institute for Research on Educational Finance and Governance.

Kottkamp, R. B., E. F. Provenzo, Jr., and M. M. Cohn. 1986. "Stability and Change in a Profession: Two Decades of Teacher Attitudes." *Phi Delta Kappan* 67 (April): 559–67.

Lawler, E. E., III. 1981. *Pay and Organization Development.* Reading, Mass.: Addison-Wesley.

Lieberman, A., and L. Miller. 1984. *Teachers, Their World and Their Work.* Alexandria, Va.: Association for Supervision and Curriculum Development.

Lieberman, M. 1985. "Educational Specialty Boards: A Way Out of the Merit Pay Morass?" *Phi Delta Kappan* 67 (October): 103–07.

Lipsky, M. 1980. *Street-Level Bureaucracy.* New York: Russell Sage.

Little, J. W. 1985. "Teachers as Teacher Advisors: The Delicacy of Collegial Leadership." *Educational Leadership* 43 (November): 34–36.

Lortie, D. C. 1964. "The Teacher and Team Teaching." In *Team Teaching,* edited by J. D. Shaplin and H. F. Olds, Jr., pp. 270–305. New York: Harper & Row.

_____. 1975. *School Teacher: A Sociological Study.* Chicago: University of Chicago Press.

_____. 1986. "Teacher Status in Dade County: A Case of Structural Strain?" *Phi Delta Kappan* 67 (April): 568–75.

Malen, B. 1986. *Career Ladder Policymaking in Utah: A State Perspective.* Paper prepared for the annual meeting of the American Educational Research Association, San Francisco.

Malen, B., and A. W. Hart. Forthcoming. "Career Ladder Reform: A Multi-Level Analysis of Initial Effects." *Educational Evaluation and Policy Analysis.*

Malen, B., and M. J. Murphy. 1985. "A Statewide Decentralized Approach to Public School Reform: The Case of Career Ladders in Utah." *Journal of Education Finance* 11 (Fall): 261–77.

Malen, B., M. J. Murphy, and A. W. Hart. 1987. *Career Ladder Reform in Utah: Evidence of Impact, Recommendations for Action.* Occasional Policy Paper 87-1. Salt Lake City: Graduate School of Education, University of Utah.

McDonnell, L. 1983. *Implementing School Improvement Strategies.* Paper prepared for the National Institute of Education Conference on State and Local Policy Implications for Effective School Research, Dingle Associated, Inc., Washington, D.C.

McDonnell, L., and A. Pascal. 1977. *Organized Teachers in American Schools.* Santa Monica, Calif.: Rand Corporation.

McLaughlin, M. W., R. S. Pfeifer, D. Swanson-Owens, and S. Yee. 1986. "Why Teachers Won't Teach." *Phi Delta Kappan* 67 (February): 420–25.

McKelvey, B., and V. Sekaran. 1977. "Toward a Career-Based Theory of Job Involvement: A Study of Scientists and Engineers." *Administrative Science Quarterly* 22: 281–305.

Mgt. of America. 1985. *A Project to Provide a Review of the Implementation of the Florida Master Teacher Program.* Tallahassee Management of America.

Miller, L. M., and E. Say. 1982. *Incentive Pay for Teachers: Impacts in an Urban District.* Paper prepared for the annual meeting of the American Educational Research Association, New York.

Mitchell, D. E. 1986. *Inducement, Incentive and Cooperation: Barnard's Concept of Work Motivation.* Paper prepared for the annual conference of the American Research Association, San Francisco.

Mitchell, D. E., and C. T. Kerchner. 1983. "Labor Relations and Teacher Policy." In *Handbook of Teaching and Policy*, edited by I. S. Schulman and G. Sykes, pp. 214–38. New York: Longman.

Mitchell, S. M. 1986. *Negotiating the Design of Professional Jobs.* Paper prepared for the annual meeting of the American Educational Research Association, San Francisco.

Moos, R. H. 1979. *Evaluating Educational Environments.* San Francisco: Jossey-Bass.

Murnane, R. J. 1985. "The Rhetoric and Reality of Merit Pay: Why Are They Different?" In *Merit, Money and Teachers' Careers*, edited by H. C. Johnson, Jr., pp. 57–76. New York: University Press of America.

_____ . 1986. "Surviving Merit Pay." *IFG Policy Notes* 6: 5–6.

Murnane, R. J., and D. K. Cohen. 1985. *Merit Pay and the Evaluation Problem: Understanding Why Most Merit Plans Fail and a Few Survive.* Palo Alto, Calif.: Stanford Institute for Research on Educational Finance and Governance.

Murphy, M. J. 1986. *Career Ladders in Utah: School District Responses.* Paper prepared for the annual meeting of the American Educational Research Association, San Francisco.

Murphy, M. J., and A. W. Hart. 1985. *Career Ladder Reforms.* Paper prepared for the California Commission on the Teaching Profession.

_____ . Forthcoming. "Career Ladder Reforms." *Teacher Education Quarterly.*

Nadler, D. A., and E. E. Lawler III. 1977. "Motivation: A Diagnostic Approach." In *Perspectives on Behavior in Organizations*, edited by J. R. Hackman, E. E. Lawler III, and L. W. Porter, pp. 26–38. New York: McGraw-Hill.

NEA Today. 1986. (November): 14.

Nelson, D. 1986. *A Statewide Survey of Teacher Opinions Concerning Utah's Career Ladder Programs.* Salt Lake City: Utah State Office of Education.

Olson, L. 1986. "Pioneering State Teacher-Incentive Plans in Florida, Tennessee Still under Attack." *Education Week* (January 15): 1, 24–25.

Patten, T. H. 1977. *Pay: Employee Compensation and Incentive Plans.* New York: Free Press.

Patton, M. O. 1986. *Utilization-Focused Evaluation*, 2d ed. Beverly Hills, Calif.: Sage.

Phillips, R. 1986. "Should the Teacher's Role Be Differentiated, and If So, What Is the Best Way to Do It?" *ASCD Update* 28 (April): 5.

Pine, P. 1983. *Merit Pay*. ERIC Clearinghouse on Teacher Education, Washington, D.C. (October): 1-2.

Powell, A. G., E. Farrar, and D. K. Cohen. 1985. *The Shopping Mall High School: Winners and Losers in the Educational Marketplace.* Boston: Houghton Mifflin.

Roberts, K. H., and W. Glick. 1981. "The Job Characteristics Approach to Task Design: A Critical Review." *Journal of Applied Psychology* 66: 193-217.

Rodman, B. 1985. "Unions Turn to Courts to Block Florida's 'Unfair' Merit-Pay Program." *Education Week* (February 20): 6.

Rosenholtz, S. 1984. *Political Myths about Educational Reform: Lessons from Research on Teaching.* Denver: Education Commission of the States.

———— . Forthcoming. "Education Reform Strategies: Will They Increase Teacher Commitment?" *American Journal of Education*: 1-55.

Rosenholtz, S. J., and M. A. Smylie. 1984. "Teacher Compensation and Career Ladders." *Elementary School Journal* 85: 149-66.

Seashore, S., and Thad J. Barnowe. 1972. "Collar Color Doesn't Count." *Psycology Today* (August): 53-56, 80-82.

Schein, E. H. 1984. "Coming to a New Awareness of Organizational Culture." *Sloan Management Review*: 3-15.

Snider, W. 1986. "Florida Scraps Master-Teacher Program." *Education Week* (June 18): 1, 20.

Stern, D. 1986. "Compensation for Teachers." In *Review of Research in Education*, edited by E. Z. Rothkopf. pp. 285-316. Washington, D.C.: American Educational Research Association.

Tennessee Education 1986.

Tennessee State Department of Education. 1985. *Tennessee Career Ladder Better Schools Program Teacher Orientation Manual.* Nashville: Tennessee Department of Education.

Utah State Office of Education. 1985. *Career Ladders in Utah: A Content Analysis of Utah's Career Ladders Plans for 1985-1986.*

Vaidero, D. 1986. "Support Teams Mandated for Teachers." *Education Week* (November 26): 8.

Vroom, V. H. 1964. *Work and Motivation.* New York: Wiley.

Wagner, L. A. 1985. "Ambiguities and Possibilities in California's Mentor Teacher Program." *Educational Leadership* 43 (November): 32-39.

Wallace, M. J., and C. H. Fay. 1982. *Compensation Theory and Practice.* Boston: Kent.

Waters, Trego & Davis. 1986. *State of South Carolina Final Report.* Dallas: Waters, Trego, & Davis, Inc.

Wise, A., and L. Darling-Hammond. 1984–85. "Teacher Evaluation and Teacher Professionalism" *Educational Leadership* 42: 28–31.

Wise, A., L. Darling-Hammond, M. McLaughlin, and H. T. Bernstein. 1984. *Teacher Evaluation: A Study of Effective Practices.* Santa Monica, Calif.: Rand Corporation.

Work in America. 1973. Report of a Special Task Force to the Secretary of Health, Education, and Welfare. Cambridge, Mass.: MIT Press.

6 MERIT PAY
Issues and Solutions

Lloyd E. Frohreich

As more school boards and state legislators search for ways to make schools more productive and the public pleased with education, the issue of merit pay once again has raised its controversial head. National crises, studies that portray a nation at risk, or comparisons with other countries that show U.S. students lagging behind other students have prompted the most recent rash of discussions about how best to make educators accountable for learning. Proposals for reform have included considerations of merit pay, differentiated staffing, and career ladders as compensation plans. It is suggested that these plans will allow school systems to pay teachers more, serve as incentives to attract and retain more teachers, and make teachers more productive. Johnson (1986) found that twenty-three states had legislated mentor teacher, master teacher, or career ladder plans as of 1985. Most states have passed or are in the process of designing comprehensive school reform legislation. Although no state has legislated the adoption of merit pay, it has been considered in one of its many forms by politicians and school boards.

A plethora of literature on the subject of merit pay exists, much of which is not based on solid research or theory. Almost every professional organization in education has taken a position on merit pay; teacher organizations generally are against it, whereas administrator and board groups support it. Polls have shown that it is supported by the public. Many teachers support it in theory but not in practice.

In this chapter merit pay is examined from a number of perspectives beginning with definition and background, followed by a presentation of related theory and merit pay issues. The chapter closes with the presentation of a proposed teacher incentive and compensation decision model. The reader is invited to read an extended discussion of the theory and practice of merit pay by Jacobson in Chapter 7 of this book.

DEFINITION AND BACKGROUND

Merit pay is a compensation plan that provides extra pay or awards for employees who have the same responsibilities and who are judged meritorious based on a performance evaluation. Merit pay or awards can assume several configurations. An employee may receive a one-time award based on superior performance. A special pay scale may be set up for merit awards. Employees may have their base salaries increased permanently. Meritorious performance also may be recognized with special awards such as sabbaticals, scholarships, travel stipends to professional meetings, or other rewards in lieu of monetary compensation.

Differentiated staffing may or may not be a merit pay system. Promotion to a higher-level position in an organization may indeed be based on performance, but if employees at the master teacher level, for example, are paid according to a schedule and not performance, then this is not a true merit pay system. Career ladder compensation plans are essentially a form of differentiated staffing and may or may not be merit systems. Career ladder plans usually imply different position-level responsibilities such as supervision, research, curriculum writing, and other nonclassroom work.

The impetus for merit pay plans and for other forms of compensating teachers seems to surface in the United States concomitantly with concerns about productivity, national security, and U.S. economic standing in comparison with other countries. National crises such as a war, a space race, and studies that portray the United States as a nation at risk invite debate on changing the way teachers are paid. Between 1918 and 1928 it was estimated that 18 to 48 percent of the districts in each state used merit pay plans (Johnson 1984).

Single salary schedules, prompted in part by collective negotiations, all but eliminated merit pay systems in the 1940s and 1950s. Sputnik revived the issue of merit pay, and perhaps as many as 10 percent of U.S. school districts adopted plans shortly thereafter.

The recent national studies highlighting the problems in education have again brought the compensation issue to the fore. Criticisms put forth in these studies claim that teacher quality is declining; quality teachers are leaving the profession; schools are attracting lower-quality teachers; students' standardized test scores are declining; students are spending less time in school and on tasks; and students are scoring below their counterparts in other countries. The argument is advanced that if schools were more productive and if educators worked harder and were more efficient, many if not all of these problems could be eliminated. Critics have suggested that the real cause of diminished productivity and student performance rests in the realm of how teachers are paid. Thus, we have numerous proposals for revising teacher compensation plans based on merit pay or on career ladder systems.

Will merit pay or other types of plans produce the desired effects? Will these plans result in higher productivity levels, more efficient operations, higher student achievement, and more productive citizens? It is hoped that the discussion that follows will shed some light on the answers to these questions.

RELATED THEORY

Johnson (1986) provides an excellent discussion of the theoretical bases for reforms to motivate individuals and to encourage greater productivity in educational institutions. The theories that are tied to the reform movement are expectancy theory, equity theory, and job enrichment theory. Expectancy theory suggests that individuals are more likely to work harder if they anticipate a valued reward, such as a bonus, promotion, or recognition. Equity theory advances the notion that individuals are dissatisfied if they perceive that they are unjustly compensated based on their performance or when compared with other individuals who perform at a lower level. Job enrichment theory purports that individuals are more productive when their work is more varied and challenging. Johnson (1986) implied that expectancy and equity theory support the concept of merit pay, whereas job enrichment theory supports differentiated staffing and career ladders.

These theories have as a base the importance of intrinsic and extrinsic rewards as ways of motivating individuals to be more productive. The distinction between intrinsic and extrinsic rewards is not always clear, but intrinsic rewards are primarily internal and refer to such factors as a sense of achievement, recognition, efficacy, and satisfaction with role and responsibilities and a feeling that one is appreciated and an integral part of an organization. Extrinsic rewards generally are material and external, such as money, promotions, material rewards in lieu of money for teaching equipment, convention trips, and released time. Most research suggests that intrinsic rewards are more important to individuals than extrinsic rewards. Still, extrinsic rewards are not irrelevant in the motivation of people. It is likely that intrinsic rewards are not sufficient to attract and to retain teachers if the extrinsic rewards (pay) are inadequate and inequitable. Either type of reward must serve as base for the other type of reward. If individuals are unhappy in their work, it is not likely that merit pay will motivate them to be more productive. It would appear that personal and family needs of individuals must be met before individuals can sense those personal accomplishments that come from intrinsic rewards.

Much more research needs to be done before definitive conclusions can be reached about what motivates teachers. Under the assumption that pay is perceived to be adequate and that teachers are reasonably satisfied with their work, are they motivated by merit pay systems that promise higher pay? If teachers' base pay is inadequate yet they are satisfied, does merit pay increase their motivation to be more productive? What combination or balance of pay and personal satisfaction is necessary to promote the highest productivity levels in teachers? There may not be definitive answers to these questions despite extensive and well-designed research. Individuals are motivated by different sets of rewards: Some are motivated by the promise of more pay, and some by praise and fulfillment rewards. The balance between intrinsic and extrinsic rewards that promote individual initiative may be an elusive target and not generalizable to groups of people such as teachers. Because each individual has his or her own set of motivational stimuli, and schools must attempt to find what works for each individual teacher much as teachers attempt to individualize how they teach students.

MERIT PAY ISSUES

The arguments for and against merit pay have continued since such plans were adopted on a large scale after World War I. Not much has been added to this debate in recent years, although some research seems to indicate that merit pay does not offer as many benefits as it was designed to present. There are more arguments against than for merit pay, but the following discussion attempts to present a balanced view of the issue.

Advocacy Positions

It is the position of supporters that *merit pay represents the American way of free enterprise.* According to this view the single salary schedule perpetuates mediocrity by penalizing those who are competitive and wish to be recognized for superior performance. Merit pay systems allow employees to rise to their levels of competence and encourages productivity, efficiency, and initiative. Merit pay recognizes those who achieve a higher level of performance and compensates them for their successes. Some evidence suggests that competition is appropriate for some individuals but that not all individuals are comfortable in a competitive environment. Competition may not be the proper incentive to encourage greater efforts especially in the profession of teaching. Furthermore, some teachers will do their best regardless of the existence of merit pay.

It is argued that *more public support would be forthcoming if teachers were paid according to their performance.* Recent polls of the public indicate that there is substantial support for merit pay and that the public believes that the quality of teaching is declining. School district costs continue to rise; enrollments are declining; test scores have declined; and the public is asking why. When asked to vote for a bond referendum or higher tax levies, the public is reluctant to support schools in the face of such negative conditions. Many citizens believe that merit pay will increase productivity and solve many of these problems. The assumption, of course, is that many teachers are lazy and that merit pay would make them work harder. There is no real evidence to support this contention, as there is no evidence to suggest that more public support would exist if schools would adopt merit pay. The basic contention of taxpayer support seems logical, but the relationship between the existence of merit pay and taxpayer support has not been proven to be causal. Indeed, if merit pay were adopted in a community, it likely would mean more financial support for bonds and tax levies because merit pay plans generally are more expensive than single salary schedules.

Merit pay would increase the level of participation in implementing such a plan and would improve the teacher evaluation process. The success of merit plans depends on the involvement of many individuals and groups. Without teacher, citizen, administrator, and school board involvement, the evidence suggests that merit pay plans are short-lived. The longevity of merit pay plans is related to teacher participation and cooperation. There also is support for the contention that the evaluation process likely would improve under a merit pay plan. The involvement of teachers, administrators, and others in designing an effective employee evaluation system likely would be an improvement over an existing process. The nature of the merit pay system demands that more attention be given to the evaluation process to make it fairer, more comprehensive, and more objective. The end result is that administrators spend more time in the classroom, communicate more with their staffs, and are better prepared to assist in staff development. Even though a merit pay system may achieve these desired effects, it must be pointed out that these results also may be realized under an effective staff development plan without merit pay.

Perhaps the most compelling argument is that *merit pay would reward, recognize, and compensate outstanding teachers.* Calhoun and Protheroe (1983) found this benefit to be most important to those districts that had merit pay. In a system where the intrinsic rewards within the classroom sustain many teachers, it may be that such rewards are not sufficient. The satisfaction that comes from the recognition by employers and by peers that an individual is meritorious cannot be underestimated. The compensation may be of only secondary importance in such a system, whereas the true motivation may come from the mere recognition of a person's worth and importance to the organization. The value of proper recognition along with adequate compensation should be considered more seriously by any school district, even with the issue of merit pay aside.

Another of the proponents' major tenets is that *merit pay will help attract and retain effective teachers and discourage ineffective teachers.* One of the more compelling arguments as to why the profession is not attracting and retaining high-quality teachers is that the reward and compensation system does not compare favorably with other professions. There is substantial evidence that beginning and average teacher salaries do not match most other professions. There seems to be little doubt that higher salaries would attract more individuals to teaching. As college students make career choices, they are aware of both salary levels and the availability of employment. It is likely that if both conditions were favorable, teaching would attract more people. Whether the level of quality would improve at the entry level is not as clear. Dissuading people from entering the profession are other factors such as pervasive negativism about education in the press and in national reports, the public's attitude toward education, the availability of alternative employment opportunities for women in the private sector, and the perception that the demands and complexities of classroom teaching are increasing.

If merit pay would raise beginning and average salaries, undoubtedly the attractiveness and the retentiveness of the profession would be increased. The truth is that a beginning teacher as the sole wage earner in a family cannot make a decent living in some communities, and all of the intrinsic rewards in existence may not be sufficient to attract and retain such a person. If a merit pay system can raise the level of both intrinsic and extrinsic rewards, then this may be the most persuasive argument for merit pay. It is possible to increase rewards without merit pay. Will merit pay cause these rewards to increase, thereby attracting and retaining more effective teachers? The answer to this question depends on the merit pay plan implemented and on many other factors. The Association for Supervision and Curriculum Development (1985) stated that the relationship between money and its motivation to encourage individuals to select and to remain in teaching has not been firmly established.

Contrary Positions

Those with contrary opinions argue that *there is no clear agreement on what constitutes effective teaching*; therefore, effective teaching cannot be measured and teachers cannot be evaluated objectively. Educational research has attempted to measure the relationship between teaching, teacher characteristics, and learning for several years. The evidence from these studies shows no clear relationship. In the early 1960s the Coleman report suggested that the effects of schooling and teachers were secondary to the importance of the socioeconomic level and influence of the home. Contrary positions to Coleman's conclusions on the effects of the home may be found in the research (Rossmiller 1986). The one teacher characteristic that has shown some consistent relationship to pupil performance is teacher verbal ability. Several studies have found that different teacher characteristics affect pupils with varying abilities differentially (Summers and Wolfe 1975). Teacher evaluations can assess knowledge of subject matter, class management, communication skills, organizational skills, ability to discipline, and the ability to individualize instruction. The question of whether those assessments are related to or have an impact on student performance is not as clear. Clearly, more research is needed on the effects of teaching and teacher characteristics before definitive conclusions may be made about this argument against merit pay or about the evaluation of teachers.

It is suggested that *merit pay systems will lower teacher morale and decrease cooperation.* If only individual accomplishments are recognized, it is argued that competition among teachers will lessen the collegiality and cooperative spirit that are necessary in an effective organization. Teachers will be less likely to share ideas, curricular innovations, and instructional methods with colleagues. If a teacher's sense of purpose becomes internalized and individualistic, then the overall purposes of the organization are compromised. If merit awards are limited to a few individuals, then those individuals not chosen may become discouraged, and merit pay may become a disincentive.

Calhoun and Protheroe (1983) found that morale problems ranked third among the major problems reported by districts that had ongoing merit pay systems. These problems can be overcome to some degree by establishing both individual and group awards, involving teachers in developing and evaluating the merit pay plan, increasing the number of individuals who receive merit awards, assuring that the evaluation plan is sound and reasonably objective, and improving the level of trust and confidence in the person doing the evaluation. Nevertheless, there will be those who do not work well in competitive environments and whose sense of worth and confidence may be diminished by any merit system.

Perhaps the most pervasive and enduring criticism of merit pay is that *most evaluation systems utilized are inequitable and subjective.* This was the most often mentioned negative comment made by districts that already have established merit plans (Calhoun and Protheroe 1983). Most studies of teacher evaluation instruments reinforce this argument. Such instruments tend to be weak with respect to comprehensiveness, reliability, validity, and level of detail. On the other hand, there are evaluation instruments developed with the cooperation of teachers and administrators which appear to be equitable and acceptable to most participants (LaDue School District 1984). Those doing the evaluation (generally principals) must be trained extensively. Merit systems encompass entire school districts, not one or two buildings. Evaluations and merit awards must be consistent and equitable across the district, not just within one building. A teacher judged to be meritorious in one building may be considered inadequate in another building because the perception of what constitutes outstanding performance may vary from one principal to another.

Even though the single salary schedule may not pay on the basis of merit, teachers argue that at least it cannot be manipulated like a merit rating (Johnson 1984). One solution that may have some value is to implement a system of multiple evaluators and evaluations. Evaluators could exchange buildings so that a principal might visit a teacher in his or her own building twice and those in two other buildings once each. A merit evaluation committee could be constituted with principals and selected staff who decide the final merit rating.

The question of the *cost and the time necessary to implement an effective merit plan* has been raised by those opposed to merit pay. The argument is that merit pay plans are not cost effective because there is no guaranty that the merit money actually will increase learning. In addition, the time needed for training administrators and doing the evaluations will be expensive and detract from more critical responsibilities. It is true that there is no evidence to support the contention that merit pay will serve as an incentive to improve instructional effectiveness and student performance. It has been shown that overall costs have increased under merit pay, but one objective of merit pay may be to increase the average level of compensation in a school district for those who are most deserving. The purpose of the merit pay incentives is to attract and to retain effective teachers. If cost effectiveness were the only criterion used to judge the worth of a program, then many instructional programs would have difficulty in maintaining their places in the curricula of schools.

A criticism of the time spent by teachers, administrators, and others in planning and implementing a merit pay system is well founded. Effective merit systems require countless hours of time in training administrators and in assessing teacher performance. In addition, an evaluator's role and responsibilities may need to be redirected. A school district must decide whether benefits such as improving teacher effectiveness, working more closely with staff, and developing staff (assuming these are products) are worth the redirected energies and time of evaluators and teachers. Again, it is necessary to point out that a more extensive evaluation system and instructional improvement program need not exist exclusively with a merit pay system. Many very effective teacher evaluation programs exist without merit pay as their main impetus.

Critics of merit pay have a litany of objections that are somewhat related to the major themes discussed above. Among the more relevant are that (1) schools may change leadership, which may cause merit plans to be refocused and teacher confidence to be diminished; (2) the complexity, extensive recordkeeping, and documentation inherent in merit systems are not worth the effort; (3) many merit pay plans are not structured adequately and lack defined goals and objectives; (4) parents may demand that their children be assigned only to meritorious teachers; (5) incentives are too low to encourage either participation or higher productivity; (6) the existence of merit quotas or artificial cutoffs will cause a majority of teachers to oppose the system and it will fail; (7) competition will cause teachers to favor and to spend more time with students who are likely to perform better on standardized tests; (8) student testing (if used as a performance criterion) does not adequately measure cognitive gains and any affective gains or creative skills of students; (9) if test scores are used as a criterion of performance, teachers may focus classroom activities mainly on those skills being tested; and (10) teachers may concentrate on those performance criteria that are known to be important to the evaluators, perhaps to the exclusion of more critical activities.

TEACHER INCENTIVE AND COMPENSATION DECISION MODEL

This chapter has discussed merit pay systems, including a definition, background, related theory, and issues. It is important to leave the

Figure 6-1. Teacher Incentive and Compensation Decision Model.

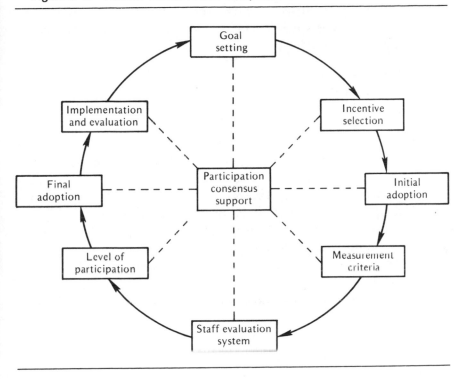

reader with some semblance of a system that might be useful to school districts as they consider the many variables and alternatives available to them regarding possible incentive and compensation plans. The teacher incentive and compensation decision model presented in Figure 6-1 was developed to assist districts in clarifying the decision process. The complexity of merit pay and other compensation and incentive plans realistically make it difficult to incorporate all of the possible factors that contribute to making such decisions. This model provides school districts with a process that identifies those components and decision points needed to select an appropriate incentive and pay program.

Goal Setting

It is essential to begin the decision process of selecting and implementing a school district incentive and compensation plan with a consideration of the goals that the district wishes to achieve with the system. Many of the goals and objectives listed below are interrelated and not mutually exclusive. The decision by the district to select one or more of these goals will affect the decisions in each of the subsequent stages of the model.

1. Attract and retain teachers.
2. Improve classroom instruction.
3. Provide a fairer pay system.
4. Improve teacher morale and satisfaction.
5. Attract teachers to perform additional assignments such as coaching, writing curricula, and advising student groups.
6. Increase public support for local schools.
7. Eliminate ineffective teachers.
8. Increase the cost effectiveness of identified programs.
9. Increase teacher productivity.
10. Increase student attendance.
11. Improve student performance in the cognitive and affective domains.
12. Improve student citizenship, creative skills, fine arts skills, and physical skills.

Incentive Selection

Goal setting is followed by a consideration of those incentives that the district believes will best encourage and motivate teachers to achieve the goals selected in the first stage. The incentives selected will provide a basis for choosing an initial incentive and compensation plan at the next stage. The following list is divided into intrinsic and extrinsic incentives.

Intrinsic Incentives

1. Shared values, culture, and collegiality
2. Sense of efficacy and accomplishment
3. Sense of belonging and contributing to an overall goal or mission
4. Recognition and celebrations of outstanding performance
5. Sense of personal worth and satisfaction

Extrinsic Incentives

1. Extra pay for additional duties and responsibilities
2. Monetary rewards based on performance

3. Monetary rewards based on personal characteristics such as degrees, course work, and longevity
4. Rewards in lieu of pay such as released time, a new title, research and writing grants, convention trips, pay for course credits, sabbaticals, and leaves of absence

Initial Selection of Compensation System

A selection of incentives is followed by a consideration of the system or combination of systems that the district believes will help promote the prescribed goals and incentives. It is important that adequate research and a review of successful plans be conducted at this stage. The whole decision process may have to be recycled at any time and a different election made if it is determined that the initial plan chosen is not feasible. The following incentive and/or compensation plans appear to be the ones most often used by school districts.

1. Single salary schedule with no merit pay provisions
2. Single salary schedule with additional merit bonuses that are either permanent or based on a year-by-year performance
3. Merit pay with multiple scales, special awards, or bonuses
4. Differentiated staffing or career ladder plans that are based on position and responsibilities
5. Additional pay for extra assignments such as coaching, curriculum writing, and research
6. Performance by objectives plan with teachers that provides for no extra compensation
7. Staff development and improvement plans that have no financial incentives
8. Magnitude of awards and distribution among financial and nonfinancial awards

Measurement Criteria

The measurement criteria that a school district chooses is probably the most important decision to be made next to the evaluation process itself. The criteria that follow are distributed among the categories of classroom performance, output measures, personal and professional growth characteristics, organizational citizenship, and community citizenship.

Classroom Performance

1. Communication skills
2. Classroom management, planning, and organization
3. Knowledge of subject matter
4. Preparation for classes
5. Discipline skills
6. Measurement and documentation of student progress
7. Utilization of available school resources
8. Behavioral objectives and expectations set for students
9. Attention to individual and group needs
10. An environment of mutual respect and trust

Output Measures

1. Student attendance
2. Student cognitive gains based on local criterion referenced tests or national standardized tests
3. Measurement of student affective behavior gains
4. Measurement of skills in the physical education and fine arts areas
5. Evidence of student demonstrations of creativeness in art, science, music, and writing

Personal and Professional Growth Characteristics

1. Education, training, and experience
2. Participation in and contribution to professional organizations
3. Writing books or articles for professional journals
4. Travel related to teaching area
5. Participation in graduate courses, inservice training, or workshops that enhance classroom effectiveness

Organizational Citizenship

1. Relationship with other teachers and administrators
2. Spirit of volunteerism and service to the school
3. Contributions to the school
4. Observation of district regulations and policies

Community Citizenship

1. Relationships to and communication with parents and community citizens
2. Contributions to the community
3. Membership in and service to community organizations
4. Utilization of community resources

EVALUATION PROCESS

The evaluation process will be determined to a large degree by the criteria chosen in the preceding phase of the model. The success of the evaluation process and the compensation plan itself will depend on the participation, planning, and agreement that is reached regarding evaluation. The decisions that relate to evaluation are enumerated below.

1. What individuals will be involved in observing the classroom performance of teachers?
2. What individuals will be requested to provide information and data about teachers?
3. What individuals or groups will actually rate and select teachers for various pay and nonpay rewards?
4. How many classroom observations will be made, at what intervals, and will they be announced or unannounced?
5. What kind and how often will feedback be provided to participants?
6. What appeal process will be set up for those who believe that they were unfairly treated, and who will serve on appeal committees?
7. To what extent will ratings, rewards, or merit pay be kept confidential?
8. Can and will evaluation instruments be developed that are fair, reliable, and valid?
9. How much and what kind of training programs will evaluators be expected to have as a condition for participation?
10. What kind of information and how will participants be informed about the criteria used and the evaluation process?
11. Can an evaluation system be developed that will have the mutual respect of participants while maintaining morale and collegiality within the organization?

Participation

1. Who and how many will be allowed to participate in the incentive and compensation system?
2. Will there be group or individual awards or both? What will be the balance of awards between groups and individuals?

3. Will there be arbitrary cutoffs and quotas placed on the number of awards?
4. Will participation be voluntary or forced? Will teachers be allowed to drop out for a given length of time?

Final Adoption

At this point a go or no-go decision must be made. A school district must decide whether the plan that has been developed is feasible and has the support of a substantial majority of the participants. If not, it may be necessary to trace back through the cycle to locate problems and then to continue the decision process from there. The following questions and criteria need to be considered at this stage.

1. What are the financial requirements for the plan chosen, and can the district raise the necessary funds?
2. Is there substantial support from the community and taxpayers for the plan?
3. Is there agreement and consensus on the part of administrators, teachers, and the school board that the plan chosen will work and should be tried?
4. Will the administration and school board provide the necessary time and leadership to make sure the plan works?

Implementation and Evaluation

The final stage in this model is the actual implementation and subsequent evaluation of the incentive and compensation plan. It may be necessary to return to the beginning of the cycle if the selected plan is not acceptable or feasible. If a monetary incentive plan is not supported, then a nonmonetary incentive plan may be the best choice. The following measures and steps need to be considered in the final stage.

1. Evaluation of the plan should include measures of teacher satisfaction, goal attainment, and cost effectiveness.
2. Those who serve on the evaluation team for assessing the plan should represent a cross-section of the school district.
3. Results of the evaluation should be communicated to all the affected participants.
4. Any recommended revisions should be approved by each group of participants.

Participation, Consensus, and Support

The final part of this decision model focuses on a theme that pervades all successful incentive and compensation plans—that is, there must be extensive participation, consensus, and support as decisions are made, whatever the level of those decisions. Numerous literature sources have cited the importance of the participation and support of affected individuals and groups in a school district. Top-down pay plans that are forced on teachers by legislatures or school boards almost always fail. These lessons should not be idly dismissed when decisions are made about how to best encourage and reward teachers.

SUMMARY

The Association for Supervision and Curriculum Development (ASCD) (1985) wrote that to argue the perceived faults and advantages of individual merit pay plans or models would result in an ideological stalemate. Nevertheless, I believe that it is important to continue this debate as long as there are those legislatures, school boards, and other groups who are concerned and prompted to promote alternative compensation plans and impose them on public employees. We must debate the merits of these compensation plans so that the best system is adopted and implemented.

The evidence presented through literature sources seems to weigh more heavily on the side of those opposed. Johnson (1986) concluded that although many change agents presume that teachers are motivated by money and are intentionally withholding their best efforts, research suggests otherwise. ASCD (1985) implied that if problems that now impede teachers remain uncorrected, pay incentives or any other systems employed to create incentives for teaching excellence will be useless. Hatry and Greiner (1984) concluded that there is little concurring evidence, one way or the other, on whether merit pay or performance-by-objectives plans have substantially affected student achievement, teacher retention rates, or the ability to attract high-quality teachers.

I believe that the outlook is not as bleak or discouraging as has been suggested in several literature sources. We cannot discount the many examples of merit pay that exist in this country. To suggest, however, that merit pay is a system that ought to be adopted by every state and school district simply is not realistic. Perhaps merit pay ought to be tied to the multiple scales of career ladder schemes. It is evident that more research is needed on several fronts. States and departments of public instruction need to sponsor systematic experiments and trials with different forms of motivational plans in a variety of settings to help prove what works. We need to increase our efforts in basic research to determine what matters to teachers, what satisfies them, and what motivates them. We also need a better sense of how participatory management relates to motivation and organizational productivity within schools. Until we have conclusive answers on these questions, the debate on motivation, incentives, rewards, and merit pay will continue to be one-sided.

REFERENCES

Association for Supervision and Curriculum Development. 1985. *Incentives for Excellence in America's Schools*. Washington, D.C.: ASCD.

Calhoun, F. S., and N. J. Protheroe. 1983. *Merit Pay Plans for Teachers*. Tyler, Tex.: Tyler Independent School District.

Hatry, H. P., and J. M. Greiner. 1984. *Issues in Teacher Incentive Plans*. Washington, D.C.: Urban Institute.

Johnson, S. M. 1984. *Pros and Cons of Merit Pay*. Bloomington, Ind.: Phi Delta Kappa Educational Foundation.

_____. 1986. "Incentives for Teachers: What Motivates, What Matters?" *Educational Administration Quarterly* 22 (3) (Summer): 54–79.

LaDue School District. 1984. *The LaDue Evaluation and Salary Program*. LaDue, Mo.: District.

Rossmiller, R. A. 1986. *Resource Utilization in Schools and Classrooms: Final Report*. Madison: Wisconsin Center for Education Research, Program Report 86–7.

Summers, A. A., and B. I. Wolfe. 1975. "Which School Resources Help Learning? Efficiency and Equity in Philadelphia Public Schools." *Business Review of the Federal Reserve Bank of Philadelphia* (February): 4–28.

7 MERIT PAY AND TEACHING AS A CAREER

Stephen L. Jacobson

When the National Commission on Excellence in Education (1983: 30) recommended that teachers' salaries would have to be "increased, professionally competitive, market-sensitive, and performanced-based" if the quality of the U.S. teacher workforce were to be improved, the Commission rekindled a debate over the merits of using merit pay in public education that has simmered since the beginning of the present century (Urban 1985).

The desire to compensate teachers on the basis of their contributions to the educational enterprise, rather than on just their years of service and educational training, remains intuitively appealing even though merit pay has a well-documented history of failure in public education (Urban 1985; Cohen and Murnane 1985; Lipsky and Bacharach 1983). Teacher union opposition, difficulties in measuring teacher performance, and the zero-sum nature of most plans are commonly cited for these past failures (Bacharach, Lipsky, and Shedd 1984; Murnane and Cohen 1986). Yet it is necessary to look no further than the content and process of teacher motivation to understand why performance-contingent salary systems generally fail to make the transition from theory into educational practice.

Merit pay proposals are often developed without a clear understanding of the rewards that teachers desire most from their employment or of how reward preferences can change with experience. Proponents of merit pay contend that teachers are no different than

161

workers in other occupations where money is effectively used as an incentive (Casey 1979). Merit pay proposals therefore typically focus only on teaching's monetary rewards, based on the following assumptions:

1. Teachers are motivated primarily by monetary incentives, and
2. The opportunity for extra compensation can be effectively used to motivate teacher behavior throughout their teaching careers.

The purpose of this chapter is to examine these assumptions by identifying the factors that influence teacher behavior, the mechanisms that link rewards to behavior, and the effect that teaching experience has on the determinants of teacher behavior. Two theoretical approaches are considered: Herzberg's two-factor theory (1966) and Vroom's expectancy theory (1964). Two recent educational reform proposals that offer alternatives to merit pay are also examined: the Holmes Group report (1986) and the report of the Carnegie Forum on Education and Economy (1986). The chapter builds on the discussion of merit pay issues and solutions developed by Frohreich in this book.

WHAT MOTIVATES TEACHERS?

When organizations seek to alter the composition of their workforce, the first changes proposed often involve rates of pay. Salary is singled out because it is the most visible and tangible component of a compensation package and, as such, the most amenable to comparison. Changes in salary enable individuals contemplating membership or those already within an organization to anticipate quantifiable dollar differences in present or future earnings. Individuals can then draw comparisons with potential earnings offered by other employment opportunities. Dyer, Schwab, and Fossum (1978: 253) contend that pay is probably the single most important reward that an organization has to offer. For some individuals, however, it is the nonpecuniary rewards intrinsic to a specific occupation that make the work attractive. Teaching is an occupation presumed to be rich in intrinsic rewards.

Intrinsic rewards such as achievement, recognition, and responsibility are nonpecuniary benefits that an individual derives from the content of his or her work. In contrast, extrinsic rewards are benefits derived from one's association with a particular employment situation and may be either pecuniary (such as salary and fringe benefits) or nonpecuniary in nature (such as relationships with other workers or general conditions within the working environment). The importance of this distinction is that proponents of recent merit pay proposals have focused primarily on increased pecuniary rewards, whereas detractors of merit pay usually cite the importance of intrinsic rewards. The following discussion highlights the importance of nonpecuniary, extrinsic rewards, particularly in terms of the labor market behavior of veteran teachers.

The Two-Factor Approach

Industrial psychology and educational studies provide several interrelated taxonomies of rewards (Spuck 1974) perhaps the best known of which is Herzberg's motivation-hygiene or two-factor theory. Two-factor theory is concerned with the content of motivation, and it identifies two types of outcomes that workers seek from their employment: *motivator* and *hygiene* factors.

Defined as rewards intrinsic to the content of work, motivators such as achievement and recognition provide the individual with the opportunity for psychological growth, a condition that Herzberg contends is necessary for employee job satisfaction and enhanced performance. In contrast, hygiene factors such as salary, which serve primarily to reduce job dissatisfaction, are rewards extrinsic to the content of work. Employee dissatisfaction is often manifest through chronic absenteeism and high rates of turnover. The two-factor approach treats job satisfaction and dissatisfaction as separate dimensions rather than as opposite ends of a single continuum. Rewards that motivate job satisfaction and performance are separate and distinct from rewards that reduce job dissatisfaction and turnover. Herzberg's theory predicts that by making work less unpleasant monetary incentives have an important role to play in improving teacher retention but that salary changes alone will not improve teacher performance. Instead, the two-factor approach suggests that compensation proposals concerned with improving teacher performance must be more attentive to making intrinsic rewards available. Focusing exclusively on pecuniary incentives can even undermine performance if these monetary rewards become more important than the intrinsic motivation of the work itself (Deci 1976: 68–69). One manifestation of this problem is "opportunistic" behavior—that is, employees' finding ways of obtaining rewards with a minimum of effort (Williamson 1975: 9). As Murnane and Cohen (1986: 16–17) suggest, using the power of money to improve teachers performance appears to be misguided.

Teacher Reward Preferences

The importance of intrinsic rewards in motivating teacher behavior is supported by a number of examinations of teacher reward preferences. Lortie (1975: 27–32), for example, asked teachers to report the factors that originally attracted them to the profession. He found, in order of preference, these five predominant themes:

1. The interpersonal theme (the desire to work with youngsters)
2. The service theme (the belief that teachers serve a special mission
3. The continuation theme (the desire to remain in a school environment
4. Material benefits (financial rewards and job security)
5. The theme of time compatibility (the work schedule in teaching)

Lortie's findings indicate that intrinsic factors represent teaching's most attractive benefits, whereas extrinsic rewards appear to be somewhat less important to teachers. Material benefits represent only the fourth most influential attraction, with just 2 to 4 percent of teachers reporting money as the primary reasons for their entering the profession.

More recently, Feistritzer (1986: 43) asked teachers to choose among the most important aspects of their work. These factors are listed by the percentage of public school teachers selecting each:

1. A chance to use your intellect and abilities (63%)
2. Change to work with young people (62%)
3. Appreciation of a job well done (54%)
4. Good salary (51%)
5. Job security (27%)
6. Medical and other benefits (16%)
7. A clean, quiet, comfortable place to work (12%)
8. Being able to retire with a good pension (10%)

Intrinsic factors were still the most important aspects of work reported, and salary remained fourth, being the only extrinsic reward selected by more than half of the 1,132 public school teachers surveyed. In contrast, Feistrizer notes that extrinsic rewards were the factors selected most often in a Louis Harris survey of 967 employed adults surveyed for *Business Week* (May 20, 1985). In that survey, only two job factors were selected by more than half the respondents, salary (63 percent) and job security (53 percent).

These findings suggest that teachers may very well be different than workers in other occupations where monetary incentives have been effectively employed. But as Lortie cautions, conclusions drawn from surveys in which teachers are asked to self-report their reward preferences must be tempered by the fact that normative expectations of teachers being dedicated professionals may inhibit teachers from acknowledging the full impact of material benefits on their behavior. Nevertheless, the findings reported bring into question the validity of the central premise of merit pay—that is, the primacy of monetary rewards as a motivator of teacher behavior. Johnson 1984: 183), for example, contends that although classroom teachers *are* concerned with the security of good salaries, they are motivated more by the content and process of their work than by the opportunity for extra compensation. Goodlad (1983: 172) argues that teachers begin their careers with a willingness to forgo high salaries because they anticipate rewards intrinsic to their work. But he cautions that if these expectations of intrinsic benefits are frustrated, salary then becomes a source of considerable dissatisfaction, ranking second as the reason teachers give for leaving the profession.

Although monetary rewards appear not to be the primary motivator of teacher behavior, the influence of salary on recruitment and retention cannot be ignored. As Frohreich (ch. 6 of this book) observes, "Intrinsic rewards are not sufficient to attract and retain teachers if extrinsic rewards (pay) are inadequate."

The discussion now shifts from the content of motivation and the factors that influence teacher behavior to the process of motivation and the mechanisms that link intrinsic and extrinsic rewards to teacher behavior.

HOW DO REWARDS MOTIVATE?

The Expectancy Approach

Perhaps the most appropriate theoretical framework from which to examine merit pay is expectancy theory (Vroom 1964). Expectancy theory describes the process of motivation through the interrelationship of three concepts:

1. Expectancy (subjective estimates of one's ability to engage successfully in particular activities)
2. Instrumentality (subjective perceptions of the connections between behavior and work outcomes)
3. Valence (the relative attractiveness of the rewards offered)

The more attractive that a reward is to an individual, the more likely it is to motivate behavior, but only if the individual perceives an instrumental link between behavior and the likelihood of obtaining the desired reward. Unlike the two-factor approach, which suggests a commonality of employee reward preferences, expectancy theory makes no a priori judgment about the attractiveness of particular rewards. Instead, the expectancy model suggests that a reward's valence is subjectively determined and is related to individual differences. The expectancy approach would therefore predict that salary incentives could motivate a teacher's behavior if the following conditions were met:

1. High expectancy (the teacher believed that improved performance could be achieved through increased effort)
2. High instrumentality (the teacher believed that improved performance would be rewarded)
3. High positive valence (the teacher found pecuniary rewards highly attractive)

Figure 7-1 represents the conditions expectancy theory requires for a reward, such as a salary increase, to motivate teacher behavior.

If a teacher perceives high instrumentality to exist between performance and reward, the availability of a highly desirable reward will motivate increased effort but not necessarily improved performance. This distinction is important because expectancy theory defines performance as a function of both effort and ability—that is,

Figure 7-1. The Expectancy Model of Merit Pay.

Effort ➡ Expectancy ➡ Behavior ➡ Instrumentality ➡ Reward ➡ Valence

(High)   (High)   (High)

Increased effort ➡ Improved performance ➡ Salary increase

a teacher's level of performance is determined as much by ability as by the desire to work harder. Proponents of merit pay argue that this distinction is important because it weeds out incompetent teachers. Teachers unable to translate increased effort into improved performance do not get rewarded and leave the profession. This argument is based on the premise that teachers will exit the profession if desired rewards are unattainable. The expectancy approach defines a reward's attractiveness as being subjectively determined and related to individual differences. The lack of monetary rewards therefore is not the only condition that can push teachers out of the classroom. The inability of teachers to attain intrinsic rewards can produce the same effect. Indeed, good teachers may be driven from the profession if they perceive that situational factors in the work environment prevent increased effort from improving performance, thereby precluding intrinsic reward. Over time, these mediating, situational factors can change subjectively determined teacher expectancy and reward preferences as well.

Experiential Feedback

The expectancy approach to motivation suggests that experience provides individuals the opportunity to reevaluate expectancy, instrumentality, and reward valence. Silver (1982) argues that teaching experience can change these subjective estimates, thereby altering teachers' motivation to perform in the future. Figure 7-2 depicts this experiential feedback loop.

Assuming that Figure 7-1 accurately represents the conditions necessary for rewards to motivate behavior, Figure 7-2 indicates that experience can change these subjective estimates in at least three ways: (1) Expectancy can be diminished, and/or (2) instrumentality can be diminished, and/or (3) valence can be diminished. Should any of these changes occur, subsequent behavior would change as well.

Figure 7-2. The Effect of Experience on Teacher Behavior.

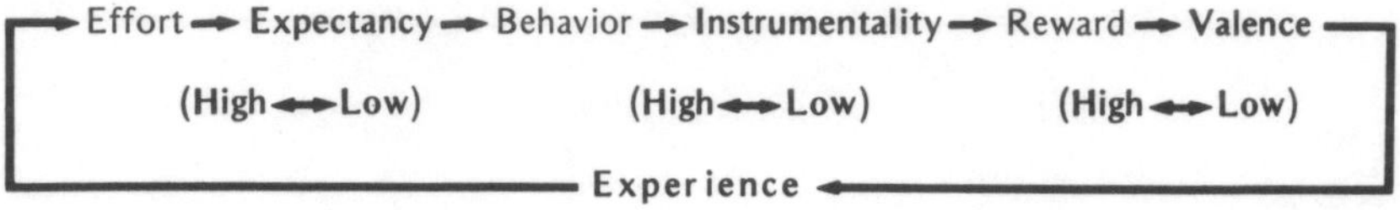

Critics of merit pay usually focus on the inability of merit pay plans to create and maintain high instrumentality between performance and reward (Lipsky and Bacharach 1983). Less attention has been paid to changes in teacher expectancy and reward valence. Merit pay proposals implicitly assume that expectancy and reward valence remain stable throughout the duration of a teacher's career. Yet observations of teacher career patterns suggest that a "typical" teacher's career passes through a series of phases, each having its own set of dynamics and determinants of behavior.

Teacher Career Phases

Charters (1964) identified three phases in a teacher's career: (1) the entry phase, (2) the sorting-out phase, and (3) the career phase. Evidence suggests that during the entry phase, when teachers are seeking their first position, they are particularly attentive to monetary rewards. Jacobson (1986), for example, examined teacher recruitment in two regions of New York state and found that districts that improved their entry-level salary, relative to the entry-level salaries offered by neighboring districts, subsequently improved their ability to recruit the most highly educated teachers available in the regional pool. Bruno (1981) examined the design of incentive systems for staffing inner-city schools and found that the opportunity for additional pay was most likely to attract young, inexperienced teachers. He concluded that the marginal value of an extra dollar of income was higher for inexperienced relative to veteran teachers. It is important to recognize that neither Jacobson's or Bruno's findings contradict the assertion that teaching's most attractive rewards are intrinsic. Rather, these findings suggest that after teaching's intrinsic benefits have influenced teachers' occupational choice, then salary differentials influence where they seek employment. As a result, administrators in school districts offering the most attractive starting salaries can be more selective when hiring teachers because they should have a larger pool of candidates from which to choose. Whether the ability to hire more selectively translates into higher-quality teachers depends on whether quality is what administrators are seeking and perhaps more important on their ability to recognize potentially high-quality teachers. To the extent that additional educational training is a proxy for teacher potential, then Jacobson's study indicates that districts offering the most attractive starting salaries can translate salary differentials into improvements in the quality of their teacher workforce.

During the sorting-out phase of a teaching career, the first five to seven years, teacher behavior is characterized by a high degree of mobility (Charters 1970; Mark and Anderson 1978). Teacher behavior during this phase is highly influenced by factors external to the work environment, such as spousal movement and/or child-rearing (Charters 1964), although salary differentials still influence inter-district migration (Pedersen 1973). In contrast, career phase teachers, teachers with seven or more years of experience, are less likely to migrate or leave teaching (Greenberg and McCall 1974; Murnane 1981; Pedersen 1973) and become more concerned with nonpecuniary factors directly related to their work environment (Charters 1964). For example, Greenberg and McCall (1974) report that when career teachers do transfer, they typically seek reassignment to schools in higher socioeconomic neighborhoods, schools perceived as offering greater nonpecuniary rewards. Similarly, Sewell (1972) found that experienced teachers were more willing to remain in inner-city schools if changes in working conditions, such as reduced class-size and/or increased paraprofessional support, were offered. These nonpecuniary, extrinsic factors become significant rewards to veteran teachers.

Teaching Experience and Reward Preference: A Synthesis of Approaches

A synthesis of the two-factor and expectancy approaches can help to explain these experience-related differences in teacher reward preferences. The two-factor model suggests that the job satisfaction of novice and veteran teachers is determined primarily by intrinsic factors, while the expectancy approach suggests that on-the-job experience enables teachers to more accurately assess the situational determinants that mediate their ability to obtain these desired rewards. Consequently, as teachers gain experience they may come to perceive their level of intrinsic job satisfaction, derived from classroom performance, as being a function of situational factors that they were less able to assess accurately as novice teachers. Based on their experience with these situational factors (class-size, paraprofessional support, student ability level, and so forth), veteran teachers will adjust their future behavior accordingly. Entry-phase teachers, on the other hand, must base future behavior on information acquired without experience. Salary differentials represent information that can be accurately assessed without experience. This argument does not suggest that salary differentials are unimportant to career teachers. Rather, the argument simply recognizes that experience provides teachers additional information about the relationships between level of effort, level of performance, and the likelihood of reward. As a result, conditions in the work environment become relatively more important to career teachers, while salary becomes relatively less important to them than to inexperienced teachers.

Feistrizer's survey (1986: 43) supports this argument. She found that salary was more important to younger teachers than to older teachers, with 58 percent of teachers ages 25 to 34 identifying a good salary as an important aspect of their job, while only 43 percent of teachers ages 55 to 64 selected salary. In contrast, the importance of a clean, quiet, comfortable place to work grew from 7 percent for teachers ages 25 to 34 to 18 percent for teachers ages 55 to 64.

Yet most incentive pay plans work to the advantage of veteran teachers, typically requiring a minimum number of years of district service before a teacher is eligible for merit rewards. As a result, prospective teachers must be willing to wait before they can capitalize on meritorious service, a bias that Monk and Jacobson (1985a: 231) report is reflected in school districts' internal salary distribution as well.

Backloaded Salary Distributions

Over the past decade, common practice has been for districts to "backload" their salary increments—that is, to add larger increments to salaries at the higher steps of the salary schedule than to those at the entry-level (NEA 1980). Data from New York state indicates that school districts distributed significantly larger percentage increases

Table 7-1. Increases in Mean Salaries of Novice and Senior Teachers in New York State, 1974–84.

	Novice[a]		Senior[b]	
	Dollars[c]	Percentage[d]	Salary	Percentage
1974	$ 9,176	100%	$16,949	100%
1984	15,520	169	30,598	181

a. Novice = teachers with less than four years of experience.

b. Senior = teachers with seventeen or more years of experience.

c. Mean salaries calculated from New York State Education Department's Personnel Master Files.

d. Percentages indexed to 1974 mean salaries.

to veteran relative to novice teachers (Monk and Jacobson 1985a; Monk and Jacobson 1985b). Table 7–1 shows that in New York, between 1974 and 1984, the mean salary of a teacher with seventeen or more years of district service increased 81 percent, while the mean salary of teachers with less than four years of experience wages grew 69 percent (Jacobson 1986: 73). As a result of these internal distribution practices, the index of salaries paid senior relative to novice teachers grew from 1.85 in 1974 to 1.97 in 1984.

Monk and Jacobson (1985b: 167) suggest that unless "the prospective teachers' time preference is such that the promise of future dollars is more important than the disadvantage of accepting an initially low starting salary," the practice of backloading salary increments may have made teaching less attractive to prospective candidates, as starting salaries lagged further behind starting salaries offered in other occupations. Implementing merit pay schemes that make monetary rewards available only to veteran teachers, who are arguably less concerned with these rewards, would do little to correct this situation. Instead, a number of compensation reform proposals issued since *A Nation at Risk* recommend that improvements in teacher performance and the quality of the workforce could be better achieved by restructuring the teaching profession and the distribution of its rewards than by implementing incentive pay plans. As Johnson (1984: 183) notes,

> While teachers unquestionably deserve higher salaries and will not remain in teaching without financial security, recent research suggests that incentive strategies for keeping our best teachers in schools should center on the workplace rather than on the pay envelope.

ALTERNATIVES TO MERIT PAY

Teacher career ladders and differentiated staffing plans are compensation reforms that propose to restructure the teaching profession and its reward system in a manner that more closely reflects experience-related differences in teacher preferences than do merit pay schemes. In *Tomorrow's Teachers: A Report of The Holmes Group* (Holmes Group 1986: 36), the deans of fourteen leading institutions of teacher education expressed the concern that teaching's flat career pattern allows ambition and accomplishment to go unrewarded:

> We need to change the career structure of teaching if we expect to improve the quality, engagement, and commitment of the teaching force. . . . Improving teaching's attraction and retention powers requires a differentiated professional teaching force able to respond to the opportunities provided by a staged career that would make and reward formal distinctions about responsibilities and degrees of autonomy.

To address teaching's "careerlessness," the Holmes Group recommends establishing a three-tiered system of teacher licensing that approximates the teacher career phases described earlier. Entry phase teachers, called *instructors*, would receive temporary, nonrenewable certificates that are good for no more than five years and would practice only under the direct supervision of certified teaching personnel. As instructors sort out their employment alternatives, those who desire to remain in the profession would have the opportunity to become *professional teachers*—the first level of professional certification. Instructors would have to earn a master's degree in teaching, complete a minimum of one full year of supervised instruction, and demonstrate competence in their area of academic instruction to be eligible to become professional teachers. From the ranks of professional teachers would come *career professionals*, those individuals "whose continued study and professional accomplishments revealed outstanding achievements as teachers, and promise as teacher educators and analysts of teaching" (Holmes Group 1986: 12). The title career professional would be the highest license awarded in teaching.

Although the Holmes Group is concerned primarily with teacher education, the three-tiered licensing system it recommends implicitly recognizes the intrinsic rewards that teachers desire. The Carnegie Forum on Education and Economy (1986: 24), on the other hand, is more explicit in addressing teachers' intrinsic needs: "Giving teachers a greater voice in the decisions that affect the school will make teaching more attractive to good teachers who are already in our schools as well as people considering teaching as a career."

In addition, the Carnegie Forum recognizes that teaching's extrinsic rewards need to be restructured as well, noting that "Higher teacher pay is an absolute prerequisite to attracting and keeping the people we want in teaching."

In *A Nation Prepared: Teachers for the 21st Century,* the Carnegie Forum (1986) recommends that teachers' salaries be differentiated on the basis of their level of certification, job function, seniority, and productivity. Teachers would progress through a sequence of licenses, certifications, and advanced certifications not unlike those proposed by the Holmes Group. Teacher certifications would be granted by a National Board of Professional Teaching Standards, and, at each new level of certification, a teacher would assume new job functions and responsibilities. As teachers progressed through these certification levels, their salaries would increase accordingly, with additional increments accruing through seniority. Increments for teacher productivity would be determined from measurements of schoolwide student performance, thereby shifting monetary incentives from the individual, as in most merit pay plans, to the instructional unit. This recommendation is intended to promote cooperation, rather than competition, among teachers. The disruptive effects of teacher competition is a problem inherent in merit pay plans that reward individual performance (Bacharach, Lipsky, and Shedd 1984).

At the pinnacle of the Carnegie Forum's teacher hierarchy, both in terms of prestige and salary, are *lead teachers*, teachers who "derive their authority primarily from the respect of their professional colleagues." Lead teachers within a school would function as a committee, "Their role would be to guide and influence the activity of others, ensuring that the skill and energy of their colleagues is drawn on as the organization improves its performance" (Carnegie Forum 1986: 25). Their responsibilities might include setting schoolwide performance criteria, development of curriculum, instructional supervision, course scheduling and assignment, and even the hiring and dismissal of personnel.

In a restructured teaching profession, as envisioned by the Holmes Group and Carnegie Forum, veteran teachers would not simply be recipients of material rewards but would be called on to identify and facilitate the availability of those intrinsic rewards that teachers find most attractive. Lead teachers would draw on their experiences to help change school environment conditions that hinder their colleagues from obtaining desired rewards. The prestige and salary that accompany the position of lead teacher would provide additional incentives for those individuals who, in the past, would have preferred to remain close to the classroom but moved instead into administration.

By broadening the definition of compensation to encompass rewards other than those just monetary in nature, the Holmes Group and Carnegie Forum move beyond the limited focus of merit pay proposals and begin to address the factors that initially attract teachers to the profession and that ultimately motivate their performance.

CONCLUSIONS

This chapter used the two-factor and expectancy approaches to employee motivation to identify the factors that influence teacher behavior and to examine the effects of teaching experience on these determinants of behavior. Contrary to merit pay's basic assumptions, teachers appear to be motivated as much by teaching's intrinsic rewards as by its monetary benefits. The influence salary differentials do have appear to be greatest early in teachers' careers (that is, after they have made their initial occupational choice) but while they are still sorting out their employment alternatives. After the first five to seven years, individuals who have decided to make teaching their career become more attentive to the conditions of their working environment. On-the-job experience enables veteran teachers to more accurately assess how these situational factors mediate their classroom performance and their ability to be rewarded by their work. Yet merit pay plans and backloaded salary distribution practices over the past decade have been more attentive to salaries paid to veteran teachers than salaries offered to beginning teachers. If educational policymakers are serious about improving recruitment, then districts must become more attentive to their starting salaries. In order to improve retention, school districts must become more attentive to the intrinsic and nonpecuniary, extrinsic rewards that veteran teachers desire. By increasing starting salaries teaching will become more attractive to talented individuals, and by increasing the profession's nonpecuniary benefits it will be more likely to retain them.

Two recent educational reform proposals by the Holmes Group and the Carnegie Forum on Education and Economy offer recommendations similar to those presented in this chapter. Both reports recommend improving teaching's material benefits so that teaching can compete more aggressively with other professions for the "best and the brightest," yet the reports move beyond the notion that waving extra dollars in front of teachers and prospective teachers will be enough to turn "the rising tide of mediocrity." Instead, the central issue raised in these reports is the need to create careers for those individuals who are willing to commit themselves to this "careerless" profession. At the heart of each report is the concern that teaching will not improve until the profession is restructured. Restructuring the profession includes restructuring teacher education, restructuring teacher field experience, restructuring teacher certification, and most important, restructuring teacher roles and responsibilities.

"Giving teachers a greater voice in the decisions that affect the school" (Carnegie Forum 1986: 24) is a far more ambitious proposal than paying teachers on the basis of their performance. Yet restructuring teaching's reward system to reflect experience-related differences in teacher preferences is more likely to effect meaningful change than merit pay schemes.

REFERENCES

Bacharach, Samuel B., David B. Lipsky, and Joseph B. Shedd. 1984. *Paying for Better Teaching: Merit Pay and Its Alternatives.* Ithaca, N.Y.: Organizational Analysis and Practice.

Bruno, James E. 1981. "Design of Incentive Systems for Staffing Racially Isolated Schools in Large Urban School Districts: Analysis of Pecuniary and Nonpecuniary Benefits." *Journal of Education Finance* 7 (Fall): 149–67.

Carnegie Forum on Education and Economy. 1986. *A Nation Prepared: Teachers for the 21st Century.* Report of the Task Force on Teaching as a Profession. New York: Carnegie Corporation.

Casey, William F., III. 1979. "Would Bear Bryant Teach in the Public Schools?" *Phi Delta Kappan* 60 (March): 500–01.

Charters, W. W. 1964. "Research in Teacher Mobility." Harvard Studies in Career Development No. 27. Cambridge, Mass.: Harvard University Press.

_____. 1970. "Some Factors Affecting Teacher Survival in School Districts." *American Educational Research Journal* 7 (January): 1–27.

David K. Cohen, and Richard J. Murnane. 1985. "The Merits of Merit Pay." Project Report No. 85–A12. Palo Alto: Stanford Education Policy Institute.

Deci, Edward L. 1976. "The Hidden Costs of Rewards." *Organizational Dynamics* 4 (Winter): 61–72.

Dyer, Lee, Donald P. Schwab, and John A. Fossum. 1978. "Impacts of Pay on Employee Behaviors and Attitudes: An Update." In *Perspectives on Personnel/Human Resource Management*, edited by H. G. Heneman and D. P. Schwab, pp. 253–59. Homewood, Ill.: Richard D. Irwin.

Feistritzer, C. Emily. 1986. *Profile of Teachers in the U.S.* Washington, D.C.: National Center for Education Information.

Goodlad, John I. 1983. *A Place Called School: Prospects for the Future* St. Louis: McGraw-Hill.

Greenberg, David, and J. McCall. 1974. "Teacher Mobility and Allocation." *Journal of Human Resources* 9 (Fall): 480–502.

Herzberg, Frederick. 1966. *Work and the Nature of Man.* New York: Crowell.

The Holmes Group. 1986. *Tomorrow's Teachers: A Report of The Holmes Group.* East Lansing, Mich.: The Holmes Group.

Jacobson, Stephen L. 1986. "Alternative Practices of Internal Salary Distribution and Their Effects on Teacher Recruitment and Retention." Unpublished dissertation, Cornell University.

Johnson, Susan Moore. 1984. "Merit Pay for Teachers: A Poor Prescription for Reform." *Harvard Educational Review* 54 (May): 175–85.

_____. 1986. "Incentives for Teachers: What Motivates, What Matters." *Educational Administration Quarterly* 22 (Summer): 54–79.

Lipsky, David B., and Samuel B. Bacharach. 1983. "The Single Salary Schedule Vs. Merit Pay: An Examination of the Debate." NEA Research Memo. Washington, D.C.: National Education Association.

Lortie, Dan C. 1975. *Schoolteacher: A Sociological Study.* Chicago: University of Chicago Press.

Mark, Jonathan H., and Barry D. Anderson. 1978. "Teacher Survival Rates: A Current Look." *American Educational Research Journal* 15 (Summer): 379–83.

Monk, David H., and Stephen L. Jacobson. 1985a. "Reforming Teacher Compensation." *Education and Urban Society* 17 (February): 223–26.

_____. 1985b. "The Distribution of Salary Increments between Veteran and Novice Teachers: Evidence from New York State." *Journal of Education Finance* 11 (Fall): 157–75.

Murnane, Richard J. 1981. "Teacher Mobility Revisited." *Journal of Human Resources* 16: 3–19.

Murnane, Richard J., and David K. Cohen. 1986. "Merit Pay and the Evaluation Problem: Why Most Merit Pay Plans Fail and a Few Survive." *Harvard Educational Review* 56 (February): 1–17.

National Commission on Excellence in Education. 1983. *A Nation at Risk.* Washington, D.C.: U.S. Government Printing Office.

National Education Association. 1980. "Salary Schedules 1979–80." NEA Research Memo. Washington, D.C.: National Education Association.

Pedersen, K. George. 1973. *The Itinerant Schoolmaster: A Socio-Economic Analysis of Teacher Turnover.* Chicago: Midwest Administration Center, University of Chicago.

Sewell, O. 1972. "Incentives for Innter City School Teachers." *Phi Delta Kappan* (October): 129.

Silver, Paula F. 1982. "Synthesis of Research on Teacher Motivation." *Educational Leadership* 39 (April): 551–54.

Spuck, Dennis W. 1974. "Rewards Structures in the Public High School." *Educational Administration Quarterly* 10 (Winter): 18–34.

Urban, Wayne J. 1985. "Old Wine, New Bottles? Merit Pay and Organized Teachers." In *Merit, Money and Teachers' Careers,* edited by Henry C. Johnson, Jr., pp. 25–38. Lanham, Md.: University Press of America.

Vroom, Victor H. 1964. *Work and Motivation.* New York: John Wiley.

Williamson, O. E. 1975. *Markets and Hierarchies: Analysis and Antitrust Implications.* New York: Free Press.

8 FUNDING OF TEACHER EDUCATION IN STATE UNIVERSITIES

Bruce A. Peseau

The U.S. governors (National Governors Association 1986) are the latest to express their distress about the quality of U.S. education. Although much of their report focuses on deficiencies within both postsecondary and K through 12 schools, it also criticizes the quality of the teacher workforce, including the preparation of teachers. The governors' agenda of needed improvements in teacher preparation, however, failed to recognize the fundamental need to assure adequate resources for teacher education. As with K through 12 education, college programs need at least minimally adequate resources to do what we expect them to do. Finding fault and defining needed changes in an area as crucial as teacher preparation is meaningless unless those programs also have the resources to do a better job and be held accountable for it. The evidence is overwhelming that "Teacher education is a poor cousin on most university campuses, underfunded and held in low regard. Expectations and rhetoric outrun resources and capacity to provide a genuinely professional education" (Sykes 1982: 2).

This chapter integrates evidence of the resource poverty of most teacher education programs in colleges and universities. First, it develops the analogy between the funding of K through 12 and higher education programs. It examines the failure of legislators to include adequate budget oversight in higher education appropriations (as is prescribed for public schools). Abundant research exists on funding and productivity relationships in higher education programs, and the chapter discusses specific studies of funding and productivity in teacher education, including national, intrastate, and intrainstitutional data. Finally, the chapter examines the causes of continuing inadequacy of funding for teacher education and the effects of this inadequacy on program quality.

THE ANALOGY BETWEEN THE FUNDING OF K THROUGH 12 AND HIGHER EDUCATION

Legislators confront complex problems in deciding how to distribute the limited resources of the state to meet the needs of its people. The amount of money available is always inadequate. Each function of government—executive, legislative, judicial, highways, law enforcement, mental health, education—competes with the other for the scarce dollars. Even in combination with federal and regional categorical funds, the total monies are less than needed to fully provide necessary government services. Fundamentally, the legislature bases its resource allocation decisions on two principles: (1) adequacy (how much is minimally necessary for each function) and (2) equity (how each agency will receive its fair share). The two concepts of adequacy and equity are closely related. Legislative oversight also requires that a system of accountability be embedded within funding authorizations to ensure that the use of state funds is consistent with legislative intent. In the case of public education, elementary and secondary schools are funded under the concept that the state pays and the community pays for educating children. Through minimum foundation programs, state monies from legislative appropriations are combined with local district taxes collected, thereby adding state funds to the local district's required effort. The intent of the legislature in authorizing funds for elementary and secondary education is to distribute the available funds to ensure that at least a minimum level will be available to every child in the state, regardless of the child's condition or location. Florida, as an example, has further differentiated need and costs through a series of weights, with grades 4 to 9 regular students as a base weight of 1.000, through forty-four levels of program costs and complexity to a maximum weight of almost 16.00 for severely handicapped. Weights are then associated to program costs, and funds authorized accordingly.

ADEQUACY

The concept of adequacy in educational funding is concerned with how much a given program should cost. These are hypothetical amounts and are often expressed in a series of relationships of programs one to another. Again, in the case of Florida elementary and secondary education, costs are classified as direct costs, school indirect costs, district indirect costs, and summed as total program costs. A proportion of those costs is provided by the state through its legislative appropriation, and the remainder must be raised through legislatively specified local district tax effort. Federal and regional categorical purpose funds (such as funds for the disadvantaged or bilingual) often supplement state and local funds. The effect of this funding formula is to guarantee that each child will have available a minimum level of funding and that some children will have more than others because of the more specialized kinds of programs required by their mental or physical conditions.

The concept of adequacy also applies in funding public higher education. Whereas elementary and secondary educational funds derive from the state appropriation and local taxes, higher education funds derive from the legislative appropriation and tuition income. In the former, the state and the community pay, and in the latter, the state and the student (through tuition) pay for the guaranteed minimum costs of programs. At all levels, other funds are potentially available to supplement those minimum costs from federal and regional sources, and especially in higher education, funds are available from additional fees for laboratory, activities, building, health services, and so forth.

Higher education also uses a weighting system to express the relative complexity and consequent cost from one program to another. Approximately thirty-five states use some variation of formula funding for higher education. These express program complexity differences by academic specialization (teacher education, engineering, nursing, law, and so forth) and by level (lower division, upper division, graduate 1, graduate 2). As with elementary and secondary, the postsecondary complexity factors and weights are derived primarily from historic experience. These program differentials undergo frequent revision, as evidence of their validity is revealed from expenditure analysis studies, national cost trend data, and requirements imposed by accrediting agencies.

How much is a minimally adequate amount of dollars for educational programs at any level? The adequate amount is influenced by two questions: (1) How much is probably available from the state treasury and the local tax or tuition source; and (2) how much is that level of funding compared to funding in other states and among peer institutions? The funding of state agencies is always constrained by the dollars available and fluctuates with economic conditions and the competing demands from government functions. The amount of dollars available is always less than ideal. This reinforces the requirement that state funds be supplemented by local taxes for elementary and secondary education and by tuition income for higher education.

Cost comparisons by educational level nationally and regionally are also a means of determining the adequacy of funding. The NEA publishes annual *Rankings of the States* (NEA 1984) studies that provide comparative data for elementary and secondary schools. In higher education, the comparative costs data are less comparable, often because of the different accounting practices and the wide variation in revenues from contracts and grants and other sources in universities. Nevertheless, certain discipline-specific studies are available from the accreditation agencies and other sources. The *Engineering Planning Factors Study* (Hemp and Brunson 1984), completed annually at the University of Florida on a national basis, is one. Another is my *Eighth Annual Academic Production and Funding Study of Teacher Education in Senior State Universities and Land-Grant Colleges* (Peseau 1986), under the sponsorship of the Association of Colleges and Schools of Education in State Universities and Land-Grant Colleges.

EQUITY

The equity concept is concerned with how each school district, each university, or each undividual is assured of its fair share of the resources available for education. Terrell Sessums, speaker of the Florida House of Representatives, believed that the test of adequacy and fairness, as spelled out in the *Serrano* case, was that the wealth of the state should stand behind each child so that state aid could compensate for differences in the wealth of local districts. Minimum foundation programs help ensure that, regardless of where a child lives, the child will receive at least a minimally adequately funded education (Sessums 1973).

Caruthers and Orwig (1979: 17) extended that concept to higher education:

> A frequent objective of budgeting in postsecondary education is to achieve equity in the funding provided. As used in these discussions, the concept of equity implies that similar resources will be provided for similar individuals, similar programs within an institution, or similar institutions within a state. One procedure used, particularly at the state level, to accomplish this purpose—formula budgeting—attempts to relate the allocations of resources to standard, consistent measures of activity.

Similar descriptions of the equity concept in higher education appear repeatedly in the literature on funding higher education (Carter 1977; Texas Higher Education Coordinating Commission 1970; Millett 1974; Stuart 1966). These reflect the fundamental principle of equity as expressed by Thomas Jefferson in his first inaugural address: "Equal and exact justice to all men, of whatever state or persuasion."

The concepts of adequacy and equity form the fundamental framework within which decisions are made to provide education or any other service to the people of a state. Legislators restrain the attempts at political favoritism and preferential treatment of some over others as they are guided by these concepts. Adequacy and equity principles have forced higher education institutions to work together rather than in competition, and state governments have created administrative mechanisms such as state boards of education and boards of regents to develop statewide approaches to addressing the needs of public education.

ACCOUNTABILITY

The adequacy of funding public education and the equitable distribution of limited resources is a constant problem demanding the attention of the legislature and its administrative agencies. Legislative oversight is a critically important means of determining whether the state's institutions have complied with the intent of the legislature that authorized the use of public funds.

A strict network of accountability from authorization to expenditure to verification has been established for elementary and secondary schools. Local school district superintendents have very little discretion over how much their schools will receive and how it might be spent. Accountability is monitored closely by the state superintendent of education and reports returned for legislative oversight reviews. The maxim that "Trust is the surrogate to control" applies much more to higher education than to elementary and secondary education throughout the United States. In higher education, although legislative decisions about funding authorizations to universities are made on the basis of enrollment data by programs and levels, university accountability in most states for expenditure reporting is categorical rather than program- or discipline-specific. Only Texas and California require a follow-up audit of their postsecondary education to verify that funds were spent consistent with legislative intent. In most states, however, there is potentially little relationship between the basis on which funds are authorized and how they are spent—that is, to ensure that an engineering student will have a minimum level of financial support or a teacher education student will have another minimum level of support regardless of which university they attend in a given state. The absence of that program-specific expenditure accountability assumes (if the legislative intent was inherent in the authorization) that university administrators who decide on funding for their academic divisions will be unbiased. That is a naive assumption.

Periodic program reviews through the board of regents, the state department of education, and accreditation agencies do reveal program strengths and weaknesses that often can be related to funding. However, most higher education programs do not begin with the same adequacy and equity premises as for elementary and secondary education—that a minimally adequate level of funding and an equitable method for its distribution is guaranteed through a weighted formula funded from state and local sources. The literature on teacher education includes numerous studies and abundant rhetoric on the status of teaching as a profession. Yet the literature fails to include minimum budget requirements, faculty/student ratios, or other indicators in accreditation standards that would enhance the development of quality programs as a departure from a beginning with essential resources.

Carter (1977: 6) has summarized the problems of adequacy and equity in funding higher education:

> The objective of equity or fairness in the distribution of state support is not easy to define or carry out. A workable definition is to provide the same resources from state appropriations to each institution of higher education for each full-time equivalent student enrolled in comparable programs of instruction. In addition, there are special circumstances of enrollment size, location, stage of development, and of clientele served which may require modification of or exceptions to this definition.
>
> What then about qualitative differences? There are such differences among institutions and among students, but there is no apparent basis for saying that high quality deserves high support or for saying that lower quality deserves lower support. For this reason the distribution of state support should be based upon equal resource support per student by program and by program level. Other sources of support can then provide the margin of difference which circumstances require. This definition of *equity* is justifiable in terms of the basic philosophy of higher education and in terms of the tradition of equality of opportunity in a democratic society.
>
> There are three primary ingredients in an operative definition of *equity*, i.e., (a) state support based upon program costs, (b) state support based upon workload, and (c) state support based upon a common definition of *available revenue*. It must be emphasized that the concept of equity does not mean a distribution of support involving the same amount of money for each institution based upon workload and program differentials. Such differences are important characteristics of a concept of equity. The essence of equity is that state institutions of higher education should be treated the same in terms of workload and in terms of program offerings.

Carter's rationale is consistent with the concepts of adequacy and equity in funding public K through 12 education, wherein the underlying concept is that the quality standard in a school district is of interest to the parents, the community, the state, and nation. State governments need to take the matter of improving the quality of teacher education as seriously as that of improving K through 12 education. Without some effective legislative oversight of state appropriations to colleges and universities, there is no assurance that the basis for funding (students in programs by levels) will ever be reflected in how the money is actually spent once it gets to our campuses.

FORMULA FUNDING FOR HIGHER EDUCATION

Minimum foundation programs, full-state funding (Benson 1975), district power equalizing (Guthrie 1975), or some other formula variation is used as a basis for determining funding appropriations to school districts throughout the nation. Formula funding variations are also used for public higher education in most states (Gross 1974). Although Moss and Gaither (1976) doubted the viability of higher education formula funding, subsequent experience has found the process to be more refined and more widely used.

Similar to the variable weights found in minimum foundation programs, higher education formula factors express the differences in program complexity and probable cost between academic programs and between levels (undergraduate, graduate 1 master's, and graduate 2 postmasters). Table 8-1 shows the higher education formula funding factors as used in Texas and Alabama.

Teacher education has among the lowest weights in most formulas. The intended use of formulas is to help legislators sort out decisions about how much of the available funds each college or university should receive for the fiscal period, based on numbers of students and credit hours produced in various academic programs, by different levels.

Despite their good intent, the entire process of allocating resources among postsecondary institutions is fundamentally flawed because it neglects to require an audit trail from appropriation to expenditure. Nevertheless, it remains as a basis for funding decisions. It will therefore be appropriate to examine evidence of the adequacy and equity of funding teacher education.

FUNDING AND PRODUCTIVITY IN TEACHER EDUCATION

The research on funding and productivity in higher education usually treats institutions as wholes, even though there is great diversity from one college to another. Although most colleges and universities provide a common set of core studies (such as English, history, math, sciences) differences among academic specializations (such as engi-

Table 8-1. Higher Education Formula Funding Weights.[a]

Academic Subdivisions	Complexity Indexes		
	Undergraduate	Graduate 1	Graduate 2
1. Business	1.12	3.27	13.45
2. General	1.00	2.73	10.33
3. Education	1.04	2.30	8.79
4. Nursing, health	2.74	4.94	17.60
5. Engineering	2.07	5.46	17.60
6. Fine arts	2.09	4.95	17.71
7. Home economics	1.39	3.34	9.31
8. Science	1.29	5.36	17.60
9. Military science	0.12	—	—
10. Law	—	1.75	—
11. Architecture	1.67	4.79	16.52
12. Agriculture	1.51	4.57	16.52
13. Veterinary medicine	—	5.77	20.53
14. Pharmacy	2.07	5.06	14.09
15. Interdisciplinary	1.26	3.23	10.33

a. Weighting factors as used in the Texas and Alabama formulas.

neering, medicine, nursing, music) translates to substantial variations in costs, when one university is compared with another. Bowen's (1981: 23) work treats higher education in this manner—at the institutional, rather than the program specialization level. Nevertheless, he concluded that

many colleges and universities are seriously underfinanced. *Even if they were operating at great efficiency, they would still lack the resources necessary for delivering acceptable high education.* . . . Several million students are served by colleges and universities with patently inadequate resources.

Bowen (1981: 120–21) further concluded that he

found astonishingly great differences—so great that one may reasonably question the rationality or equity in the allocation of resources among [and with-

in] higher education institutions. This state of affairs may be tolerated because so little is known about the relationship between the amount of resources and educational outcomes.

Higher levels of funding do not assure high quality of programs. However, minimally adequate funding is essential for minimally adequate staffing, faculty loads, supervision of clinical learning, and other conditions necessary for preparation in the professions.

Bloom (1983) analyzed three years of data (credit hours produced by academic discipline and level, and credit hours produced per FTE faculty) from twenty-two academic disciplines in twenty-one major public universities and calculated complexity/cost weights for each using an optimizing technique. He found a good to excellent fit of data to the generated weights in fourteen of twenty-one universities, with the exception of some programs, including teacher education. He acknowledged that the weights he derived were generally lower, especially at the graduate level, than weights used in other studies (Board of Regents 1978; Coleman and Bolte 1976; Keating 1983; Ryland 1978). Bloom (1983: 191) concluded that the weight model that he developed "states that teaching differs by academic discipline and by level of instruction," but that teacher education and some other disciplines do not fit the model.

Hemp and Brunson (1984) produce annual national studies of engineering education under the sponsorship of the American Society for Engineering Education. Although their research collects and analyzes data on many of the same variables as in my annual studies on teacher education, a principal difference is that all credit hours produced are treated the same, as if there is no cost difference between undergraduate and graduate studies.

Teacher Education

The primary motive for analyzing cost and productivity data from academic programs is to identify peer institutions and to compare the status of various programs. For that reason, cost and productivity data are often described as planning data. They are intended to assist deans and department heads in their efforts to obtain reasonable levels of resources for what a program attempts to produce.

Feldman and Fisher (1982) presented their cluster analysis approach to identifying peer programs for teacher education. Although their research included variables such as cost per credit hour, some other variables (percentage of students receiving teaching positions, whether or not the program included a laboratory school, and program requirements such as English and speech) have very questionable relevance to cost and productivity relationships. They identified four clusters of institutions, characterized as groups of teacher education programs of (1) private colleges with very small undergraduate and little or no graduate enrollments, (2) public universities with large undergraduate and graduate enrollments, (3) public universities with larger undergraduate and graduate enrollments than the private institutions in cluster 1, but smaller than those in cluster 2, and (4) public universities with very large undergraduate and graduate enrollments. The Feldman and Fisher study only marginally explored any cost and productivity relationships.

The Association of Colleges and Schools of Education in State Universities and Land-Grant Colleges (ACSESULGC) has sponsored research on its member institutions for several years. The eighth annual study (Peseau 1986) of this effort was recently disseminated. Data from that research and other published material (Orr and Peseau 1979; Peseau and Orr 1980; Peseau 1982; Peseau 1984) will be used to develop this section, in which evidence on the inadequacy and inequity of funding teacher education will be shown.

The ACSESULGC studies analyze what colleges of teacher education produce with the resources they have. The 1986 study included data from seventy-five (110 possible) major public universities in thirty-two states[1] with programs through the doctorate. The data analyses help those deans judge the relative adequacy and equity of their resources in relation to productivity and to develop budget justifications intended to help their programs receive their fair share of available resources. The studies were motivated by the lack of quantitative standards in the National Commission on the Accreditation of Teacher Education (NCATE) standards. In the absence of quantitative standards, the accreditation process tends to become highly subjective, based on abstract assumptions. This increases the probability that, as accreditation terms change from one site visit to another, a given program will be judged according to the idiosyncrasies of the team members more than by the available objective evidence. As with minimum foundation programs and formula funding methods, a design of quantitative relationships helps reduce political influence and individual biases substantially. Quantitative indicators do not substitute for expert judgment; data provide the basis for input/output relationships; and the nuances of expert judgment build on and refine analysis from that base of facts and data.

The participating programs submitted data for the 1984–85 fiscal year on 214 variables; another seventy variables were calculated from the data. Areas of the data included headcount and FTE faculty, budgets from university and external sources by function with corresponding FTE assignments, faculty salaries by academic rank, credit hours produced by levels (undergraduate, graduate 1 master's and graduate 2 postmaster's), degrees awarded, FTE support staff and graduate assistants, and tuition and fees charged.

Other variables were calculated from the data supplied, such as weighted credit hours, cost per weighted credit hour, FTE students by level, class size by level, student/faculty and faculty/support staff ratios, productivity per FTE faculty, an institutional complexity index (expresses the relative program mix of undergraduate, graduate 1, and graduate 2 productivity), tuition as a percentage of direct costs, and operations funds per FTE faculty.

The eight years of research on ACSESULGC teacher education programs have resulted in the identification of five resource variables and eight productivity variables as the principal indicators of the condition of teacher education. Note that all of the variables are independent of institutional size or urban/suburban location.

Resource variables:

AYPROFD: academic year full professor's salary
UNOPDFTE: university funds for operations per FTE faculty
PERFTEUD: total university funds (including salaries) per FTE faculty
FACOSUP: ratio of FTE faculty to FTE support staff
AVGGASAL: average (.5 FTE) graduate assistant salary

Productivity variables:

FACWCHPR: weighted credit hours per FTE faculty (twelve months)
AYUGCLSZ: average academic year undergraduate class size
FTESFTIF: ratio of FTE students to FTE instructional faculty
G2WCHPCT: percentage graduate 2 level weighted credit hours of total produced
GRDEGPCT: percentage graduate degrees of total produced
COMPINDX: institutional complexity index (program mix by level)
COSTWSCH: cost per weighted credit hour produced
TUPCTCST: tuition cost as percent of academic year direct cost

Table 8-2. Principal Resource Variables, Forty-three Teacher Education Programs, 1984–85.

Region	Average Full Professor Salary	Operations Funds per FTE Faculty	Total Funds per FTE Faculty	Ratio of FTE Faculty to FTE Support Staff	Average Graduate Assistant Salary
II (Southeast)					
N = 20					
Average	$37,310	$3,329	$43,568	3.60	$ 6,286
Standard deviation	3,608	1,943	6,660	0.93	2,163
High	46,292	7,057	56,862	5.45	12,949
Low	30,428	1,058	33,264	1.57	3,000
III (Ohio Valley)					
N = 11					
Average	40,195	4,074	43,595	3.33	8,442
Standard deviation	5,408	1,889	7,744	1.32	3,430
High	48,473	7,472	59,770	6.44	14,368
Low	30,306	1,666	35,192	1.55	4,208
V (South Central)					
N = 16					
Average	36,816	2,420	38,488	4.70	5,458
Standard deviation	3,974	1,401	5,804	2.16	2,309
High	45,194	6,804	52,812	9.69	12,332
Low	33,180	749	29,098	1.94	2,405

Table 8-3. Principal Productivity Variables, Forty-three Teacher Education Programs, 1984–85.

Region	Weighted Credit Hours per FTE Faculty	Average Undergraduate Class Size	Ratio of FTE Students to FTE Faculty
II (Southeast)			
N = 20			
Average	1,089	20.60	17
Standard deviation	501	5.71	4
High	2,495	41.54	22
Low	484	14.00	11
III (Ohio Valley)			
N = 11			
Average	973	21.76	18
Standard deviation	330	7.08	7
High	1,531	35.54	32
Low	557	11.65	8
V (South Central)			
N = 16			
Average	1,023	22.27	19
Standard deviation	230	6.76	5
High	1,551	44.24	33
Low	744	13.11	13

Because of the quantity of data and the large number (seventy-five) of participating teacher education programs, the following analyses will include those programs from only zones II (southeast), III (Ohio Valley), and V (south central). The same data relationships were also found for programs in regions I, IV, and VI, however.

Table 8-2 shows the averages of resource variable data for forty-seven universities from the three regions. Teacher education program data averages from zone II are shown first, followed by zone III, the zone V. Although the variables tended to be somewhat more favorable in zone III (higher professor's salaries, lower ratios of support staff to FTE faculty), there is no consistent pattern. Within a zone, there are extremes within any variable. It cannot be concluded that one zone has more favorable levels of resources to support their teacher education programs than another zone. Moreover, there is no

Table 8-3. continued

Percentage Graduate 2 Level Credit Hours	Percentage Graduate Degrees Awarded	Institutional Complexity Index	Cost Per Weighted Credit Hour	Tuition as Percent of Direct Cost
44.52	57.05	2.61	51.47	88
23.03	14.58	1.09	15.62	57
85.35	87.63	5.43	76.75	299
7.97	26.90	1.67	15.42	28
44.48	47.48	2.36	52.10	114
17.89	14.98	0.55	15.42	39
71.13	75.40	3.33	82.31	198
14.53	29.41	1.28	36.96	57
41.26	49.72	2.35	40.55	73
15.87	13.38	0.50	9.11	42
62.53	76.02	3.34	59.36	162
18.12	26.42	1.55	25.43	13

pattern of higher levels of resources for teacher education programs in urban areas, as is often the case with K through 12 systems.

Table 8-3 shows the eight productivity variables for the forty-seven universities. Again, note the great variation for these teacher education programs, both nationally and within each of the three regions.

Although we would expect some urban advantage to show up in productivity data due to the larger population mass and more convenient course scheduling, there is no such consistent pattern. Therefore, it must be assumed that some teacher education programs are carried out with proportionally much less resources than other programs, to the detriment of some program quality. Great differences (of more than 5 to 1) are apparent among several of the productivity variables. However, the evidence of underfunding in relation to productivity is most compelling in the data for the last variable: how much of their direct program costs that students pay from their tuition. Direct teacher education program costs are those in the academic division's budget, including all faculty and support staff salaries, operating expenses such as supplies, travel, and communications, and fringe benefits. They exclude the costs of capital outlay. On the average for all academic programs in all disciplines, Bowen (1981) reported that tuition pays for about 40 percent of direct program costs. Among these fortyseven teacher education programs, only five paid for less than 40 percent of direct costs from tuition, and three of these were in Texas, where students pay very low tuition in public universities. In seventeen of the forty-seven teacher education programs, students' tuition paid for 100 percent or more of direct program costs—as if the state appropriation did not help fund their programs.

Intrastate Comparisons

Funding for academic programs in public higher education institutions within a given state is probably more standardized than for K through 12 education. Whereas local school districts depend on community-generated taxes (ad valorem, usually) to complement the state's appropriation, higher education's funding is from tuition and the state appropriation. Community-generated taxes are based on some ability-to-pay formula and therefore vary substantially from one district to another; tuition rates for colleges and universities are usually very consistent among the four-year public institutions within any state. Therefore, if there are substantial differences in resources provided for academic programs among the public universities within individual states, it must be due to administrative decisions internal to the institution about funding of each of its academic programs—not some consistent amount provided from the legislative appropriation for similar programs among the state's public universities. Such administrative discretion is generally allowed in the expenditure of state funds (including tuition income), since legislative oversight is generally absent.

The 1986 ACSESULGC study included (1984–85) data for two or more universities in six states of zone I (AL, FL, GA, NC, TN, VA), four states of zone III (IN, KY, OH, PA) and five states of zone V (KA, LA, MO, OK, TX). These totaled forty-three universities. Figures 8-1 through 8-5 show the intrastate comparisons of the resource variables of teacher education programs in those fifteen states. The vertical high/low bar for each state includes a teacher education program plotted at each end of the bar, and any other programs in that state plotted with other symbols.

An examination of the five graphs reveals that the resources were most consistent between the two teacher education programs in Louisiana universities and relatively similar for the two programs in Tennessee. However, the most extreme differences are found in the resources for the six programs in Texas and the four programs in Ohio universities. The resources also varied greatly for the four Florida programs and the three North Carolina programs. Among the other nine states (AL, GA, VA, IN, KY, PA, KS, MO, OK), there also appear substantial differences among these resource variables. It must be emphasized that although these differences sometimes appear insignificant when shown on a unit basis, they become greatly magnified when calculated on the basis of a hundred or more FTE faculty.

These substantial, unexplainable variations of resources available to teacher education programs within individual states become more meaningful when a comparative resource model is developed. Table 8-4 shows the comparative resources that would be available if the resource distribution were fully equitable among the four teacher education programs in Florida. This hypothetically equitable level of resources would be based on the existing differences (in program size, credit hours produced, enrollments) among programs, and therefore would not produce the same funding, but instead equitable resources as a function of program size and level. Assuming that each

Table 8-4. Hypothetical Level of Resources, Based on Actual Data for Four Florida Teacher Education Programs.

Institution	Professional Salaries	Op'ns Funds for Faculty	Total Funds for Faculty	FTE Support Staff	Graduate Assistant Salaries
209	$3,042,800	$142,900	$3,783,200	26.60	$120,000
245	3,673,200	105,800	3,922,200	25.64	237,800
251	3,574,100	422,200	5,019,600	24.39	231,760
289	3,751,500	115,800	3,722,600	63.69	300,080

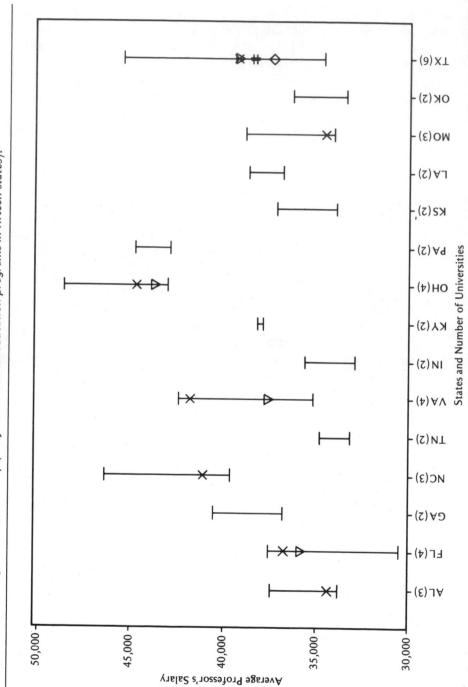

Figure 8-1. Average Professor's Salary *(forty-three teacher education programs in fifteen states).*

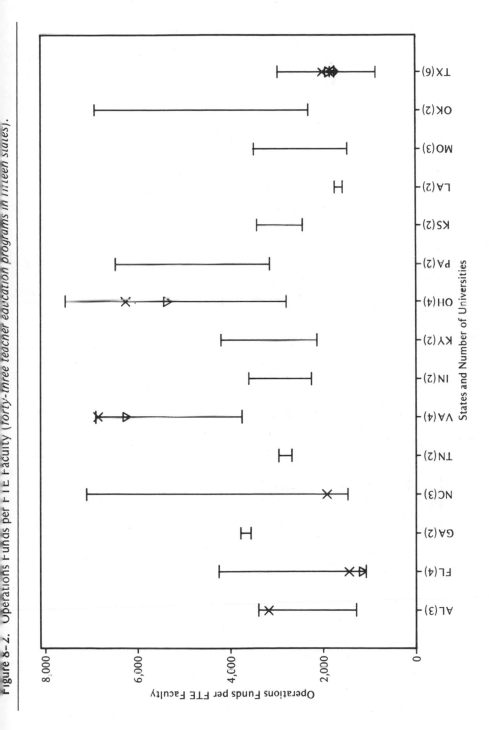

Figure 8–2. Operations Funds per FTE Faculty (forty-three teacher education programs in fifteen states).

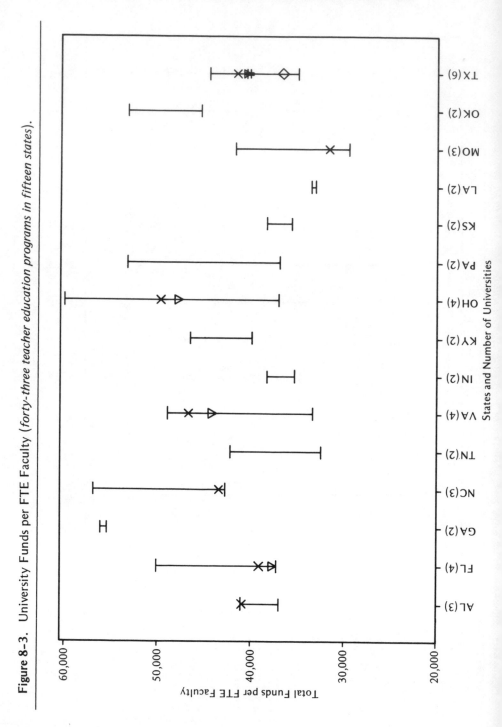

Figure 8-3. University Funds per FTE Faculty (*forty-three teacher education programs in fifteen states*).

Figure 8–4. FTE Faculty: Support Staff Ratio *(forty-three teacher education programs in fifteen states)*.

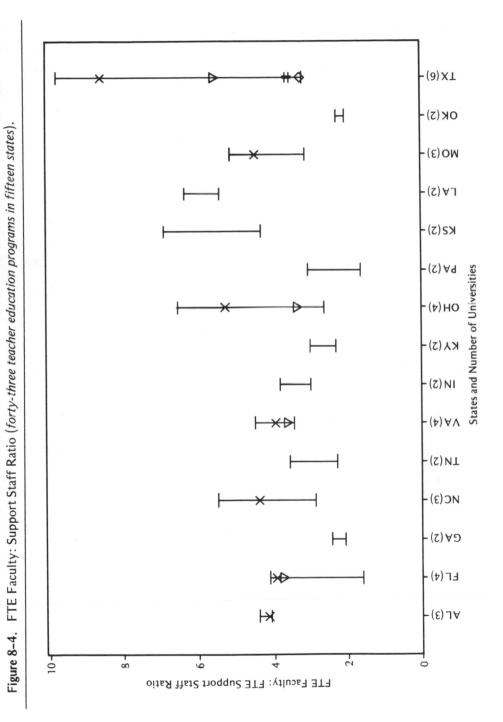

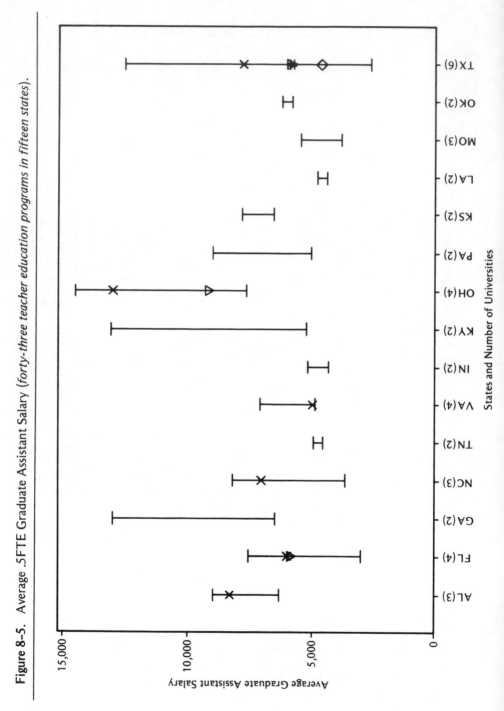

Figure 8-5. Average .5FTE Graduate Assistant Salary (forty-three teacher education programs in fifteen states).

of these programs had 100 FTE faculty (the actual national average from the 1986 ACSESULGC study was 110 FTE faculty for the seventy-five universities) and forty graduate assistants at .5 FTE each (the actual national average was 42), how would the funding and personnel resources differ between these four programs?

If the resources were distributed among these teacher education programs on a strictly equitable basis, the funds available for faculty salaries, college and departmental operations and graduate assistant salaries would be reasonably the same, and the number of FTE support staff to assist faculty also would be reasonably the same. Instead, based on actual 1984–85 data, the resources differ greatly among the four programs. One program has 23 percent more funds for faculty salaries, four times as much for operations, and two and one-half times more for secretarial staff and for the graduate assistants. This model does not infer by any means that I propose a single-salary schedule for these university faculty. Instead, it means that the resource base would be the same for each program, and internal merit performance processes could distribute those funds for salaries differentially among their 100 FTE faculty—but the base would be a function of the relative size of other teacher education programs in that state. It would, as Carter (1977: 6) proposed, "provide the same resources from state appropriations [and tuition] to each institution of higher education for each full-time equivalent student enrolled in comparable programs of instruction." By providing equitable resources to academic programs, it helps ensure equitable educational quality to the student, regardless of the institution attended.

Intrainstitutional Comparison

How does teacher education fare internally in our colleges and universities? Berlinger (1984) reported that at the University of Arizona it costs the state about $15,000 for the four years of a liberal arts undergraduate (who takes courses in literature, history, psychology, and so forth), and only $13,000 for four years of a teacher education student. I reported (Peseau 1984) on the comparative funding and productivity of teacher education, engineering, and business administration in a major southeastern public university. Table 8–5 summarizes the data for four resource variables and four productivity variables, using 1982–83 data.

Table 8–5. Comparative Resources and Productivity, 1984–85.

Variable	Teacher Education	Engineering	Business
Resources:			
Average faculty salary	$31,801	$36,956	$39,729
Opn's funds per FTE faculty	$ 1,732	$ 3,479	$ 2,739
Faculty per support ratio	3.51	2.74	3.29
Graduate assistant salary	$ 8,746	$19,350	$12,010
Productivity:			
Weighted SCH per FTE faculty	815	1019	901
Prog. complexity index	2.59	2.39	1.43
Cost per weighted SCH	$ 44.14	$ 46.43	$ 51.08
Tuition as percentage of cost	72.15	34.47	57.51

Among the resource variables, faculty average salaries are much higher for engineering and business, perhaps as a function of market competition. However, those colleges have much more resources than does teacher education for operations funds per FTE faculty, for support staff assistance (the lower ratio is better), and for graduate assistant salaries.

In terms of productivity, both engineering and business have higher credit hour weights (Table 8–1) than teacher education. In this decade of high student demand for engineering and business and a great decline of teacher education enrollments, the faculty productivity is about 20 percent less in the latter discipline. Teacher education has a much larger proportion of its productivity at the graduate level (the higher complexity index), but its cost per weighted credit hour is the lowest of the three colleges. However, due to lower program funding, the student's tuition as a percentage of direct program costs is higher.

My judgment is that other teacher education programs across the nation fare about the same as in this case. Despite the fact that the relative complexity of the disciplines (the weights in funding formulas) always places teacher education at the low end of the scale, its faculty productivity compares favorably; its programs are much more graduate level; its weighted credit hour and per-student direct costs are lower; and students (or their parents) pay for a larger share of their educational costs than in the two other disciplines. Warner (1986: 96) reports some hope for the future of teacher education, at least in Texas: "the Governor's Select Committee on Public Education (SCOPE) recommends that the formula for teacher education be raised to the same level as other professional programs. The cost to implement that . . . is estimated to be $99.6 million in the first year and $101.2 million in the second year."

TEACHER EDUCATION AND K THROUGH 12 EDUCATION COSTS

The problem of severely underfunded teacher education is national in scope, and it is a national disgrace. Great effort has been made to ensure that the intent of the adequacy and equity concepts are translated into policy and practice for K through 12 education. The results are still imperfect, but conscious and effective improvement continues. When the findings of the ACSESULGC national studies of teacher education in major public universities are compared to the K through 12 per pupil cost data (NEA 1984) and to the NEA reports for prior years, the relative status for teacher education is distressing (Table 8-6).

The NEA cost-per-student data are for current expenditures. It has been estimated that 85 to 90 percent of public school current ex-

Table 8-6. Comparative Public School and Teacher Education Costs per FTE Student.

	1978-79	1979-80	1980-81	1981-82	1982-83	1983-84	1984-85
Public school cost	$1,658	$1,906	$2,156	$2,354	$2,566	$2,785	$2,986
Teacher education cost	1,091	1,534	1,319	1,331	1,848	1,518	1,590
Teacher education as percentage of public school cost	66%	81%	62%	57%	72%	55%	53%

Sources: NEA, *The Cost of Public Education* (for each year from 1978–79 through 1984–85); Bruce Peseau, *Annual Studies of Resources and Productivity in Teacher Education Programs in State Universities and Land-Grant Colleges* (for each year from 1978–79 through 1984–85).

penditures are classified as "direct cost"—that is, they include the costs of instruction, administration, materials, and so forth. Therefore, the NEA total current expenditure figures were multiplied by 87.5 percent to derive the direct cost estimates. The direct costs of teacher education from these studies were then calculated as a percentage of the direct costs for an average public school child. In all cases, the direct costs for an undergraduate in teacher education in these—the senior U.S. public universities—were much less than for the average public school child. Some of the fluctuations in the teacher education costs can be attributed to the fact that the population of participating universities in these studies varied a little from year to year. In all cases, some new university teacher education programs participated each following year, but a few also dropped out or failed to provide complete data for a particular year.

Nevertheless, the pattern is obvious. The condition of teacher education relative to the public schools deteriorated by 19 percent between 1982–83 and 1984–85, and the teacher education direct cost is now at the lowest proportional relationship to public school cost per student in the eight years of these studies. Although there are antagonists to the value and legitimacy of teacher education, the argument has not been made that a year of preparation for teacher education majors should cost less than for a year of educating a child in third grade, seventh grade, or eleventh grade.

THE PROBLEM AND ITS CONSEQUENCES

The current criticism of teacher education is probably long overdue. When the target of the public's condemnation was limited to K through 12 education, significant reforms resulted—better funding, higher salaries, structural and curriculum redesign, pass/fail standards, effective schools research—and these continue. Now the relatively poor preparation of teachers has been recognized as part of the problem. It has probably contributed to the problem of poor schools and poor learning for a long time. Teacher education reform has also occurred: earlier and more clinical experiences, more equitable participation by the schools in teacher preparation, better definition of the knowledge base and curriculum redesign, and more cooperative follow-up during the new teachers' first years. However, these changes have virtually ignored the fact that teacher education generally operates at a poverty level in our colleges and universities. There are two primary reasons for this: The lack of effective quantitative standards and the lack of effective expenditure oversight.

Despite the recent NCATE redesign of teacher education accreditation policies and procedures, the standards still avoid the issue of any relationship between program quality and the adequacy and equity of a program's funding. The accreditation standards for medicine, nursing, engineering, and business all include quantifiable indicators, whether in terms of student/faculty ratio, class size, or direct expenditures per student. In the absence of such clout from external program review agencies, and in the absence of rigidly enforced legislative audit oversight of how higher education actually spends state appropriations, campus administrators will continue to fund teacher education at its current inadequate level. The quality of preservice teacher preparation is vitally important to the quality of education in this nation. Without effective quantitative standards and audit controls, the quality of education will continue to be at the mercy of the biases and prejudices of university administrators who undervalue and underfund teacher education.

NOTES

1. The teacher education programs in the 1986 study included, by AACTE geographic region:

   Zone I University of Delaware, University of Maine, University of Maryland, University of Massachusetts, SUNY/Buffalo, SUNY/Potsdam, Rutgers University

   Zone II University of Alabama, University of Alabama/Birmingham, Auburn University, University of Florida, Florida Atlantic University, Florida State University, University of South Florida, University of Georgia, Georgia State University, Memphis State University, University of Southern Mississippi, University of North Carolina/Greensboro, North Carolina State University, University of South Carolina, University of Tennessee, University of Virginia, Virginia Polytechnic and State University, Virginia Commonwealth University, University of North Carolina/Chapel Hill, College of William and Mary

   Zone III Indiana University, Indiana State University, University of Kentucky, University of Louisville, Miami University of Ohio, Ohio University, Ohio State University, Pennsylvania State University, University of Pittsburgh, West Virginia University

Zone IV   University of Iowa, Iowa State University, University of Minnesota/Minneapolis, Northern Illinois University, Southern Illinois University, Wayne State University, University of Wisconsin/Milwaukee

Zone V   University of Arkansas, East Texas State University, University of Houston, University of Kansas, Kansas State University, Louisiana State University, University of New Orleans, University of Missouri/Columbia, University of Missouri/St. Louis, North Texas State University, University of Oklahoma, Oklahoma State University, University of Texas, Texas A&M University, Texas Tech University

Zone VI   University of Alaska, University of Arizona, Colorado State University, University of Hawaii, University of Montana, Montana State University, University of Nebraska, University of Nevada/Las Vegas, University of Nevada/Reno, University of New Mexico, New Mexico State University, Oregon State University, Utah State University, University of Washington, Washington State University, University of Wyoming

REFERENCES

Benson, Charles. 1975. *Equity in School Financing: Full State Funding.* PDK Fastback 56. Bloomington, Ind.: Phi Delta Kappa Educational Foundation.

Berlinger, David. 1984. "Making the Right Changes in Preservice Teacher Education." *Phi Delta Kappan* (October): 94–96.

Bloom, Allan. 1983. "Differential Instructional Productivity Indices." *Research in Higher Education* 18(2): 179–93.

Board of Regents. 1978. "Executive Summary of the Study Conducted by the Regent's Task Force on Funding." Topeka: March. Mimeo.

Bowen, Howard. 1981. *The Costs of Higher Education: How Much Do Colleges and Universities Spend and How Much Should They Spend?* San Francisco: Jossey-Bass.

Carter, David. 1977. "Program Funding by Formula of the Unrestricted Current Fund Operation of Kentucky's Public Higher Education Institutions." Knoxville: Kentucky Council of Public Higher Education. Mimeo.

Caruthers, J. Kent, and Melvin Orwig. 1979. *Budgeting in Higher Education.* Washington, D.C.: American Association of Higher Education.

Coleman, D.R., and James Bolte. 1976. "A Theoretical Approach for the Internal Allocation of Academic Personnel Resources." In *Conflicting Pressures in Postsecondary Education*, edited by R.H. Fenske, pp. 26–32. Tallahassee, Fla.: Association for Institutional Research.

Coordinating Board. 1970. "Designation of Formulas." Austin: Coordinating Board of the Texas College and University System. Mimeo.

Feldman, Marilyn, and Robert Fisher. 1982. "The Role of Cluster Analysis in Comparing Teacher Education Programs among Similar Institutions." Paper presented at the Annual Meeting of the American Association of Colleges for Teacher Education, Houston, February 17-20.

Gross, Bertram. 1974. "The Use of Formulas for State Appropriations for Higher Education." Ph.D. dissertation, University of Tennessee.

Guthrie, James. 1975. *Equity in School Financing: District Power Equalizing.* PDK Fastback 56. Bloomington, Ind.: Phi Delta Kappa Educational Foundation.

Hemp, Gene, and Jim Brunson. 1984. *1982-83 Planning Factors in Engineering National Study.* Gainesville, Fla.: American Society for Engineering Education.

Keating, J. C. 1983. *The Cost of Higher Education in Virginia 1977-79.* Richmond, Va.: Council of Higher Education.

Millett, John. 1979. *The Budget Formula as a Basis for State Appropriations in Support of Higher Education.* Washington, D.C.: Academy for Educational Development.

Moss, C. E., and G. H. Gaither. 1976. "Formula Budgeting Requiem or Renaissance?" *Journal of Higher Education* 47(5): 543-64.

National Governors Association. 1986. *Time for Results: The Governor's 1991 Report on Education.* Washington, D.C.: NGA.

National Education Association. Various years. *The Cost of Public Education.* Washington, D.C.: NEA.

_____ . 1984. *Rankings of the States.* Washington, D.C.: NEA.

Orr, Paul, and Bruce Peseau. 1979. "Formula Funding Is Not the Problem in Teacher Education." *Peabody Journal of Education* 57(1) (October).

Peseau, Bruce. 1982. "Developing an Adequate Resource Base for Teacher Education." *Journal of Teacher Education* 33(4) (July/August): 13-15.

Peseau, Bruce. 1984. "Resources Allocated to Teacher Education in State Universities and Land-Grant Colleges." Paper prepared for the National Commission for Excellence in Teacher Education, Atlanta.

Peseau, Bruce. 1986. *Eighth Annual Study of Funding and Academic Production of Teacher Education in State Colleges and Universities.* University, Ala.: Association for Colleges and Schools of Education in State Universities and Land-Grant Colleges.

_____ . Various years. *Annual Studies of Resources and Productivity in Teacher Education Programs in State Universities and Land-Grant Colleges.*

Peseau, Bruce, and Paul Orr. 1980. "The Outrageous Underfunding of Teacher Education." *Phi Delta Kappan* 62(2): 100-102.

Sessums, Terrell. 1973. "Adequate and Equitable." In *A Potpourri of Institutional Research Studies,* Proceedings of the Sixth Statewide Invitational Conference on Institutional Research, pp. 74-75, Tampa, Fla., June 28-29.

Stuart, Douglas. 1966. *The Application of Formula and Cost-Analysis Procedures to the Budgeting of Academic Departments.* Ph.D. dissertation, Michigan State University.

Sykes, Gary. 1982. Statement presented at the Public Hearing on Teaching and Teacher Education, Georgia State University, Atlanta, May 12. Mimeo.

Texas Higher Education Coordinating Commission. 1970.

Warner, Allen. 1986. "On Scapegoating Teacher Education." *NASSP Bulletin* (May): 94-97.

Yeager, John, and Cynthia Linhart. 1978. "Adequacy of Formulas for Balancing Institutional Needs and Resources in Non-Growth Periods." ERIC ED 161333. Paper presented at the Annual AIR Forum, Houston, May 21-25.

9 JUDICIAL REQUIREMENTS FOR EQUAL PAY

Joseph C. Beckham

Federal statute laws mandating wage and salary equity, designed with the intent to prohibit discrimination in compensation based on sex, have not been judicially interpreted to compel widespread reform of wage inequities among professional employees in educational institutions. Difficulty in establishing proof of discriminatory intent and judicial acceptance of employer defenses predicated on the influence of "market forces" in setting wages and salaries have effectively eliminated discrimination suits based on theories of comparable worth. However, legislative initiatives at the state level may define new standards of judicial review in cases involving wage and salary disparities and lead to reform of pay inequities based largely on the legacies of social role sex stereotypes.

FEDERAL STATUTES MANDATING EQUAL PAY

In 1963 section six of the Fair Labor Standards act was amended to include one additional fair labor standard—equal pay for equal work regardless of sex. In order to establish a prima facie case under this amended provision, known as the Equal Pay Act, the employee must establish that the employer is paying workers of one sex more than workers of the opposite sex in a situation where both sexes are performing the same or similar work.[1] The similarity of work is established by demonstrating that the skill, effort, and responsibility of both jobs are equal and performed under similar working conditions.[2]

One year after the Equal Pay Act was enacted, Congress passed Title VII of the Civil Rights Act of 1964. Title VII forbids employers "to fail or refuse to hire or to discharge any individual, or otherwise discriminate against any individual with respect to his compensation, terms, conditions, or privileges of employment, because of such individual's race, color, religion, sex, or national origin."[3] Title VII prohibits both intentional discriminatory treatment of employees based on impermissible criteria,[4] and facially neutral policies that have discriminatory impacts but that are not justified by business necessity.[5] However, employers are allowed to differentiate on the basis of sex in establishing wage rates as long as the differentiation is within the exceptions of the Equal Pay Act.[6]

To harmonize with the two provisions, Congress enacted the Bennett Amendment to Title VII. The text of the Bennett Amendment provides that it shall not be an unlawful practice under Title VII for an employer to differentiate on the basis of sex in determining the amount of wages or compensation paid to employees if such differentiation is authorized by the Equal Pay Act.[7]

BURDEN OF PROOF

An employee alleging a violation of the Equal Pay Act bears the initial burden of establishing a prima facie case of wage or salary discrimination based on sex. The employee must show that the employer paid more to employees of the opposite sex for the performance, under similar working conditions, of a job requiring substantially equal skill, effort, and responsibility.[8] The employee does not have the initial burden of proving that the pay differential was based on sex.[9]

Once a prima facie case is established, the burden shifts to the defendant to prove as an affirmative defense that the pay disparity is based on a particular factor other than sex. The employer may demonstrate that one of four statutory exceptions accounts for the salary discrepancy. The four exceptions, all affirmative defenses, include (1) a seniority system, (2) a merit system, (3) a system that measures earning by quantity or quality of production, or (4) a differential based on any factor other than sex.[10]

Substantially Equal

In 1974 the Supreme Court adopted the "substantially equal" test in *Corning Glass Works v. Brennan*.[11] *Corning* defined a plaintiff's burden of proof under the Equal Pay Act as proof by a preponderance of the evidence that an employer pays unequal wages to male and female employees for equal or substantially equal work.[12]

Courts have interpreted the term *equal* to refer to the nature of the job, not its value to an employer. In *Hodgson v. Miller Brewing Co.*,[13] the Court of Appeals for the Seventh Circuit held that Congress intended only jobs of the same character to be compared in Equal Pay Act cases. This interpretation of the act precludes comparison of jobs in different occupational categories.

The broadening of the equal work standard to substantially equal work in Equal Pay Act cases was of little help to underpaid employees in jobs of differing occupations. Wage differentials remained the same because the Equal Pay Act was too narrow to cover certain discriminatory practices of employers. For example, employers could escape liability under the act simply by assigning different job titles to predominately female jobs and predominately male jobs and by paying the men more than women, despite the similar identity of the jobs.[14]

To remedy the limited applications of claims under the Equal Pay Act, employees have asserted that traditional means of proving discrimination are equally effective in proving sex-based wage discrimination. A showing of discriminatory job assignments, classifications, or other practices in the administration of an employment relationship provides circumstantial evidence of an intent to discriminate.

Under Title VII's disparate treatment model, discriminatory intent can be proved in two ways. First, the inference arises when difference treatment is accorded two employees performing substantially equal jobs. Second, discriminatory intent is imputed to the employer where the disparity in pay is more likely than not the result of intentional sex-based discrimination.[15]

In contrast to the disparate treatment theory, the plaintiff need not provide discriminatory intent on the employer's part in a disparate impact case. To establish a prima facie disparate impact case, a plaintiff must show that an employer's "facially neutral employment practice" has a substantially disproportionate impact on a group protected by Title VII.[16] Once a plaintiff has shown the existence and impact of such a practice, the employer will be held liable unless the practice can be justified by "business necessity."[17] If this showing is made, plaintiffs are entitled to show that alternative practices would fulfill the "business necessity" with a less discriminatory impact.[18]

The two standards offer alternative bases for establishing a claim of wage or salary discrimination. With disparate impact analysis, an employment practice that is facially neutral is nonetheless impermissible discriminatory if it has a disproportionately adverse impact on a protected group, provided that such practice is not justified by any business necessity.[19] An employment practice fails the disparate treatment test if it is animated by a discriminatory intent—that is, if the practice is selected "at least in part 'because of' and not merely 'in spite of' its adverse effects upon an identifiable group."[20]

In *County of Washington v. Gunther*,[21] the U.S. Supreme Court sought to decide the narrow issue of whether the Bennett Amendment precluded Title VII claims on unequal work. In *Gunther* female jail guards challenged a county pay scheme that paid them only 70 percent of what male guards received. The women argued that the county violated the Equal Pay Act because their work was substantially equal to that of male guards. In the alternative, they alleged intentional sex discrimination under Title VII.

The Supreme Court found that the females' jobs were not substantially equal to the males' because the female guards spent much of their time performing less valuable clerical work, but the Court allowed the Title VII claim, holding that the Bennett Amendment did not restrict Title VII claims to those that comply with the equal work standard of the Equal Pay Act.[22] Instead, the Court interpreted the Bennett Amendment to incorporate the four affirmative defenses of the Equal Pay Act.[23] These four defenses available to an employer under the Equal Pay Act are merit, seniority, productivity, or any factor other than sex.[24]

Comparable Worth

In *American Federation of State, County, & Municipal Employees (AFSCME) v. Washington*,[25] a three-judge panel of the U.S. Court of

Appeals for the Ninth Circuit unanimously refused to recognize a theory of comparable worth in Title VII's ban on gender-based discrimination. In so doing, the court reversed a district court ruling that the state of Washington had discriminated on the basis of gender by compensating employees in jobs traditionally held by women at lower rates than employees in jobs mostly held by men, even through a management study judged the positions to be of comparable worth.

The court dismissed the theory held by both AFSCME and the district court: that the state of Washington's practice of paying employees at market rates was impermissibly discriminatory. Furthermore, the court noted, "We find nothing in the language of Title VII or its legislative history to indicate Congress intended to abrogate fundamental economic principles such as the laws of supply and demand or to prevent employers from competing in the labor market."[26] This decision, which rejected comparable worth as a judicially mandated standard, left the option of enacting a comparable worth statute to the Washington state legislature.[27]

The Ninth Circuit panel rejected comparable worth under Title VII on two grounds. First, the court stated that "disparate impact analysis is confined to cases which challenge a specific, clearly delineated employment practice applied at a single point in the job selection process."[28] By contrast, the employment practice at issue—namely, taking market forces into consideration when setting wage levels—"involves an assessment of a number of complex factors not easily ascertainable, an assessment too multifaceted to be appropriate for disparate impact analysis."[29] As for disparate treatment, the court ruled that mere reliance on market forces did not supply the necessary discriminatory animus, particularly because the state did not create the market-based disparities and because it was not shown that the state perpetuated these disparities with any intent to discriminate on the basis of gender.

A REPRESENTATIVE CASE

In a case in which both the Equal Pay Act and Title VII claims were addressed, faculty members of the University of Washington School of Nursing filed suit against the university for sex-based wage discrimination. The faculty members submitted statistical and anecdotal evidence to support their charges that the university paid them disproportionately lower salaries compared to the salaries received by faculty in similar schools within the university. The university based its wage rates for each school on the current market wage rates. The Ninth Circuit Court of Appeals dismissed these claims under both the Equal Pay Act and Title VII in *Spaulding v. University of Washington.*[30]

The Equal Pay Act requires that the nursing faculty state a prima facie case by showing that its members "did not receive equal pay for equal work."[31] The plaintiffs tried to establish substantial job equality between their department and higher-paying comparator departments. They argued that the jobs within each department called for equal responsibility, skill, and effort and that the jobs were performed under similar working conditions. The court, however, was unpersuaded. It reasoned that the jobs were not substantially equal because various comparator departments placed different degrees of importance on research, training, and community services.[32] It also found the evidence unpersuasive because it did not account for earlier job experience, multiple degrees, or rank, and it did not sufficiently evaluate the work actually performed by faculty members.[33] Although the evidence presented may have demonstrated a disparity in pay, that disparity alone did not establish a prima facie violation of the Equal Pay Act because the compared jobs were not substantially equal.

In order to establish a claim of disparate treatment, the nursing faculty offered salary statistics as circumstantial evidence of discriminatory animus, but the court held that such circumstantial proof, standing alone, is evidence only of disparate impact.[34] The statistical evidence was insufficient as circumstantial evidence because the court found that the nursing faculty did not represent an adequate statistical analysis.[35] The comparator faculty members were selected without acknowledgment of the fact that not all degrees are equal and without regard to previous job experience and daily job responsibilities. Furthermore, the nursing faculty's salaries were never compared to female faculty wages from other departments, so the study did not determine how much disparity was due to sex discrimination and how much was due to the discipline itself. Thus, the statistical findings did not take into account the individual differences that could have justified the unequal treatment received among the faculty members.

In *Spaulding* the nursing faculty's claim under the disparate impact model of Title VII also failed. The court held that it was not the purpose of the disparate impact model to wage a "full scale assault on the employer's salary practices," as the nursing faculty was attempting to do.[36] "The discriminatory impact model . . . is not . . . the appropriate vehicle from which to launch a wide-ranging attack on the cumulative effect of a company's employment practices."[37] Examination of the substance of the policy, the court instructed, was necessary to see if it is a "non-job-related pretext to shield an individious judgment." The court found that employers are "price-takers," in that they must look to market values in determining labor costs and salaries.[38] Title VII is geared to proscribe discriminatory policies based on culpable intentions but is not intended to prohibit a policy such as setting salaries according to market conditions.

CIRCUMSTANTIAL EVIDENCE OF WAGE DISCRIMINATION

The use of direct evidence of discrimination is the most persuasive. Direct evidence of discrimination—such as discriminatory statements made by an employer, sexual stereotyping, and corporate hostility toward women—has consistently been regarded as the best evidence of a violation of federal laws prohibiting discrimination.

Although direct evidence of discriminatory intent provides a stronger case for a disparate treatment claim, the U.S. Supreme Court has held that circumstantial evidence may be used to infer intent in a disparate treatment case.[39] Courts differ on the weight assigned to circumstantial evidence but have been inclined to allow a variety of types of circumstantial evidence to infer intent. Plaintiffs have produced inferences of discrimination using pairing, multiple regression techniques, and job evaluation studies.

Pairing and Regression Analysis

The techniques for generating data applicable to Equal Pay and Title VII disparate treatment and disparate impact claims are pairing and multiple regression analysis. Under a paired comparison, a female employee selects a "comparator"—a male employee who performs a comparable job—and demonstrates to the court that the jobs are substantially equal and that the male receives greater pay.[40]

Another method used by plaintiffs to produce evidence required to carry the burden of proof is multiple regression analysis. Through this statistical device a quantitative estimate is made about the effects of independent variables on a single dependent variable—salary.[41] Independent variables such as degree, years of experience, institution from which degree was received, publications, and other matters are used to "predict" a salary for individuals of like characteristics. Predicted salaries and actual salaries are compared for the individuals who allege sex discrimination. Regression analysis is primarily used in class action lawsuits.[42]

The use of paired comparisons has its pitfalls. If the employee fails to select comparators who performed "substantially equal jobs," no showing of a salary differential would be significant. Differences in level of skills between jobs could influence a finding that the pairing was improper.[43] Similarly, distinguishable duties such as number of employees supervised[44] or length of contract could invalidate a comparison.[45]

However, use of a pairing technique has been sustained as a proper method for establishing a salary or wage disparity. When comparisons are made between faculty in the same department[46] or when comparisons involve faculty with the same level of training, experience, education, and ability,[47] courts have recognized the employee's prima facie case.

Multiple regression analysis is particularly useful in class action wage discrimination suits because it permits the courts to examine the average effect of a given employment qualification on employment outcomes for an entire group.[48] Because the technique is relatively sophisticated as a means of determining the effects of different factors on a particular variable, expert testimony is often required. Arguments over whether relevant variables were included in the analysis often involve disputations between opposing expert's representing the parties. In *Spaulding* the nursing faculty's statistical evidence was successfully attacked because, in the court's view, the analysis failed to account for faculty experience, rank, and distinguishing duties.[49]

Spaulding set strict standards for a statistical analysis presented by a plaintiff seeking to make a Title VII claim under the disparate treatment model.[50] It also required additional evidence of discriminatory animus to supplement the circumstantial evidence.[51] Furthermore, in a case decided subsequent to *Spaulding,* a federal district court created additional burdens for plaintiffs in waged discrimination suits; the court emphasized that the plaintiff may not rely on data supplied by the employer as to wage and salaries and that he or she must carry the burden to verify the accuracy of the information provided.[52]

Despite the limits on statistical analysis imposed by courts, regression analysis has been utilized to establish a prima facie case of sex discrimination in wage and salary practices.[53] Although such an analysis deals with composite experiences rather than individual cases, the circumstantial evidence provided where comparison groups are performing work that is substantially similar has been adopted by federal courts.[54]

Job Evaluation Studies

Sex-based deviation from job evaluation studies in the establishment of wage rates can be probative of intentional discrimination.[55] In *Gunther* the Supreme Court made it clear that proof of intentional discrimination in violation of Title VII could be inferred from an employer's deviation from job evaluation results.[56] Similarly, in *International Union of Electrical Workers v. Westinghouse Electric Corp.,*[57] the U.S. Court of Appeals for the Third Circuit held that sex-based wage differentials would violate Title VII where the employer deviated from job evaluation results along pronounced sex-based lines for jobs involving comparable worth.[58]

However, the plaintiff's case is strongest when based on an employer's job evaluation study rather than on one arranged by the plaintiff. The plaintiff's task of proving the comparability of different jobs is already accomplished if an employer has conducted the job evaluation study. The employer is less likely to assert the invalidity of results if the employer has sanctioned the job evaluation study. However, if it is the plaintiff's own job evaluation, the employer can contest the results.

EMPLOYER'S AFFIRMATIVE DEFENSE

Employers must pay male and female employees the same wage for equal or substantially equal work, unless the disparity results from a seniority system, merit system, a system based on quality or quantity of work product, or a differential based on a factor other than sex. When a plaintiff makes out a prima facie case of sex discrimination, the burden shifts to the employer who must submit evidence to establish that one of the four affirmative defenses applies and accounts for the difference in salary. The most common defenses for employers involve a showing of a merit or incentive system or evidence that market factors account for the difference in pay.

A pay differential based on factors other than sex has met judicial standards for an affirmative defense in several cases. An Oregon school district established that teacher performance standards and qualifications were properly considered in establishing pay differentials.[59] A university successfully asserted a merit system related to teaching and research as a basis for pay differentials when defendants established that the merit system had been formalized in the university's personnel policies and that faculty members were aware of its focus.[60] In a "market forces" defense, Brown University demonstrated that it was compelled to raise the salary of one instructor in order to retain the employee who had received an offer of employment from another institution.[61]

Affirmative defenses require the employer to carry the burden to justify salary or wage differentials. The burden imposed on the employer in an educational institution would appear to require the producing of that documentation that would support the articulated affirmative defense. This restriction would require the institution to clearly define the requirements of positions, specify and apply job-related criteria in the evaluation of employee performance for merit or incentive purposes, and demonstrate what market factors compelled salary differentials between employees.

CONCLUSION

Congress enacted the Equal Pay Act in an effort to eradicate the notion that one sex, because of societal role expectations and tradition, should be compensated more generously than another. The primary intent of the law was to compel equal dollars for equal, or substantially equal work, irrespective of gender. The law has particular significance for women. In the words of one federal court judge,

The Act was intended as a broad charter of women's rights in the economic field. It sought to overcome the age-old belief in women's inferiority and to eliminate the depressing effect on living standards of reduced wages for female workers and the economic and social consequences which flow from it.[62]

The Equal Pay Act was not a panacea, and it was followed by the more comprehensive provisions of Title VII. Title VII prohibited discrimination in compensation, terms, conditions, or privileges of employment on the basis of race, color, religions, sex, or national origin.[63] Recognizing that discrimination in the workplace could take many forms, Title VII sought to eliminate intentional discrimination in the form of disparate treatment and practices fair in form but discriminatory in impact.[64] The two laws were to be read *in pari materia* regarding discrimination in compensation based on sex with neither provision undermining the intent of the other.[65]

Title VII did not initially extend to the faculty of educational institutions, and, prior to amendment in 1972, the Equal Pay Act did not apply to professional employees of educational institutions. In 1972 Congress passed the Equal Employment Opportunity Act and the Education Amendments of 1972. Read together, these two laws removed the Title VII exemption for faculty and added Title IX, subjecting educational institutions to the provisions of the Equal Pay Act.[66]

Although the judicial standards recognize federal statutes as prohibiting different pay for substantially equal work, the laws have not been interpreted to extend to a claim of comparable worth.[67] The acceptance of a market forces defense to claims of discrimination based on comparable worth theories has effectively eliminated this basis for establishing a prima facie case of wage or salary discrimination.

Various state laws, executive orders, and agency regulations have embellished existing federal statutes. Statutes specifying comparable worth as the standard for resolution of sex-based disputes have been enacted in several states, and Congress has periodically introduced comparable worth bills.[68] Sex-based wage discrimination is frequently an issue in collective bargaining negotiations, and comprehensive studies of pay equity are underway in a number of jurisdictions.[69]

No court has yet held that evidence of unequal pay for work of comparable worth is irrelevant, although federal courts have not been willing to rule that such evidence is sufficient to establish a claim of sex-based wage or salary discrimination. Studies of comparable worth continue to be commissioned by employers and state legislatures concerned with resolving a history of gender-based discrimination. Ultimately, the initiative for reform of wage inequities based on the legacies of traditional social roles must rest with new legislative state and federal initiatives that define new legal standards and specify appropriate remedies.

NOTES

1. Corning Glass Works v. Brennan, 417 U.S. 188 (1974).
2. 29 U.S.C. §206(d)(1) (1985).
3. 42 U.S.C. §2000e-2(a) (1985).
4. McDonnell Douglas v. Green, 411 U.S. 792 (1973).
5. Griggs v. Duke Power Co., 401 U.S. 424 (1971).
6. *See* Gunter v. County of Washington, 452 U.S. 161, 168–70 (1981).
7. 42 U.S.C. §2000e-2(h).
8. Corning Glass Works v. Brennan, 417 U.S. 188, 195 (1974).
9. *See* Danielson v. De Page Area Vocational Education Authority, 595 F. Supp. 27, 31 (D. Ill. 1984). Female teachers in vocational-technical school alleged facts sufficient to state a claim under Equal Pay Act by asserting male teachers in equal or equivalent positions received more favorable terms or conditions of employment.
10. *See* Ende v. Board of Regents of Regency Universities, 757 F.2d 176 (8th Cir. 1985). A salary increase that restores a victim of past discrimination to the salary level that he or she would have enjoyed absent discrimination qualifies as a defense under (4), even where the discrimination itself was based upon sex. *But see* Lyon v. Temple University, 543 F. Supp. 1372 (E.D. Pa. 1982). Affirmative action program would not justify wage inequities such that a defendant's motion for summary judgment would be affirmed.
11. 417 U.S. 188 (1974).
12. *Id.* at 196.
13. 457 F.2d 221 (7th Cir. 1972).
14. *See* J. O'Hara, "An Overview of the Theory of Comparable Worth," 22 *Educ. L. Rptr.* 1073–84 (1986).
15. McDonnell Douglas Corp. v. Green, 411 U.S. 792 (1973).
16. Griggs v. Duke Power Co., 401 U.S. 424 (1971). The purpose of disparate impact theory is to remedy "practices that are fair in form, but discriminatory in operation." *Id.* at 431.
17. *Id.* at 432.

18. Dothard v. Rawlinson, 433 U.S. 321, 329 (1977).

19. *Id.* at 328-29 (1977). *See also* Griggs v. Duke Power Co., 401 U.S. 424, 430-31 (1971).

20. Personnel Administration of Massachusetts v. Feeney, 442 U.S. 256, 279 (1979).

21. 452 U.S. 161 (1981).

22. *Id.* at 178-80.

23. *Id.* at 178.

24. 29 U.S. §206(d)(1) (1982).

25. 770 F.2d 1401 (9th Cir. 1985).

26. *Id.* at 1407.

27. "The Washington legislature may have the discretion to enact a comparable worth plan if it chooses to do so." *Id.* at 1407.

28. *Id.* at 1405.

29. *Id.* at 1406.

30. 740 F.2d. 686, 692 (9th Cir.), *cert. denied,* 105 S. Ct. 511 (1984).

31. 29 U.S.C. 206(d)(1).

32. *Spaulding, supra* note 30, 740 F.2d at 697-98.

33. *Id.* at 698.

34. *Id.* at 703.

35. *Id.* at 704.

36. *Id.* at 708.

37. *Id.* at 707.

38. *Id.* at 708.

39. *Id.*

40. International Brotherhood of Teamsters, 431 U.S. 324, 325 (1977).

41. Jacobs v. College of William & Mary, 517 F. Supp. 791 (E.D. Va. 1980), *aff'd,* 661 F.2d 922 (4th Cir. 1980), *cert. denied,* 454 U.S. 1044 (1981).

42. EEOC v. McCarthy, 578 F. Supp. 45, 47 (D. Mass. 1983).

43. *Id. See also* Wilkins v. University of Houston, 654 F.2d 388 (5th Cir. 1981), *cert. denied,* 459 U.S. 822 (1982) (Title VII class action); Sobel v. Yeshiva University, 566 F. Supp. 1167 (S.D.N.Y. 1983) (Title VII class action).

44. Hein v. Oregon College of Education, 718 F.2d 910 (9th Cir. 1983).

45. Orahood v. Board of Trustees, 645 F.2d 651 (8th Cir. 1981).

46. *Jacobs, supra* note 41, 517 F. Supp. at 797-98.

47. Melanson v. Rantoul, 536 F. Supp. 271 (D.R.I. 1985).

48. Marshal v. Georgia Southwestern College, 489 F. Supp. 1322 (M.D. Ga. 1980).

49. Fisher, "Multiple Regression in Legal Proceedings," 80 *Colum. L. Rev.* 702 (1980).

50. 740 F.2d 686, 698. The court rejected the nursing faculties' contention that "teaching is teaching" as appealing but superficial.

51. *Id.* at 704.
52. *Id.* at 703.
53. Penk v. Oregon State Board of Higher Education, 604 F. Supp. 715 (D. Or. 1986).
54. Ende v. Board of Regents, 757 F.2d 176, 180 (8th Cir. 1985).
55. *See* EEOC v. McCarthy, 578 F. Supp. 45 (D. Mass. 1985).
56. *See* Bellace, "Comparable Worth: Proving Sex-Based Wage Discrimination," 69 *Iowa L. Rev.* 655, 703 (1984).
57. 452 U.S. 161.
58. 631 F.2d 1094 (3d Cir. 1980), *cert. denied*, 452 U.S. 967 (1981).
59. *Id.* at 1096-97.
60. Smith v. Bull Run School District, 722 P.2d 27 (Or. App. 1986). The school district offered evidence that complaints about the performance of plaintiff/teachers justified the lower pay as an incentive to improve performance.
61. EEOC v. Cleveland State University, 29 Empl. Prac. Dec. (CCH) 32, 783. *But see* EEOC v. McCarthy, 578 F. Supp. 45. The college's merit pay system was informal and the college failed to carry burden to demonstrate merit could adequately account for pay differentials.
62. Winkles v. Brown University, 747 F.2d 792 (1st Cir. 1984).
63. Shultz v. Wheaton Glass Co., 421 F.2d 259 (3d Cir. 1970), *cert. denied*, 398 U.S. 905 (1970).
64. 42 U.S.C. §2000e-2(a)(1) (1982).
65. International Brotherhood of Teamsters v. United States, 431 U.S. 324, 339 (1977).
66. *See* Laffey v. Northwest Airlines, 567 F.2d 429, 446 (D.C. Cir. 1978), *cert. denied*, 434 U.S. 1086 (1978).
67. *See* Powell v. Syracuse University, 580 F.2d 1150 (2nd Cir. 1987), *cert. denied*, 439 U.S. 984 (1978).
68. *See* J. O'Hara, "An Overview of the Theory of Comparable Worth," 22 *Educ. L. Rptr.* 1073-84 (1986).
69. *See* S. 1900, 98th Cong., 1st Sess. (1983) and H.R. 5092, 98th Cong., 2d Sess. (1984).

10 THE CHANGING CONDITIONS OF TEACHER RETIREMENT SYSTEMS
A Certain Past, a Tenuous Present, an Uncertain Future

Eugene P. McLoone

Financing teacher retirement systems in the past was relatively simple. The major purpose of retirement systems was to provide funds for career teachers who after retirement were unable to meet living costs in an inflationary period. Retirement systems also helped rid schools of elderly teachers who were unable to perform satisfactorily and helped retain a career teaching force. Retirement system financing was guided by these goals in first half of the twentieth century. Teachers employed before the 1950s did not benefit from the economic expansion generated by World War II. For those teachers the equalizing difference hypothesis (that workers trade liberal pension benefits for low wages) seems to apply; the equalizing difference hypothesis does not seem to apply to private pensions, however.

Beginning in 1951, when Social Security was extended to public employees, retirement system administrators and policymakers who deal with retirement systems faced challenges from external forces. Should policy for retirement systems be made from the standpoint of its members or from the standpoint of some outside imperative? How should the divergent viewpoints be reconciled? These policy imperatives came not only from national policy toward Social Security but also from the return available from private providers of retirement plans, from the economy in terms of inflation, from the varied views of appropriate corporate social policy, from the changing relationship of aged dependent population to working population, from changing views of prudent investment behavior, and from drives to make retirement plans nondiscriminatory in terms of sex. Each of these social issues demanded—and continues to demand—that retirement plan administrators and policymakers look beyond the narrow scope of member concerns. The two major sections of this chapter discuss historical background and major studies of retirement plans as well as current issues and problems.

HISTORICAL BACKGROUND AND MAJOR STUDIES OF FINANCING RETIREMENT SYSTEMS

Retirement systems and their financing can be viewed from the perspective of state or local public employees' systems for elementary and secondary school teachers and Teacher Insurance and Annuity Association (TIAA) for college and university teachers. More broadly, the financing of retirement systems can be viewed to include Social Security (as Old Age, Survivors, Disability, and Health Insurance (OASDHI) are commonly called). Also included are Individual Retirement Accounts (IRAs), section 403(b) tax-deferred annuity plans, and the host of private providers of retirement plans. The choice of perspective yields different answers to similar questions. The broader perspective is needed to understand the general social, economic, demographic, and political climate within which decisions have been and are being made about publicly financed retirement systems.

To set the stage for current issues of financing retirement systems for teachers, this chapter presents broad stages in the development of retirement plans, a general picture of state and local government employee plans, including specific information on teacher plans when available, and a review of significant dates and changes in the history of retirement plans. Generally available data on financing and related issues in the *Census of Governments* and special studies appearing irregularly are discussed. Major studies of state and local retirement plans and their financing are then reviewed, and finally, some issues related to financing are covered.

Stages in the Financing of Retirement Systems

Prior to 1920 retirement plans were simple arrangements that were established without an idea of ultimate cost. Often they were handled on a pay-as-you-go basis and financed without reference to actuarial findings. During the 1920s, however, actuarially funded systems were established. Contributions under these plans were generally required from employees. After World War II benefits were increased to include guarantees of total benefits based on final salary. Money-purchase or defined contribution plans as well as pay-as-you-go funding of retiree pensions all but disappeared during this time in state/local retirement systems. Social Security, when extended to public employees in 1951, further raised total benefits. Cost-of-living adjustments were made to the benefits received in the 1960s. In the 1970s concerns with funding costs for existing benefits led some states to seek integration of social security and state/local employee retirement benefits.

The 1950s not only witnessed the growth of retirement plans for employees in the private sector but also the growth of a private sector with a large number of plans for personal savings for retirement. Prior to the 1950s almost the only vehicle for private saving for retirement was annuities offered by insurance companies. During the late 1970s these privately provided plans briefly came to the forefront with the establishment of individual retirement accounts (IRAs).

Current state/local employee retirement systems are considered within the broad context of income plans for the elderly that include personal savings, Social Security, and private pensions as part of a total package or as a part of the effect of retirement incomes on the total economy, work effort, and labor force participation. Financing retirement plans today are considered in the broadest social, economic, and political context.

Although attention here is directed to the financing of teacher retirement systems, those systems must be examined within some larger context. In part, the larger context results from the availability of data, with this data limitation providing only one reason for teacher retirement plans' being reviewed within the broader context. Many of the recent studies have examined policy issues extending beyond the confines of a single retirement system or a retirement system for a single group of employees, whether teachers or some other class of public employees. Attention has been directed at an income policy for the elderly, the effect of investment of retirement fund assets on capital markets and the economy, the need for integration of Social Security with other retirement plans, and the effect of retirement plans on early retirement and work incentives. In addition, questions have been raised concerning the role of individual saving for retirement: Should each person provide for herself or himself? Are employee-sponsored retirement plans and Social Security a disincentive for private savings? Increased interest in these large questions has brought scholars from many fields into the study of retirement systems. As a result of this increased attention, terminology has changed. Although the *Census of Governments* publications still refer to state and local government *employee-retirement systems*, other authors are apt to refer to *pension plans.* Terminology varies with authors despite the efforts of a Committee on Pension and Profit-Sharing Terminology, under the joint auspices of the Commission on Insurance Terminology and of the Pension Research Council of the Wharton School at the University of Pennsylvania.

General Overview of Teacher Retirement Plans

It is difficult to develop a general overview of teacher retirement systems, as can be ascertained from the many detailed footnotes and careful pictures provided in Bleakney (1972), Tilove (1976), and Greenough and King (1976) and from the cautions given there about generalizations. This overview attempts to place retirement plans in a societal perspective and presents both terminology and data requirements for analysis.

The general picture of state/local retirement plans—of which teacher retirement plans are a part and with which teacher retirement plans generally share the same characteristics—is one that does not restrict entrance on the basis of either age, service, or some age and service combination. State/local retirement plans almost always use cliff vesting, which entitles individuals to retirement benefits after a given period of service, usually five years.

Virtually all state/local plans are defined benefit contributory plans that use past earnings to compute retirement benefits. To a large extent, for almost two-thirds of the plan participants in state-administered plans, a unit benefit formula determines benefits as a fixed percentage of a specified salary base multiplied by the length of service. The usual formula provides for approximately one-half of final compensation (defined as final three- or five-year average or as high three- or five-year average) with either twenty-five or thirty years of service at normal retirement age 60. Some plans permit earlier retirement at age 55 with thirty years of service.

This use of final compensation in public plans differs from private plans that, when they use earnings-based benefits, rely on career average of earnings. This difference in earnings base leads to public employees' receiving an annual benefit equal to 57 percent of final salary and private employees' receiving only 29 percent of salary (based on a hypothetical worker retiring in 1977 with a final salary of $20,000) (Kotlikoff and Smith 1983: 10–11). Tilove (1976) points out that if allowance is made for the contributory nature of public pensions and for the fact that almost 40 percent of members of public retirement systems do not participate in Social Security, then the difference between public and private pensions is modest.

Census of Governments data for monthly payments to beneficiaries reveal the same pattern for teachers as compared with other state/local employees. Teachers received $808 in monthly benefits compared to $440 for all recipients of state/local retirement systems in fiscal 1982. One contributing factor to the difference is that teachers are more likely to be career employees, whereas other public employees are hired at ages 40 to 50.

The contribution rate to teacher retirement plans is usually about 6 percent of salary. When teachers are covered by Social Security, the percentage of salary declines to 4 percent of salary. When teachers are not covered by Social Security, the percentage often increases to 8 percent of salary. When step rates were used in place of a uniform rate on total salary, the rate varied from 3 to 6 percent of salary on a $10,000 salary in 1972. When age/sex contribution rates are based on time of entry for a female at age 25 the percentage of salary is above 6 but less than 8 percent of salary.

For every dollar of receipts of state/local retirement plans, 40.8 cents come from investment earnings; 41.6 cents come from governments with the state providing 23.5 cents and localities, 18.1 cents; 17.6 cents come from employees. For every dollar invested state and local retirement systems placed 24.0 cents in government bonds; 34.3 cents in corporate bonds; 22.1 cents in corporate stocks; 7.7 cents in mortgages; 7.8 cents in other securities; 1.9 cents in other investments; and 2.2 cents in cash.

As a percentage of state and local employee payroll, state and local retirement fund contributions remained about 10 percent from the 1950s until fiscal 1982. From 1973 to 1979 state and local contributions increased from 11 to 13 percent but remained at 11 percent in fiscal 1982 (Kotlikoff and Smith 1983: 14):

> While public pension plans in the aggregate appear fairly well funded in terms of total accrued liabilities, there is considerable heterogeneity across pension plans. Based on an 8 percent interest rate, for example, seven state plans are less than 50 percent funded with respect to total accrued liabilities, twelve states have funding ratios between .5 and .75, eighteen fall between .75 and 1, and thirteen states are more than fully funded.

The details of the procedure use by Kotlikoff and Smith (1983) as well as their assumptions will be discussed later. In addition to the conceptual questions about the appropriate measure of liabilities of retirement funds, measurement of liability is highly sensitive to the interest rate used to discount future benefit streams, to projected rates of employee wage growth, and to assumptions about worker longevity and employment separation. Employee separation may be a function of the benefit level of the retirement plan. The two concepts of retirement system liability used are explained here.

First, accrued liabilities, which are based solely on past experience, can be viewed as the liabilities that a plan would face if it were shut down. These liabilities equal the benefit obligations that a plan would face if it terminated operation and paid off vested and (in the case of total accrued liabilities) unvested benefits using only past service and past levels of earnings to compute benefits. Second, projected liabilities equal present expected value of benefits payable to current participants, assuming that the plan continues in operation and that service and earnings of active participants increase at projected rates.

Kotlikoff and Smith (1983) needed to make such assumptions because state plans do not routinely report fund liabilities. Available information cannot be consistently compared across states because of the differences in actuarial procedures and assumptions.

History of Retirement Plans

The first public retirement plan was begun for police officers in New York City in 1857. The first private retirement plan was offered by American Express in 1875. Toward the end of the nineteenth century private pension plans generally grew among regulated industries such as railroads and public utilities. Among nonregulated industries, only in the oil industry did pensions assume importance. The first public school pension plan was established in Chicago in 1893, and New Jersey was the first state to enact provisions for a statewide retirement system for teachers in 1896. The creation of statewide teacher-retirement systems, as a rule, followed the breakdown of local systems. Multiemployer plans were first established for granite workers in 1905. The Teacher Insurance and Annuity Association (TIAA) for college and university professors was established in 1918, and its companion fund, College Retirement Equities Fund (CREF), was established in 1952. Both funds for professors sought to help that impoverished class battle inflation—TIAA by providing a retirement plan and CREF by providing a retirement fund that would grow with inflation. The movement toward providing retirement plans was not always one of continued progress. In 1929 Idaho abandoned its teacher retirement system, which was established in 1921. In 1917 twenty-two states had established a retirement plan for teachers (Studensky 1920). By 1934 twenty-four of the forty-eight states had a statewide teacher-retirement system (Keesecker 1934). Between 1936 and 1940 thirteen states created retirement plans for teachers. By 1950 all states had retirement plans for teachers (Mackin 1971). By 1967 all fifty states had plans for public employees; sixteen of these systems for public employees covered teachers, and another eleven also included other educational personnel (Mackin 1971). Private retirement plans or pensions began their growth during World War II; restrictions on wage increases that did not apply to fringe benefits gave the impetus for their growth. Wage and price controls allowed payment of funds into welfare plans on behalf of workers. Such payments, in addition, were not subjected to federal income taxation. In 1948 the National Labor Relations Board (in the case of the United Steel Workers) allowed unions to bargain for retirement plans.

Census of Governments

The census of governments in years ending in a two or seven provides data on employee retirement systems of state and local governments since 1952 (U.S. Department of Commerce 1983). The report contains information on membership, benefit payments, and cash and security holdings of state and local government employee retirement systems throughout the nation. Although 2,559 systems were reported in the 1982 census of governments, about 95 percent of the persons participating in state and local government retirement systems belong to the largest 171—those reporting a membership of 5,000 or more. Since 1950 the census of governments annually has reported the same information on the largest retirement systems in *Finances of State and Local Employee Retirement Systems.*

Fifty-seven school employee or teacher retirement system operate in thirty-one states. Eight states maintain separate retirement systems for teachers and for other school employees. Seven retirement systems exist for teachers alone in large cities (Boston, Chicago, Duluth, New York City, Portland, St. Paul, and Washington, D.C.). Eight other local retirement systems are operated for all school employees (Arlington County, Virginia, Denver, Fulton County, Georgia, Kansas City, Minnesota, Minneapolis, Omaha, St. Louis, and Wichita). In data analysis and reporting, these fifteen retirement systems often are referred to as the fifteen large local government retirement systems for teachers.

The distinctions of the government's Division of the Bureau of the Census in the census of governments reporting are important because the Census provides the only consistent and regularly published data about retirement systems. Therefore, analyses follow the definitions of the Bureau of the Census. In some instances, teachers are members of "general coverage" systems, and in other instances, they are members of "limited coverage" systems that "comprise both (a) very broadly based systems applying to school employees generally (including clerical and custodial employees, bus drivers, etc.), and (b) systems for school employees other than teachers." Furthermore, some states have separate plans for elementary and secondary teachers and for college and university teachers. Seventy-two of the state/local plans cover college and university professors; only fifteen of these seventy-two do not provide for Social Security or TIAA as either an alternative or a supplemental plan.

In some instances, local school systems supplement statewide plans, and teachers have bargained for the right to invest their tax-deferred payments in a variety of private plans. Although the total variety of retirement plan provisions and their financing should be covered, available data usually limit coverage to those plans reported by the Bureau of Census. Only in census of governments years are all state and local government retirement systems covered. In non-census of governments years, only the large membership plans are covered.

Other Data Required for Financing Retirement Plans

The census of governments publications provide membership, benefit payments, and cash and security holdings of state and local employee-retirement systems. Data on the necessary qualifications for membership, contribution rates, benefit formulas and provisions for normal retirement, survivors, disability, death, and early retirement are not centrally provided on a regular basis. Retirement systems and state teacher associations provided such data for their members. School systems as employers often have such data available for their employees. Although often difficult to summarize over plans and among states in a meaningful way, these data are vital to anyone planning the financing of retirement systems. Special surveys provide such data from time to time.

Financing of retirement systems requires such data to cost the benefits based on the actuarial assumptions applied to the benefits. Actuaries begin with the benefit formula and make assumptions about mortality rates among present workers and retirees, the turnover of the workforce, the return on assets invested, present and future compensation scales, retirement rates and ages, and disability experience to determine the cost of retirement plans. These data are known only by retirement system administrators and their actuaries and only occasionally are collected for use by researchers.

Finally, information on investment strategies and legal restrictions placed on retirement plan administrators by state law is desirable. Data on administrative practices of state and local retirement systems assist in comparisons. These data affect the financing and the cost of funding retirement systems in the following manner. The annual contribution made by a government is the sum of the administrative costs and the contribution level necessary to finance benefit level, minus the return on investments. Often local governments and state agencies through their personnel offices absorb some of the administrative costs of retirement systems by providing employee counseling and assistance with completion of required documents. Thus, retirement plans and states may vary in administrative costs as they do in return on investments. As a result, annual contributions to retirement systems vary and the degree of unfunded liabilities varies not only because of differences in benefits but also because of differences in either investment return or administrative costs.

Significant Studies of State/Local Retirement Plans

Almost all the desired data on state and local retirement systems were gathered and analyzed during the 1970s. These studies, however, fall short of the detailed data that are available on retirement systems and often offer a less than comprehensive analysis of financing. Because retirement systems have been subject to changing economic conditions, plan benefits, and age/sex composition of plan members, more frequent collection of these data on a regular schedule is desirable.

Four institutions have extensively engaged in research about retirement plans: the Pension Research Council, Wharton School, University of Pennsylvania; the National Bureau of Economic Research's Project on the Economics of Pensions; the Brookings Institution's Studies in Social Economics; and the Employer Benefit Research Institute. Bleakney (1972), in a publication of the Pension Research Council, comprehensively covers state and local employee retirement systems, including those for teachers. He presents various methods of financing public employee retirement systema and pays attention to implications for inflation. Kotlikoff and Smith (1983), as part of the ongoing studies conducted by the National Bureau of Economic Research, comprehensively cover both public and private plans as of 1978 and discuss almost all studies done through 1982. Their study does not give separate attention to teacher retirement plans but covers them as part of all state/local plans. Their study provides a comprehensive overview of present financial condition and future potential problems.

Greenough and King (1976) give a history of retirement plans and Social Security and describe the types of plans, their size, and the coverage under both private and public employee retirement systems. Current investment practices and trends in these practices are described. Greenough and King give this background for their analysis of public policy issues of private and public retirement plans and their policy prescriptions within a context of an income support system for the elderly. They surveyed seventy-two public higher education retirement systems found among the 123 systems covering 90 percent of all state and local employees in the *1962 Census of Governments*. They recommend integration of pension plans with Social Security. Despite the fact that adjustments to pensions plans for inflation are generally unsatisfactory or costly, pension plans must develop such compensation precautions for inflation.

Graebner (1984) gives an excellent history of retirement plans. He shows that the reason for retirement plans are often multipurpose and that policy from the standpoint of a single viewpoint may seem strange until a more complete view of purposes served by retirement plans is taken.

Tilove (1976) describes in detail the characteristics of public employee retirement plans for separate teacher plans and for those plans that include either teachers or all school employees in general public employee plans. He raises the major public policy questions affecting the plans and evaluates solutions to them. He also reviews almost all previous studies on financing retirement plans.

Mackin (1971) presents historical data to indicate past failures of retirement systems from the standpoint of the retiree. Mackin, Bleakney (1972), and Tilove (1976) discuss many of the same issues and recommendations. Mackin does so from his perspective of the effects of inflation on the real income of the retiree.

The U.S. House (1978: 3) *Pension Task Force Report* on public employee retirement systems examined the areas covered by Bleakney (1972) and found serious deficiencies with regard to funding, financial disclosure, and fiduciary responsibility. The House Committee on Labor and Education found that "the benefit levels and benefits provisions of public employee retirement systems compare favorably with those found under private sector pension systems." The report paid particular attention to vesting and portability of retirement rights, plan termination provisions, reporting to members, and administration—all items of concern under the Employee Retirement Income and Security Act of 1974 (ERISA).

Schmitt (1976), responding to the mandate of ERISA for a congressional study of public retirement plans, discusses the areas of interest delineated by Congress and the problems facing state and local retirement plans. These problems include the higher benefit level of public versus private plans, the liberalization of benefit formulas and their increased cost, incidences of fiduciary irresponsibility on the part of plan trustees and administrators, and the pay-as-you-go nature of funding of most public plans. Schmitt indicates that serious problems will result if present trends continue. Taxpayers may refuse to bear the burden if costs become oppressive. Government workers with Social Security benefits may retire with disposable income greater than that derived from their working salary.

These same problems are identified in other studies. Munnell and Connolly (1976; 1979) do simulations of the financial operations of state and local employee retirement systems. Jump gives a review essay on collective bargaining, wages, and retirement plans in Municipal Finance Officers Association (1978). Although most attention is given to the local retirement systems in the volume, many of the principles apply to state plans as well. SRI International (1982) provides most the recent comprehensive information on local retirements plans including those offered by large school systems on a local basis. Jump (1981) continued his study of state and local retirement systems in Urban Institute, Winklevoss and Associates, Government Finance Research Center, and Dr. Bernard Jump, Jr. (1981), which deal with the future of state and local pensions. The Municipal Finance Officers Association Committee on Public Employee Retirement Administration (1977) deals with design and administering local retirement systems. In this chapter, most of these problems are approached in terms of Kotlikoff and Smith (1983), the latest report that contains references to almost all previous studies and that develop its own projection of funding needs.

Studensky (1920), Keesecker (1934), and Schmid (1971) provide historical information on teacher retirement systems and data on the systems. They discuss many of the problems of current retirement systems, although the context in which the problems are placed is different.

Kotlikoff and Smith (1983) analyzed the census of government data and made actuarial assumptions about the members of the systems and the benefits. Arnold (1982) gathered information on all state-administered pension plans with over 500 participants. The Frank Arnold STPS (1982) data base covers 144 state-administered pension plans. The file contains summary plan descriptions for each state plan and other information on the plan's finances, the number of participants, and the demographic characteristics of covered employees. Kotlikoff and Smith (1983) used the STPS data in conjunction with the census of governments' data to construct unfunded liabilities of state-administered retirement systems.

Pope (1986), taking the census of government data base as a starting point, sent a separate survey to the large public retirement systems. His 20 percent response rate is typical of such surveys. He found that for the retirement systems responding there were economies of scale in larger administrative units and that smaller retirement systems should be combined for administrative purposes.

The paucity of studies from which generalizations can be made about financing retirement systems and the wealth of data and studies about the broader questions of financing systems from the standpoint of the individual lead to the procedure followed here. The major questions about financing retirement systems for teachers are best viewed from the standpoint of the individual and from the standpoint of the broad economy. Studies conducted on Social Security or privately provided plans should be replicated in the public sector for state and local plans. Nonetheless, although replication is desirable, such replication may not be done due to the lack of any ongoing systematic data collection. For this reason, it is more likely that research will be done on a retirement system basis. Members of retirement systems need to assure themselves that their plan meets their own goals.

Generalizations about retirement systems seem to remain the same; the following quote could have been made in the 1920s as well as today (Lynn 1983: 9):

> Criticisms leveled at pension systems include the following: (1) some are underfunded or unfunded (these are pay-as-you-go systems), and therefore offer little assurance of pension payments in the long run, although they are a source of pensions now. (2) Pensions originating in plans presupposing a stable currency prove inadequate when prices of goods and services rise. (3) In cases arising with noticeable frequency, pension systems (sometimes several in concert) pay pensions that exceed preretirement, earned income or that are inadequate. (4) Accumulated funds are used by bankers or insurers or other fund managers as a means of exercising inappropriate economic, social, or political power. (5) Many systems, such as social security, originate in a tax or a payroll deduction or a deferred wage that is involuntary; thus these systems are supported by some (for example, the independently wealthy) who might prefer not to support them at all. (6) Some systems are abused or corrupted.

POLICY QUESTIONS ABOUT RETIREMENT SYSTEM FUNDING

Although the questions about individual retirement plans are best raised and answered by the plan members and plan administrators, large overriding questions about every plan are raised in the many studies conducted. These questions are external to the plans and their members. Yet these questions—about integration of retirement plans with Social Security generally and in particular with regard to benefit levels, about role of appropriate corporate social policy in investments, about the degree of portability and vesting, about who should be protected from inflation, and about the relationship between present and future generations—are being asked of retirement system administrators and state legislatures. Policy about retirement systems seems to be moving into a context beyond that of the retirement system and its members; this movement toward a broader social and economic context is creating the uncertain future.

Integration of Social Security and Retirement Plans for Public Employees

Since January 1, 1984, newly hired federal employees are required to join Social Security. Yet 43 percent of active members of state and local public employee retirement systems in fiscal 1982 were not members of Social Security. The percentage of state and local public employees not belonging to Social Security has increased over the decade from fiscal 1972 through fiscal 1982.

The national imperative that no one should be excused from paying his or her fair share of the taxes for the social policy represented by Social Security has largely been ignored by policymakers for public retirement systems. Furthermore, policymakers were faced with a need to choose between following this national policy imperative or following policies that seem best for members of the retirement system.

Male teachers usually qualified for Social Security by summer and other part-time employment. Married female teachers saw little gain from their separate Social Security account when comparison was made with their spousal allowance. In 1987 the difference could be as little as $1,000 annually in benefits.

Social Security can create equity problems between single and married teachers. Assuming a retirement system that provides 50 percent of final salary, a single person receiving payment from Social Security and the retirement system will have approximately 71 percent of salary, and a married person qualifying for spousal allowance will receive approximately 87 percent of salary. For which group of individuals should retirement systems be planned?

Since Social Security was extended to public employees in 1951, policymakers and administrators of retirement systems for public employees including teachers have faced at least the following two dilemmas: (1) benefit levels set by two different decisionmakers without either being sure of future benefits under the other system and (2) a need to consider policies beyond those of the retirement system and its members in determining retirement system decisions.

The need to integrate Social Security and the retirement plans is clear as a policy issue; the means are not. The several states have given different answers. Future planned benefits of Social Security as the maximum creditable earnings increase can threaten the existence of supplemental retirement plans for low-income workers as benefits provide replacement for a large percentage of previous earnings. Future Social Security benefits levels depend on the Consumer Price Index (CPI), increases in wages, and changes in maximum creditable earnings. The percentage of final earnings paid as benefits depends on the relationship of growth in wages to CPI. If wages increase at 5 percent per year, the replacement percentage at the maximum earning level can increase from the present approximately 20 percent to nearly 50 percent in the twenty-first century at the 4 percent CPI increase versus a 35 percent level for 3 percent increase in CPI. Below the maximum earning level, similar increases will take place. Planning for future benefits from retirement plans integrated with Social Security requires estimating the change in CPI, wages, and the ratio of the salary of teachers to maximum Social Security creditable earnings.

The Benefit Level

It is not unusual to find that benefit payments to state and local public employees exceed benefit payments to members of private pension plans, nor is it unusual to find that teachers receive larger payments than other public employees. The public employee receives a larger percentage of final salary, or a larger dollar payment, than the private employee. The *1980 Current Population Survey* indicates average benefits of $3,850 for 65- to 69-year-old private pension recipients and $4,654 for corresponding state and local pension recipients. For female recipients in this age group, private pension recipients average $1,789, compared with public benefits for females of $3,850.

Census of Governments data for monthly payments to beneficiaries reveal the same pattern of more generous benefits for teachers as compared to other state and local employees. Teachers receive $808 monthly compared to $404 for all recipients of state/local retirement systems in 1981 through 1982. Based on this monthly data, the annual benefit for teachers would be $9,696, compared with $5,280 for all state and local employees.

These data are often used to raise questions about the benefit level of public employee retirement systems and in particular about the benefit level of teacher retirement plans. Several questions that can be raised about these comparisons: (1) whether or not the comparison of benefit levels between plans is appropriate; (2) the extent to which the available data permit adequate and accurate comparisons; and (3) why these differences exist and whether or not they are appropriate for future retirement policy.

Two important reasons for the differences between private and public pensions are coverage by Social Security and employee contributions to retirement plans. Approximately 40 percent of state/local retirement system participants are not members of the Social Security system. As a result, many state and local employees receive only their state/local retirement payment. In the past, when present retirees were working, most public employee retirement plans required employee contributions; most private plans did not require employee contributions. Both public and private plans today may require contributions, but private and public plans differed in the past. When Tilove (1976) made allowances for these conditions, public retirement plans remain more generous than private plans but not to a large extent.

Generalizations about retirement plans and comparisons between plans need to be made cautiously with attention to anomalies among plans. Retirement plans for teachers often exclude other school employees such as janitors, clerical staff, and bus drivers; these plans often include administrative and other certified personnel. In some states, teachers are members of a general employee retirement system. Thus, the data for teachers compared with other public employees are confounded by the classifications. Furthermore, teachers, more than other public employees, are likely to have served for a long tenure. Public employees generally are hired when they are age forty to fifty.

Comparisons of payments to presently retired workers are most useful when the groups compared have had similar past records of work experience and retirement plan participation. Workers hired in the 1960s and later may so qualify. Thus, comparisons of anticipated benefits by age cohorts for a single retirement system and among retirement systems may be useful. In order to plan for financing retirement systems, the benefit levels of both present and the near future retirees, and of a 22-year-old hired today and retiring at age 65 in the year 2030 must be known.

Comparisons of benefit levels among plans of presently retired workers give a view of the past but not necessarily of the present or future. For the past, it was not unreasonable to expect a career teacher to retire with twenty-five to thirty years of service at 50 percent of final compensation. This standard for benefit levels may be viewed as excessive, especially if teachers are not compensated near the maximum earning level of Social Security; it may be viewed as less desirable than provisions of vesting and portability by other than career teachers.

Portability and Vesting

Retirement benefits should be portable—that is, employees should be able to retain their rights as they change employers. Statewide systems achieve this for teachers, and general coverage retirement systems for all state employees achieve it for employees switching between education and other public employment.

From the standpoint of the employer, retirement plans have assured a permanent cadre of workers. Retirement plans, at least in the public sector, have been based on the idea of a lifetime career with one employer. In the absence of a single statewide plan, credit for service elsewhere in the state and transfer of credits and funds among plans achieve the same result of permitting employee mobility and a larger labor pool for a given job. The question of exchanging credits among and between states and either the federal government or the private sector remains unanswered. Mobility of workers is therefore restricted, and the supply of available workers is constricted. From the standpoint of an individual, the question raised is the portability of pension benefits and the degree of vesting.

Vesting in the public sector is usually cliff vesting. No partial credit is given before that time for a lesser period of service. Therefore, a person must make a commitment of five years of service with a single public employer in order to earn retirement benefits. The vested benefit remains for the employee to use on reaching normal retirement age. The vested benefit, even in plans with the same general benefit schedule, will affect the retirement payments of a mobile worker with more than a single employer.

Assuming that salaries increase 5 percent per year, a person entitled to a retirement benefit of 50 percent of final salary after thirty years of service with one change of employer after fifteen years will receive 37 percent of final salary or a 26 percent reduction in benefits. The portion of retirement benefits from the first employer will not take into account subsequent salary increases. Vesting provides only partial protection. Permitting the transfer of credited funds and benefits from the first to the second employer or making benefits portable would help. Although the solution of portability of rights clearly would assist the individual member of the retirement system, no clear method is available that will also protect the system and its members who remain.

Questions of portability of benefits and vesting loom large for school systems when retirement benefits are considered in the context of personnel policies and changing demographic conditions of school enrollments. If employment policies call for consideration of three-, five-, or ten-year term employment, then portability of pension benefits may be as important as salary. If declining enrollment makes staff reductions a necessity, portability of benefits as well as provisions for early retirement or retirement buyouts can become a central issue for personnel management. With changing economic conditions of states and regions within states and their concomitant population shifts, lifetime careers in education within a state may not be possible. Portability of benefits can become increasingly important.

Investment Policy

Portability could be easily achieved if all retirement systems had the same benefit formulas, investment policies, and contribution rate and if workers were identical as to age/sex composition, mortality, turnover, and present and future compensation rates. Investment policy standards could be uniform, and the status of present funding could be easily determined and compared.

Three major issues arise with regard to investment policy: (1) whether or not retirement systems are adequately funded to pay present or future liabilities to their members; (2) whether the investments are earning the maximum rate of return possible; and (3) whether, in conflict with the second question and in partial conflict with the first, investments are made in accordance with appropriate corporate social policy or even broader social policy goals. The first question has been continuously asked since 1920 when retirement plans first relied on actuarial estimation of plan fund requirements. The second question has always followed from the first because member contributions as well as employer contributions are affected by the rate of return. The second question became increasingly important as private providers of retirement plans indicated potential for rates of return beyond those rates achieved by retirement system administrators. The third question of appropriate corporate social policy and investments seems to be most important for the future.

The pervasiveness of pension plan investments in industries and companies invited special interest groups to seek change in corporate or industry policy through the channeling of their retirement plan investment funds to industries and companies in agreement with the interest group's view of responsible corporate social policy. The 1980s saw investments restricted by state or local law in companies dealing with South Africa or guilty of discrimination in Northern Ireland.

The appropriate corporate social policy includes issues of nuclear power, sex and race discrimination, air and water pollution, defense contractors and specific war materials, unionization, women's issues, and the foreign policy issues already mentioned. The effect of pursuing these policies on the rate of return in the long run is not clear. Some mutual funds for private investors appear able to offer a competitive rate of return while paying attention to the investor's desire for appropriate corporate social policy. The major effect of appropriate corporate social policy is that citizens at large or vocal special interest groups will determine investment policy. Invdstment policy will not be left to professional investors or to the members of the retirement system through their board of directors. Both of the latter groups are more likely to be concerned with the rate of return.

The rate of return on investments is crucial to the members of a retirement system and to their employer. The annual contribution made by a government is the sum of the administrative costs and the contribution level necessary to finance the benefit level, minus the return on investments. When this formulation requires increasing governmental contributions, either benefit levels or employee contribution levels are changed. When this formulation indicates no need for a change in a governmental contribution or a lower governmental contribution as evidenced in the 1960s, benefit formulas and levels often are liberalized. When the rate of returned lags behind the rate of inflation, as in the 1970s, questions are raised about the adequacy of funding and the ability of a retirement system to provide adequate payments in the future. The financial condition of state/local retirement plans depends on the assumed rate of return and on the measurement of liabilities.

The effect of the assumption about the rate of return on the soundness of retirement plan financing is now considered. Kotlikoff and Smith (1983) assumed either a 5 or 9 percent increase in inflation so that the rate of return was the rate of inflation plus 3 percent. Thus, their interest rates were 8 and 12 percent. Nominal wages were assumed to grow at 2.7 percent plus the inflation rate, with 2.0 percent economy growth in productivity and 0.7 percent growth in real wage association with increased years of service. Thus, wages increase at either 7.7 or 11.7 percent, nominal wages plus the rate of inflation.

Higher inflation, although associated with larger increases in wages and retirement benefits because of their effect on investment returns, makes funding the retirement system easier than does a lower rate of inflation. Should the nineteen states—those with a ratio below .75— feel a need to improve their contributions to achieve a better funding level of the retirement system? The answer is not clear. The seven states with a ratio below .50 probably should look at their funding. Some of the differences among states is partially a result of using the same age/sex/service profile for all systems. Although there was little difference in the effect on funding requirements among the thirteen age/sex/service profiles collected, it is not clear that such profiles are that similar among states and their retirement plans. This study by Kotlikoff and Smith (1983) is one of the most carefully done studies giving attention to many variables not previously considered; nonetheless, some of the differences among states must be discounted because neither state nor retirement system specific data were available.

Using state- or system-specific data does not always ensure accurate comparisons. Governmental contributions based on actuarial principles need not yield a single correct amount as the annual contribution rate. Whether a deficiency should be amortized over twenty-five, thirty, or forty years should illustrate the point that more than one amount can be correct for full funding. Whether the retirement system will decrease, remain stable, or increase in membership should also illustrate the point. All retirement systems are not alike on these and other aspects. Without such contextual knowledge, system-specific information can mislead. The study of Kotlikoff and Smith (1983) provides a basis for the seven states with ratios below .50 and for the thirteen states that are fully funded to examine their plans. The study also provides a basis for believing that funding of state/local retirement plans is not too serious an issue. Governmental contributions generally seem at an adequate level for benefits.

Whether or not state/local retirement systems can achieve the rate of return on investments projected in the study under the economic conditions outlined is open to question. The potential restraining effect on the rate of return of demands to pursue responsible corporate social policy in investing has already been noted. Retirement systems may not be able to properly time or switch investments to achieve the maximum going rate. Both legal requirements as to proper prudent investments and boards of directors wishing to approve investments may inhibit prompt action on certain types of investments. The time horizon chosen as appropriate for the retirement system likewise may interfere. If the long-term view of thirty years is taken, then investments may be made mainly in bonds to capture rates of return over that thirty-year period. Short-term rates greater than the long-term rate may be overlooked. Volatile rates of return will be viewed with suspicion. Retirement systems may have different policies with regard to the risk that they are willing to endure. Rates of return are apt to differ from the norm assumed, and thus the degree to which retirement plans are funded or not for liabilities may differ.

In periods of high inflation, more than 5 percent on the CPI, retirement systems will prefer short-term to long-term investments for the basic reason that investments are not locked into interest rates below those now attainable. The prudent long-term view becomes more and more short-term. The appropriate investment policy also becomes challenged as the age/sex composition of the retirement system members changes. Young members may prefer somewhat greater risk to achieve long-term appreciation in value, whereas older members may prefer conservation of capital with a continued yield. The younger group may prefer growth stocks of emerging companies, whereas the older group prefers utility stocks. How one reconciles the differing views brought on by inflation or by the future time horizon of members that changes as members age is unclear for investment policy. A variety of options seems the best alternative. The increased choice, however, is liable to decrease the influence on professional management of investments. A large portion of the investment choice becomes that of the member and thus raises the question of whether plan administrators ought not to offer individual choice of investments. The next logical step would seem to be a defined contribution plan rather than a defined benefit plan.

The broad policy outlines are clear: seek the maximum rate of return and keep the retirement system rully financed for potential liabilities. Which investments a retirement system should pursue and the degree to which corporate social policy should affect investments are less clear. Still less clear is whether the general public or members of retirement systems should have final say on investment policy. When pursuit of investment policy decreases the rate of return, should taxpayers or members through their contribution provide the loss? The future appears to contain many instances where social policy rather than the rate of return may become the central question.

Inflation and Retirement Plans

Inflation affects benefit level, required contributions by both governments and members, rate of return on investments, and salary increases. Social Security provides for benefits to increase with the changes in the CPI. Some states follow this method; other states have a flat allowance (for example, 2 percent a year), for inflation. The latter method permits better planning of future costs than does the former. When the CPI is used, future costs are beyond the control of the retirement system. Funding is based on an historical average of, for example, 3 percent. As long as the CPI remains at or below that level, funding is adequate. An occasional rise above the level is manageable as long as there are periods below the assumed long-term increase in CPI. Several years in succession or a long period of time above the assumed change in CPI creates funding problems. State/local retirement systems generally have these problems of funding because most public systems provide some measure of protection to members against increases in CPI or inflation.

Once again, the policy choice is clear: Retirees need some protection against inflation. Neither adjustment of benefits based on CPI nor a constant percentage solves the inflation problems of either the retiree or the retirement system caused. Protecting the retiree from inflation means that the retirement system has uncertain funding. Providing certainty in funding by allowing a constant percentage increase in benefits means that the retiree is not protected from inflation. Having experienced relatively stable prices in the 1960s and 1980s but double-digit inflation in the 1970s, members of retirement systems may have conflicting desires as to the worth of inflation protection. Unlimited increases to match increases in CPI of the 1970s may be too costly. Matched increases in CPI capped at approximately 3 percent may not be significantly better than a constant increase, which would be less costly to fund and more acceptable during times like the 1960s or 1980s. Protection of retirees from lost purchasing power due to inflation does not have the same appeal today as it did in the 1960s. Only the future can indicate if the importance of protecting retirees from inflation will increase or decrease. Social Security payments, indexed to CPI as maximum creditable earnings under Social Security rise to a higher percentage of final salary, can decrease the importance of other retirement plans' being fully indexed.

Ratio of Dependent Aged to Working Population

The ratio of working population to retired dependent population will decrease from three workers for each retired person today to two workers for each retired persons in the twenty-first century. Therefore, if resources were shared equally among the total population of workers and retirees, today workers could keep three-fourths of production while they will be able to keep only two-third of production in the twenty-first century. Which workers make the sacrifice for the retirees or the distribution of the burden of retirement can depend on the method of financing whether pay-as-you-go from taxes on earnings in Social Security or return on investments in funded retirement plans. The increased portion of economic goods claimed by the retirees may change the attitude of society toward benefit level needed by retirees.

SUMMARY

The major policy issues for retirement systems seem clear when viewed apart from a retirement system and its members, but these issues are not clear when viewed from the standpoint of the retirement system and its members. The major question is whether policy will be made in the narrow context of retirement systems and their members or in the broader social and economic context.

Means to achieve policy imperatives are less clear than the goals. A shift from defined benefit plans to defined contribution plans seems the route to solve vesting, portability, investment policy, inflation, and equity concerns of members. If there is a shift to defined contribution plans, then the future will be a dramatic change from the present and past. Yet such a change seems to address the many challenges of the present. A defined contribution plan appears to solve the patchwork benefits available within a state to persons employed in the same profession; such a plan would also assist local school systems, which are employers that could have a greater voice than now in retirement plan operation, especially if states shift more of the financial burden to localities.

Five or six plans or benefit formulas for teachers may exist within a given state. Sometimes, the retirement plan has a new name; often, the options within a single plan are increased. Recently hired employees may usually join only the latest plan. At the time of adoption of the new plan and sometimes later, employees can choose between their present coverage and the new plan. Sometimes the choice for present employees is between variations of the old plan. That choice may be between (1) retaining the old plan and benefit level for a higher employee contribution rate than the present contribution rate and (2) a new plan and lower benefit formula with the same contribution rate as in the past. The employer contribution rate may vary among plans; the varied plans may affect employer policy with regard to hiring, compensating, and retaining employees. The local school system as employer, however, often has little input into the decisions of the retirement plan because these decisions are affected by retirement administrators and retirement system members. Defined contribution plans could provide local school systems control over funding requirements.

The percentage of salary under the defined contribution plan provided by the employer can become the maximum provided under a defined benefit plan because the employee is required to provide the funds necessary beyond the employer paid percentage of salary in a defined contribution plan. Alternately, benefit levels can be lowered to match the funds available at present contribution rates. These choices and others mark the uncertain future of retirement plans and their funding. Unwieldy costs, too generous benefits, employee and employer share of cost, investment policy, and the question of who should bear the burden of inflation are all policy questions that are most likely to be solved by forces external to retirement systems and their members. The greatest uncertainty is the extent to which retirement system members will be part of the policy debate. Members of retirement systems will need to voice their concerns more and more to the public at large.

REFERENCES

Arnold, Frank S. 1982. *Estimation of State-administered Public Employee Pension Funds: Theory and Evidence.* Ph.D. dissertation, Harvard University, Cambridge, Mass.

Bleakney, Thomas P. 1972. *Retirement System for Public Employees.* Homewood, Ill.: Irwin, for the Pension Research Council.

Graebner, William A. 1984. *A History of Retirement: The Meaning and Function of an American Institution, 1885–1978.* New Haven: Yale University Press.

Greenough, William, and Francis King. 1976. *Pension Plans and Public Policy.* New York: Columbia University Press.

Keesecker, Ward W. 1934. *Teacher-Retirement Systems: Principal Provisions of State Systems.* Washington: U.S. Department of Interior, Office of Education Bulletin No. 6.

Kotlikoff, Laurence J., and Danile E. Smith. 1983. *Pensions in the American Economy.* A National Bureau of Economic Research Monograph. Chicago: University of Chicago Press.

Lynn, Robert J. 1983. *The Pension Crisis.* Lexington, Mass.: Lexington Books.

Mackin, John P. 1971. *Protecting Purchasing Power in Retirement.* New York: Fleet Academic Editions, Inc.

Municipal Finance Officers Association. 1978. *State and Local Finance and Financial Management: A Compendium of Current Research.* Washington, D.C.: Municipal Finance Officers Association.

Municipal Finance Officers Association Committee on Public Employee Retirement Administration. 1977. *Public Employee Retirement Administration.* Washington, D.C.: Municipal Finance Officers Association.

Munnell, Alicia H., and Ann M. Connolly. 1976. "Funding Government Pensions: State-Local, Civil Service and Military." In Federal Reserve Bank of Boston, *Funding Pensions: Issues and Implications for Financial Markets.* Conference Series No. 16. Boston: Federal Reserve Bank of Boston.

_____. 1979. *Pensions for Public Employees.* Washington, D.C.: National Planning Association.

Pope, Ralph A. 1986. "Economies of Scale in Large State and Municipal Retirement Systems." *Public Budgeting and Finance* 6, no. 3: 70–80.

Schmid, W. William. 1971. *Retirement Systems of the American Teacher.* New York: Fleet Academic Editions, Inc.

Schmitt, Raymond. 1976. *Retirement Systems of State and Local Governments—Dimensions of the Pension Problem.* Washington, D.C.: Library of Congress, Congressional Research Service, Report No. 76-24 ED.

Studensky, Paul. 1920. *Teachers Pension Systems in the United States.* New York: D. Appleton and Company.

SRI International. 1982. *Local Public Employee Pension Plans—Current Condition and Prospects for the Future.* Menlo Park, Calif.: SRI.

Tilove, Robert. 1976. *Public Employee Pension Funds: A Twentieth Century Fund Report.* New York: Columbia University Press.

U.S. Department of Commerce, Bureau of Census. 1983. *Finances of Employee Retirement Systems of State and Local Government, 1981-1982.* Washington, D.C.: Government Printing Office.

U.S. House Committee on Education and Labor. 1978. *Pension Task Force Report on Public Employee Retirement Systems.* Washington, D.C.: U.S. Government Printing Office.

Urban Institute, Winklevoss and Associates, Government Finance Research Center, and Dr. Bernard Jump, Jr. 1981. *The Future of State and Local Pensions.* Final Report to the Department of Housing and Urban Development. Washington, D.C.: U.S. Department of Housing and Urban Development.

11 TEACHER SALARIES
Progress over the Decade

Richard G. Salmon

Many contend that the quality of public education should not be determined by the salaries paid professional personnel. Because most statistical studies have reported only tenuous relationships between teacher compensation and pupil achievement, the use of teacher salary data for interstate or interdistrict comparisons is felt to be an inappropriate quality criterion. On the other hand, some people advocate additional compensation for professional personnel as the only mechanism that can immediately improve the public schools. Proponents of this argument often point to occasional state or school district increases in pupil achievement scores relative to contiguous states or school districts to justify their requests for additional teacher compensation.

Perhaps it is a mistake to argue either end of this continuum. Although most research studies have failed to identify a strong relationship between teacher compensation and various output measures of pupil performance, few personnel officers would argue that levels of teacher compensation are unrelated to their recruitment efforts. It is equally fallacious to contend that small incremental and spasmodic changes in pupil achievement can be attributed directly to recent increases or decreases in state or school district appropriations.

The salaries paid professional personnel, however, do indicate the economic health of the profession. It generally is agreed that the most important determinant in providing an effective educational system is the quality of the classroom teachers. It also is generally true that in our society a person's status in the community is determined largely by accumulated wealth or level of income generated. Anticipated financial compensation is one of several factors that are considered by people who confront career choice decisions. Research studies have documented that the teaching profession recruits personnel from the lowest academic quartile and that the highest percentage of teachers who abandon the profession come from the ranks of those with the greatest level of academic skill. Even within the teaching profession, long-term financial benefits accrue to classroom teachers who leave their classrooms for administrative or supervisory positions (Barker 1987).

Many of the recent national, regional, and state studies of public education predict that current levels of teacher compensation may prove inadequate to attract and retain sufficient numbers of high-quality teachers in the future (National Commission on Excellence in Education 1983). This chapter describes how the nation and its geographical regions have responded to the demands for increases in salaries for public school teachers during the recent era of public school reform, 1976–77 to 1986–87. The salaries of teachers were adjusted through use of the Consumer Price Index (CPI) in order to neutralize the effects of inflation. Salaries paid to teachers were contrasted with the salaries paid to those in other professions for the purpose of determining whether relative changes have occurred.

CLASSROOM TEACHER SALARIES: CURRENT DOLLAR TRENDS

As is shown in Table 11–1, the national average annual salaries paid classroom teachers rose from $13,357 in 1976–77 to $26,704 in 1986–87, yielding a total increase of $13,347. Increases in average annual salaries paid classroom teachers ranged from a low of $834 in 1978–79 to a high of $1,678 in 1984–85. Annual percentage increases ranged from 5.9 percent for 1978–79 and 1986–87 to 10.5 percent in 1980–81. From 1976–77 to 1986–87, the average salaries paid classroom teachers increased 100 percent (NEA 1978, 1987).

Table 11–2 displays similar classroom teacher salary data for the eight geographical regions of the United States. The relative rankings among the eight geographical regions changed little from 1976–77

Table 11-1. Average Annual Salaries Paid Classroom Teachers, School Years, 1976–77 to 1986–87.

School Year	Average Annual Classroom Teacher Salary	Dollar Increase	% Increase
1976–77	$13,357	—	—
1977–78	14,198	$ 841	6.3
1978–79	15,032	834	5.9
1979–80	15,970	938	6.2
1980–81	17,644	1,674	10.5
1981–82	19,274	1,630	9.2
1982–83	20,693	1,419	7.4
1983–84	21,917	1,224	5.9
1984–85	23,595	1,678	7.7
1985–86	25,206	1,611	6.8
1986–87	26,704	1,498	5.9
1977–87		13,347	100.0

Sources: National Education Association (1978, 1987).

Table 11-2. Average Annual Classroom Teacher Salaries for the Eight Geographical Regions and United States, 1976–77 to 1986–87.

Geographical Area	Average Annual Classroom Teacher Salary		Dollar Increase	% Increase
	1976–77	1986–87		
New England	$13,403	$27,154	$13,751	102.6
Mideast	15,338	30,198	14,860	96.9
Southeast	11,122	23,100	11,978	107.7
Great Lakes	14,006	28,139	14,133	100.9
Plains	12,119	24,207	12,088	99.7
Southwest	11,582	24,894	13,312	114.9
Rocky Mountains	12,480	25,158	12,678	101.6
Far West	15,743	30,236	14,493	92.1
United States	13,357	26,704	13,347	99.9

Sources: National Education Association (1978, 1987).

to 1986–87. Only the geographical regions of the Plains and Southwest showed any movement, with Plains moving from sixth to seventh place and Southwest moving from seventh to sixth place. The Far West recorded the highest average annual salaries for classroom teacher for both 1976–77 and 1986–87—$15,743 and $30,236, respectively. The Southeast had the dubious distinction of registering the lowest average annual classroom teacher salaries for both years—$11,122 and $23,100, respectively. The largest increase in average annual classroom teacher salaries was made by the Mideast, which registered an increase of $14,860. The smallest increase was made by the Southeast with an increase of $11,978. However, the largest percentage gain in average annual classroom teacher salaries was made by the Southwest, which showed an increase of 114.9 percent. The smallest increase, 92.1 percent, was made by the Far West. There is evidence that some progress is being made in reducing the range in average salaries paid classroom teachers among the eight geographical regions. In 1976–77 the ratio of high to low average annual classroom teacher salaries among the eight regions was 1.4 to 1, and by 1986–87 the ratio had fallen to 1.3 to 1. Nevertheless, the range in average annual salaries paid classroom teachers remained nearly constant among the fifty states during the eleven-year period. In 1976–77 the ratio in average annual salaries paid classroom teachers between Alaska, the state with the highest average annual salary, and Mississippi, the state with the lowest average annual salary, was 2.2 to 1. In 1986–87 the ratio between Alaska, again the state with the highest average annual salaries for classroom teachers, and South Dakota, the state with the lowest average annual salaries, had increased to 2.3 to 1 (NEA 1978, 1987).

Displayed in Table 11–3 are the five highest and five lowest states ranked by annual average salaries paid classroom teachers for both 1976–77 and 1986–87. There is considerable consistency among states regarding the level of salary funding provided the classroom teachers. Four of the five highest-ranked states in 1976–77 also were ranked among the five highest in 1986–87. Similar consistency was shown among the five lowest-ranked states: Three of the five lowest-ranked states in 1976–77 repeated among the five lowest-ranked states in 1986–87. A Pearson product-moment coefficient of correlation between 1976–77 and 1986–87 average annual salaries of classroom teachers for the fifty states yielded an $r = .93$, significant at $p > .01$.

Table 11-3. The Five Highest- and Lowest-Ranked States Regarding Annual Average Salaries Paid Classroom Teachers, 1976-77 and 1986-87.

| | School Year | | | |
| | 1976-77 | | 1986-87 | |
Rank	State	Average Salary	State	Average Salary
1	Alaska	$20,878	Alaska	$43,970
2	New York	17,150	New York	32,620
3	California	16,317	Michigan	31,500
4	Michigan	16,216	California	31,170
5	Washington	14,921	Rhode Island	31,079
46	South Carolina	10,507	Louisiana	21,280
47	New Hampshire	10,250	Maine	21,257
48	South Dakota	10,183	Arkansas	19,951
49	Arkansas	9,733	Mississippi	19,575
50	Mississippi	9,399	South Dakota	18,781

Sources: National Education Association (1978, 1987).

CLASSROOM TEACHER SALARIES: ADJUSTED FOR INFLATION

In Table 11-4 are annual average salaries paid to classroom teachers from 1976-77 through 1986-87, adjusted for price inflation through use of the CPI. When price inflation is taken into consideration, the real gain in average annual salaries paid classroom teachers is modest during the period. In fact, from 1976-77 to 1980-81 classroom teachers actually experienced a decline in purchasing power; they lost a total of $1,476 or 11.05 percent in real dollars. In 1981-82 and continuing through 1986-87, however, classroom teachers saw their average annual salaries increase faster than the costs of inflation. Over the eleven-year period 1976-77 to 1986-87 the average annual salaries paid to classroom teachers have increased from $13,357 to $14,152, representing an increase of $795, or a 5.95 percent gain in real dollars (NEA 1978, 1987).

In Table 11-5 the average annual salaries paid classroom teachers for 1976-77 and 1986-87 are listed by geographical region. Among

Table 11-4. Average Annual Salaries Paid Classroom Teachers, Adjusted for Price Inflation, 1976–77 to 1986–87.

School Year	Current Average Annual Salary	Real Average Annual Salary	Real Increase or Decrease	% Change
1976–77	$13,357	$13,357	—	—
1977–78	14,198	13,282	($75)	-0.56
1978–79	15,032	12,782	(500)	-3.76
1979–80	15,970	11,963	(819)	-6.41
1980–81	17,644	11,881	(82)	-0.69
1981–82	19,274	12,024	143	1.20
1982–83	20,693	12,451	427	3.55
1983–84	21,917	12,683	232	1.86
1984–85	23,595	13,160	477	3.76
1985–86	25,206	13,706	546	4.15
1986–87	26,704	14,152	446	3.25
1977–87			795	5.95

Sources: National Education Association (1978, 1987).
Note: Real average annual salaries of classroom teachers adjusted to 1976–77 dollars based on the Consumer Price Index.

the eight geographical regions, the Southwest showed the largest increase, both in total real dollars and percentage increase, with a real increase of $1,610, or a 13.9 percent gain. The Far West experienced the smallest increase in real dollars, with a gain of only $280, or a 1.78 percent increase. Despite recording the smallest increase among the eight geographical regions, the Far West continued to lead the nation in regard to average annual salaries paid classroom teachers (NEA 1978, 1987).

CLASSROOM TEACHER SALARIES: CONTRASTED WITH OTHER OCCUPATIONS

Historically, the average annual salaries paid to classroom teachers have not compared favorably with salaries paid those in other professional occupations. Despite the recent attention given by numerous public school reform efforts to the chronically low salaries paid to classroom teachers, the relationship between the salaries paid class-

Table 11-5. Average Annual Salaries Paid Classroom Teachers, Adjusted for Price Inflation, by Geographical Region, 1976-77 to 1986-87.

Geographical Region	Average Annual Classroom Teacher Salary				
	Current 1976-77	Current 1986-87	Real 1986-87	Dollar Increase	% Increase
New England	$13,403	$27,154	$14,390	$ 987	7.36
Mideast	15,338	30,198	16,003	665	4.34
Southeast	11,122	23,100	12,241	1,119	10.07
Great Lakes	14,006	28,139	14,912	906	6.47
Plains	12,119	24,207	12,828	709	5.85
Southwest	11,582	24,894	13,192	1,610	13.90
Rocky Mountains	12,480	25,158	13,332	852	6.83
Far West	15,743	30,236	16,023	280	1.78
United States	13,357	26,704	14,152	795	5.95

Sources: National Education Association (1978, 1987).
Note: Real average annual salaries of classroom teachers adjusted to 1976-77 dollars based on the Consumer Price Index.

room teachers and those in other professional groups has remained constant. Table 11-6 lists the average annual salaries for classroom teachers contrasted with average annual salaries paid members of several other professional and technical occupations for selected years, 1977-78 to 1985-86. It is difficult for several reasons to equate salaries paid to classroom teachers with the salaries paid other occupations: diversity of technical skills, dissimilarity of contractual conditions, and varying lengths of work years. Nevertheless, it is appropriate to examine the salary positions that classroom teachers have experienced relative to the salaries of selected occupations over a period of years. According to Table 11-6, in 1977-78 classroom teachers ranked last among the professional occupations and slightly above the technical occupations. The ratio between the average annual salaries paid the combined selected occupations and the average annual salaries paid classroom teachers was 1.5 to 1. By 1979-80 classroom teachers again ranked last among the professional occupations and approximately midpoint among the technical occupations. The ratio between the average annual salaries paid the combined

Table 11-6. Average Annual Salaries for Classroom Teachers Contrasted with Average Annual Salaries for Selected Occupations, Selected Years, 1978 to 1986.

	Years				
Occupations	*1977–78*	*1979–80*	*1981–82*	*1983–84*	*1985–86*
Professional					
Accountants III	$18,115	$21,299	$25,673	$28,721	$31,143
Auditors III	18,756	22,026	26,502	30,209	32,121
Attorneys IV	33,547	40,864	49,818	55,462	63,933
Buyers III	19,590	22,904	27,424	30,610	33,580
Chemists	28,494	33,793	40,207	45,614	50,678
Engineers V	28,001	33,141	40,677	46,349	50,769
Technical					
Engineering Technicians III	14,062	16,756	20,219	22,351	23,896
Drafters III	13,709	14,308	17,046	19,098	20,201
Computers Operators IV	13,737	16,050	19,325	23,107	24,550
Selected Occupational Average	21,259	25,278	30,979	35,514	38,626
Classroom Teachers	14,198	15,970	19,274	21,917	25,206
Ratio (selected occupational average to classroom teacher average)	1.5:1	1.6:1	1.6:1	1.6:1	1.5:1

Sources: National Education Association (1987); U.S. Department of Labor, Bureau of Labor Statistics (1978, 1980, 1984, 1986).

selected occupations and the average annual salaries paid classroom teachers had increased to 1.6 to 1. The pattern established in 1979–80 persisted until 1985–86. In 1985–86 the average annual salaries paid classroom teachers slightly exceeded the average annual salaries paid the technical occupations; however, the salaries paid classroom teachers still ranked last among professional occupations (NEA 1978, 1987; U.S. Department of Labor 1978, 1980, 1982, 1984, 1986). In essence, despite considerable rhetoric indicating the need for increased status and financial remuneration for classroom teachers, little relative change has occurred in the fiscal priority assigned to classroom teachers by society.

CLASSROOM TEACHERS SALARIES: FISCAL EFFORT GENERATED

Displayed in Table 11-7 by geographical region and the nation are current expenditure percentages of personal income, percentages of salaries paid classroom teachers of current expenditure, and percentages salaries paid classroom teachers of personal income for 1976-77 and 1986-87. Current expenditures of public elementary and secondary education calculated as percentages of personal income of states, regions, or the nation are often used as measures of fiscal effort generated for the current operation of public schools. As is evident by an examination of Table 11-7, the fiscal effort for current

Table 11-7. Percentage of Current Expenditures of Personal Income, Percentage of Salaries Paid Classroom Teachers of Current Expenditures, and Percentage of Salaries Paid Classroom Teachers of Personal Income, by Geographic Region, 1976-77 and 1986-87.

Geographic Region	% Cur. Exp. of Per. Inc.		% Class. Tchr. Sal. of Cur. Exp.		% Class. Tchr. Sal. of Per. Inc.	
	1977	1987	1977	1987	1977	1987
New England	5.1	3.9	45.3	42.0	2.3	1.6
Mideast	5.2	4.5	42.4	38.1	2.2	1.7
Southeast	4.3	4.1	47.1	42.0	2.0	1.7
Great Lakes	4.7	4.2	45.3	42.5	2.1	1.8
Plains	4.8	4.1	46.2	43.5	2.2	1.8
Southwest	4.2	4.4	53.2	45.5	2.2	2.0
Rocky Mountains	5.2	5.0	45.4	39.9	2.4	2.0
Far West	4.6	3.8	43.5	36.6	2.0	1.4
United States	4.7	4.2	45.4	40.8	2.1	1.7

Sources: National Education Association (1978, 1987); U.S. Department of Commerce, Bureau of Economic Analysis (1977, 1987).

operation generated by all geographical regions and the nation declined from 1976–77 to 1986–87. All geographical regions experienced a decline in fiscal effort generated for current operation, ranging from a decline of 1.2 percentage points for New England to .2 percentage points for Southeast. The nation as a whole experienced a decline in fiscal effort from 4.7 to 4.2 percent, a decline of .5 percentage points (NEA 1978, 1987: U.S. Department of Commerce 1977, 1987).

Concurrently, salaries paid classroom teachers calculated as percentages of current expenditures of public elementary and secondary education also declined from 1976–77 to 1986–87. All geographical regions and the nation experienced this shift in expenditure pattern, with a decline of 7.7 percentage points for the Southwest to 2.7 percentage points for the Plains. For the entire nation 45.4 percent of current expenditures was allocated for salaries paid classroom teachers in 1976–77. In 1986–87, 40.8 percent of current expenditures was allocated for salaries paid classroom teachers, a decline of 4.6 percentage points (NEA 1978, 1987).

In addition to the decline in fiscal effort made to fund current expenditures of public elementary and secondary education, there was also a noticeable decline in the fiscal effort made to fund the salaries of classroom teachers from 1976–77 to 1986–87. In 1976–77 the highest fiscal effort for salaries of classroom teachers, 2.4 percent, was generated by the Rocky Mountains region, and the lowest fiscal effort, 2.0 percent, was recorded by the Southeast and the Far West regions. The nation recorded a fiscal effort for salaries of classroom teachers of 2.1 percent in 1976–77. By 1986–87 the average fiscal effort generated by the nation for salaries paid classroom teachers had fallen to 1.7 percent, a decline of .4 percentage points. Among the eight geographical regions, the highest fiscal efforts for salaries of classroom teachers, 2.0 percent, were recorded by the Southwest and Rocky Mountains regions. The lowest fiscal effort made for salaries of classroom teachers in 1986–87, 1.4 percent, was registered by the Far West region (NEA 1978, 1987; U.S. Department of Commerce 1977, 1987).

Throughout the period 1976–77 to 1986–87, the Rocky Mountains region recorded the highest fiscal effort for funding current expenditures of public elementary and secondary education and for funding salaries of classroom teachers. Considerable relative improvement in fiscal effort made for funding current expenditures and salaries of classroom teachers was made by the Southwest region during the eleven-year period. At the other end of the continuum, the Far West region reduced its relative fiscal effort to fund current expenditures and salaries of classroom teachers from 1976–77 to 1986–87, ranking last among the eight geographical regions. Additionally, a considerable relative decline in fiscal effort made both for funding current expenditures and for funding salaries of classroom teachers was apparent for the New England region over the eleven-year period (NEA 1978, 1987; U.S. Department of Commerce 1977, 1987).

SUMMARY AND OBSERVATIONS

From 1976–77 to 1986–87 the average annual salaries paid classroom teachers approximately doubled. Unfortunately, classroom teachers, similar to most occupations, lost most of their salary increases to price inflation. When price inflation was taken into consideration through use of the CPI, the real increase was a modest $795, or 5.95 percent. Although the range in average annual salaries paid classroom teachers among the eight geographical regions declined slightly during the eleven-year period, the range between the states at the extreme ends of the salary continuum remained constant.

The average annual salaries paid classroom teachers have increased significantly over the period 1976–77 to 1986–87, but salaries of other occupations also have increased proportionally. The fiscal position occupied by classroom teachers relative to other occupational groups, both professional and technical, has remained virtually unchanged during the eleven-year period. In 1977–78 the ratio between average annual salaries of selected occupational groups and the average annual salaries of classroom teachers was 1.5 to 1, precisely the ratio derived for 1985–86. A case could also be made that the average annual salaries paid to classroom teachers are more comparable with salaries paid to technical occupational groups than with those paid the professional occupational groups.

Despite the considerable attention given to public elementary and secondary education during the past decade and the generally observed need for society to increase the salaries of classroom teachers, the fiscal effort generated by the nation for both current expenditures and salaries of classroom teachers declined from 1976–77 to 1986–87. Concurrent with the decline in fiscal effort to fund the salaries of classroom teachers has been the decline in the percentage of current expenditures allocated to the salaries of classroom teachers.

The decline in fiscal effort for current expenditures and salaries of classroom teachers and the expenditure pattern shift away from teacher salaries has been apparent in most states and all geographical regions.

During the past decade many state legislatures and local school boards have been conscientious in their attempts to increase dramatically the salaries they pay their classroom teachers and other school personnel. However, ample evidence exists, as discussed above, that little progress has been achieved. Why has there been little real gain in increasing the average annual salaries paid classroom teachers or in reducing the salary distance between classroom teachers and other occupational groups? There is no simple answer to this complex question. Reasons for not making better gains in raising the salaries of classroom teachers vary across states and school districts throughout the country.

During the period 1976–77 to 1986–87, some states and school districts experienced enormous fiscal stress, which virtually prohibited them from increasing significantly the salaries of public employees. Although the economic climate improved for most of the country during the latter years of the analysis, several states, most noticeably the oil-dependent states, were still encountering significant fiscal difficulties. Simultaneously, the federal government, faced with mounting budget deficits, began transferring greater fiscal responsibility to the states. Competition among various state governmental agencies for fiscal resources became more pronounced as health, welfare, transportation, and other state agencies struggled to meet their commitments.

The size of the public education establishment also made it difficult for states to increase dramatically the salaries of public school personnel. Public elementary and secondary education usually is the largest single agency funded by state and local governments. The weight of employee numbers has resulted in the establishment of influential state and national professional organizations. These organizations have been more effective in achieving job security and in protecting membership reitrement benefits, however, than they have been in raising the salaries of classroom teachers significantly. Classroom teachers are unable to convince state legislatures and local school boards to substantially increase their salaries rests partially because the public perceives the professional organizations to be intransigent. For example, alternatives to the single salary schedule, such as merit pay, career ladders, and differentiated staffing, are perceived by legislatures and local school boards to be an anathema to most professional organizations. Those persons already opposed to additional resource allocation to public elementary schools often join forces with persons frustrated by the reluctance of professional organizations to accept alternatives to the single-salary schedule. Such alliances usually have defeated efforts to significantly improve the salaries of classroom teachers.

Without question, the salaries of classroom teachers need to be increased significantly in most states of the nation. As the occupational choices of women broaden, public elementary and secondary education are deprived of a ready supply of qualified classroom teachers. Several studies have indicated that a severe shortage of qualified classroom teachers will exist by 1990 (Feistritzer 1984). If public elementary and secondary education is to attract quality personnel who can provide the level of instructional services that we need to remain competitive internationally, the United States will have to make a great fiscal effort.

REFERENCES

Barker, Edlow G. 1987. *A Cost-Benefit Analysis of Investment in Graduate Education by Virginia Public School Teachers*. Ed. D. dissertation. Blacksburg, Va.: Virginia Polytechnic Institute and State University.

Feistritzer, C. Emily. 1984. *The Making of a Teacher*. Washington, D.C.: National Center for Education Information.

National Commission on Excellence in Education. 1983. *A Nation at Risk: The Imperative for Educational Reform*. Washington, D.C.: U.S. Government Printing Office.

National Education Association. 1978. *Estimates of School Statistics, 1977-78*. Washington, D.C.: NEA.

_____. 1987. *Estimates of School Statistics, 1986-87*. Washington, D.C.: NEA.

U.S. Department of Commerce, Bureau of Economic Analysis. 1977. "Total and Per Capita Personal Income for States and Regions, 1970-76." *Survey of Current Business*. 57 (October): 18.

_____. 1987. "Total and Per Capita Personal Income for States and Regions, 1980-86." *Survey of Current Business 67* (April): 34.

U.S. Department of Labor, Bureau of Labor Statistics. 1978, 1980, 1982, 1984, 1986. *National Survey of Professional, Administrative, Technical, and Clerical Pay*. Washington, D.C.: U.S. Government Printing Office.

NAME INDEX

SUBJECT INDEX

ABOUT THE EDITORS

Kern Alexander is president and professor at Western Kentucky University and president-elect of the American Education Finance Association. Previously he served as professor of educational administration and director of the Institute for Educational Finance at the University of Florida and as director of the National Education Finance Project. Earlier he worked as an administrator in the United States Office of Education and consulted with state agencies and state legislatures to formulate new laws relating to education and school finance. Dr. Alexander received his doctorate from Indiana University and completed postdoctoral studies with distinction at the University of Oxford, Pembroke College, Oxford, England. He is the founder and executive editor of the *Journal of Education Finance*. Included among his numerous books are *The Economics and Financing of Education, Constitutional Reform of School Finance, American Public School Law*, and *College and University Law*.

David H. Monk is associate professor of educational administration at Cornell University. He joined the Cornell faculty in 1979 after earning his Ph.D. at the University of Chicago. In addition to having been an elementary school teacher, he has taught at the University of Rochester, the International Institute for Educational Planning in Paris, and Institut de Recherche sur l'Economie de l'Education at the

University of Burgundy in Dijon, France. His interests in the economics and financing of education are reflected in numerous research articles that have appeared in professional journals. He is currently writing a book on resource allocation problems in education.

ABOUT THE CONTRIBUTORS

Patricia Anthony is an assistant professor of education at the University of Massachusetts-Amherst, where she teaches school finance and school law. She holds a Ph.D. in educational administration from the University of Florida, Gainesville. She is the editor of the *Journal of Education Finance* and currently serves on the board of the American Education Finance Association. Dr. Anthony has recently been funded to study the status of teacher salaries in the Commonwealth of Massachusetts through a research grant for the 1987–88 academic year. She has published in both the school law and school finance areas, her most recent contributions being a chapter in *Principles of School Business Management* and an analysis of state funding in Massachusetts for the series, *Public School Finance Programs*.

Joseph C. Beckham is a member of the faculty in the College of Education at Florida State University. A graduate of the University of Florida's Holland Law Center, he has served as a consultant and counselor on matters of law and education to school districts, institutions of higher education, state departments of education, and various national organizations. Prior to his completion of the Ph.D. in educational administration, he was state director of a comprehensive educational program for Connecticut juvenile offenders. Dr. Beckham is a former director of Florida State University's Institute for Studies in Higher Education and served as a member of the board of the

National Organization on Legal Problems of Education. His legal research studies have been published in law reviews and numerous professional education journals. He summarizes appellate decisions involving public schools for the quarterly law reporter, *Schools and Courts*, and annually writes the Educational Research Service's series on *School Officials and the Courts*. His publications include an edited book entitled *Legal Issues in Public School Employment* and several monographs, including *Legal Aspects of Teacher Evaluation, Legal Aspects of Employee Assessment and Selection in Public Schools*, and *Faculty/Staff Dismissal for Cause in Institutions of Higher Education*.

James N. Fox is a senior economist in the Office of Research of the U.S. Department of Education. Previously he served as a policy analyst and school finance adviser to the assistant secretary for education in the U.S. Department of Health, Education, and Welfare and was an adjunct professor at Virginia Tech. He holds a B.A. in economics from Stanford University and an M.A. in economics (public finance) from UCLA. He completed his coursework at UCLA for the Ph.D. in educational policy, planning, and administration with specialties in quantitative methods and school finance, and a cognate in economics. Dr. Fox is on the board of directors of the American Education Finance Association and on the editorial review board of the *Journal of Education Finance*. He designs and conducts research in the areas of education policy, education productivity, the economics of education, and school finance.

Lloyd E. Frohreich is a professor of educational administration at the University of Wisconsin-Madison and specializes in school business administration, educational finance, and education facilities. Currently he serves on the editorial advisory board for the *Journal of Education Finance*; he has also served on the board of directors for the American Education Finance Association. He recently completed a book entitled *Creating and Maintaining Educational Facilities*. Prior to receiving his Ph.D. degree from Purdue University, he was a teacher and school business administrator in Indiana.

Ann Weaver Hart is an assistant professor in the Department of Educational Administration at the University of Utah. Formerly she was a junior high school principal in Utah. Dr. Hart received the

Ph.D. in organizational theory, job redesign, and principalship from the University of Utah. She has published articles in several journals, including the *American Educational Research Journal, Journal of Educational Administration, Journal of Research and Development in Education, Journal of Teacher Education, and Education Evaluation and Policy Analysis.* Her current research focuses on the redesign of teaching.

Stephen L. Jacobson is an assistant professor of educational organization, administration, and policy at the State University of New York at Buffalo. Prior to receiving a Ph.D. from Cornell University, he taught special education for the New York City Board of Education, working primarily with drug abusers. He has published articles on teacher compensation in the *Journal of Educational Finance* and *Education and Urban Society* and has written a chapter in *Crisis in Teaching.*

K. Forbis Jordan is the senior specialist in education with the Congressional Research at the Library of Congress, where his recent work has included tracking the school reform movement and analyzing teacher education proposals. He has been actively involved in the reauthorization of federal programs for elementary and secondary education as well as higher education. Previously he was the executive secretary of the Commission on Schools of the North Central Association and a professor of school administration at Indiana University and the University of Florida. Jordan's primary research interests have been in the field of state school finance programs. He has published over ten books and numerous monographs and articles in the fields of school finance, school business administration, and general school administration, and was the senior editor of the second AEFA yearbook. His undergraduate and master's degrees are from Western Kentucky University, and his doctorate is from Indiana University.

Stephen B. Lawton is a professor of educational administration at the Ontario Institute for Studies in Education. The author of *The Price of Quality: The Public Finance of Elementary and Secondary Education in Canada* and numerous articles on school finance in Canada, he is currently the principal investigator on studies of the cost of adult continuing education and regional cost differences in the provision of educational services in Ontario. He is a member of the AEFA board of directors and former vice-president and program chair of the Canadian Association for the Study of Educational Administration; in 1988 he will be the program chair for Division A of the American Educational Research Association. A former high school mathematics teacher with a B.A. in mathematics and history, he completed his Ph.D. at the University of California, Berkeley.

Eugene P. McLoone is a professor in the Department of Education Policy, Planning, and Administration, and an associate professor in the Department of Economics, both at the University of Maryland, College Park. He has a B.A. from La Salle College, a M.S.G.M. from the University of Denver, and a Ph.D. from the University of Illinois. Prior to teaching at the University of Maryland, he served as the research director for School Finance in the Research Division of National Education Association, senior research associate for the State-Local Finance Project at The George Washington University, a member of the School Finance Sector of the U.S. Office of Education, and a research assistant and associate in the Bureau of Education Research, University of Illinois. He is a member of the National Research Council Panel on Statistics on the Supply and Demand of Pre-collegiate Teachers of Science and Mathematics and research vice-chairperson of the University Contact Research Committee of Association of School Business Officials. Previously he served on the Governor of Maryland's Task Force on the Funding of Special Education, the Intergovernmental Relations and Property Committees of the National Tax Association, the Advisory Panel for National Education Finance Project, and committees on the development of the *Financial Reporting Handbook II* and its revisions, and has participated in the revision of state aid formulas in over ten states. Dr. LcLoone has written almost 100 articles on school finance and two books.

Betty Malen is an assistant professor in the Department of Educational Administration at the University of Utah. She also serves on the board of directors of AEFA. She received the Ph.D. in the politics of education and education policy and finance from the University of Minnesota. Formerly Dr. Malen was a school administrator in North Dakota and Michigan. Her articles have been published in the *Journal of Education Finance, Education Evaluation and Policy Analysis, and Educational Administration Quarterly.* Her current research focuses on the politics of educational reform, site-based governance, and career-ladder adoption and implementation.

Michael J. Murphy is an associate professor in the Department of Educational Administration at the University of Utah, the director of the State Education Policy Seminar, and a staff associate at the Center for Educational Policy, Far West Laboratory. Formerly he was an assistant professor in the Teachers College at Columbia University. He received the Ph.D. in labor economics from Claremont Graduate School. His articles have been published in the *Journal of Education Finance, Public Budgeting and Finance, National Forum, and Theory into Practice.* His current research focuses on employment relations, teacher wage and incentive systems, and staff utilization.

Bruce A. Peseau is a professor of administration and planning in the area of educational leadership and program chair of higher education administration at The University of Alabama. He earned a bachelor's degree in education at San Jose State University, a master's degree in school administation at Sacramento State University, and a Ph.D. degree in administration and supervision at the University of Kentucky. His educational experience includes service as an elementary and a secondary schoolteacher; an elementary and junior high school principal; a curriculum specialist; a superintendent of schools for the Creold Petroleum Corporation in Venezuela; and an assistant dean for administration, area head of educational leadership programs, and an associate dean for graduate programs and planning at The University of Alabama. He also worked as a planning consultant to the Ministry of Education in Venezuela. Dr. Peseau has published more than fifty journal articles, chapters in books, and monographs and has conducted an annual research project on resources and productivity in teacher education. Articles summarizing the financial plight of teacher education have been published in *The Journal of Teacher Education, Peabody Journal of Education, Kappan*, and *Action in Teacher Education.*

Richard G. Salmon is an associate professor in educational administration at Virginia Polytechnic Institute and State University. He has conducted research studies in the areas of school finance and business management for local, state, and federal agencies. He has published articles in several journals and is the managing editor of the

Journal of Education Finance. He recently co-authored a graduate textbook entitled *School Business Administration*, and he is completing the American Education Finance Association collaborative publication, *Public School Finance Systems of the United States and Canada.*

AMERICAN EDUCATION FINANCE ASSOCIATION OFFICERS 1987-88

Officers

President	William E. Sparkmen
President-Elect	Kern Alexander
Secretary-Treasurer and Executive Director	George R. Babigian
Immediate Past President	James G. Ward

Directors

Robert Berne	Bettye MacPhail-Wilcox
William E. Camp	Van D. Mueller
Koy Floyd	Julie Underwood O'Hara
James Fox	Robert Perlman
Lloyd E. Frohreich	James Rose
Suzanne Langston	Joan Scheuer
Stephen B. Lawton	Deborah Verstegen
Kent McGuire	

Editor, Journal of Education Finance

Kern Alexander

Sustaining Members

American Association of School Administrators
American Federation of Teachers
National Education Association
National School Boards Association